Seeing in the Dark

The Poetry of Phyllis Webb

Pauline Butling

Wilfrid Laurier University Press

This book has been published with the help of a grant from the Humanities and Social Sciences Federation of Canada, using funds provided by the Social Sciences and Humanities Research Council of Canada.

Canadian Cataloguing in Publication Data

Butling, Pauline
   Seeing in the dark : the poetry of Phyllis Webb

Includes bibliographical references and index.
ISBN 0-88920-271-0

1. Webb, Phyllis, 1927- − Criticism and interpretation. I. Title.

PS8545.E222 1997   C811'.54   C96-930966-X
PR9199.3.W422 1997

Copyright © 1997
WILFRID LAURIER UNIVERSITY PRESS
Waterloo, Ontario, Canada   N2L 3C5

Cover design by Leslie Macredie,
using "Open Here," a photo-collage
by Phyllis Webb

Printed in Canada

This book is dedicated to the memory of

my mother, Helen Butling, who showed by example

that anything was possible,

and

my father, G.A. Butling, who read me Blake's songs

Contents

Preface

Phyllis Webb's poetry offers the reader many pleasures. As a lyricist, she delights the ear, eye, and heart. Her work is playful, reflective, sensual, sonorous, formally inventive, and intellectually complex. She also addresses compelling ethical and political questions such as social injustices, the use and abuse of power, and the relation between the personal and the political. Indeed, her work challenges social and epistemological paradigms, especially in the realm of gender constructs. But when I first began reading Webb's poetry in the 1960s, I was unaware of these social and political complexities. I had been trained as a "New Critical" reader to look to poetry only for aesthetic pleasures and humanistic affirmations, to value beauty of form and complexity of thought "for its own sake," as we used to say so glibly without any idea of what we meant. I had accepted the ahistorical viewpoint that disturbances in poetry were aesthetic, not social or political; that poetry's only social function was to intensify perception and sensitivity. The rebelliousness of young writers was safely contained within the Freudian construct of young writers necessarily rebelling against their literary fathers. I was rapidly advancing, or so I thought, toward the higher realm of aestheticized sensibility where truth and beauty became self-evident.

Outside the classroom, however, my experiences with poetry were quite different. While I was a student at the University of British Columbia (1957-63), I was part of a literary community of jazz-loving "beats," rebellious writer/students, and radical young professors. Reading, writing, and talking about poetry were part of our daily lives; radical writing was connected to a radical politics of initiating social and political change. The constant discussions, arguments, poetry readings, literary festivals, and publishing activities helped shape the anger and frustration of a largely working-class group (most of the group were the first members of their families to attend university) into a populist challenge to upper-middle-class, aesthetic, and social norms. We started magazines (such as *Tish*) that were deliberately cheap, unpolished, and community based, to reach non-establishment local and international readers; we organized discussion groups, poetry readings, and literary festivals as part of counter-culture politics and poetics; we learned that literature was contemporary, alive, and vital to the community.

It has taken me some thirty years to integrate these socio-political experiences of poetry into my critical practice and even now my formalist academic training often demands that I edit out personal pleasures and political concerns, that my social self go into hiding. This book thus represents an uneasy blend of formalist and the more politically engaged methodologies of feminist and post-colonial critical practices. I combine politicized readings of Webb's work—suggesting various ways that her poetry offers interventions in epistemological and social contexts—while also offering formalist analyses of particular poems.

In the first five chapters, I discuss Webb's work from several overlapping perspectives. I argue that Webb's is an interventionist, feminist poetics—a "seeing in the dark" that opens up "darknesses" in the symbolic order by strategies of subversion, re-vision, and reversal. Chapter 1 focusses mainly on Webb's poetry of the 1950s and 1960s, but also includes an outline of her writing strategies in the later books. *Naked Poems* is discussed in detail as a pivotal book which reconfigures the discourse of romance by articulating a lesbian erotic within pleasurable darknesses. Chapter 2 foregrounds my own struggle to find ways of reading Webb's *Water and Light* that recognize the book's disjunctiveness while tracing its feminist trajectories. I use Webb's section title "Middle Distance," together with James Clifford's notion of necessary oscillations between "metanarratives . . . of homogenization . . . and emergence" (Clifford, 1988, 17), to characterize the mottled truths and clustered meanings that I find in *Water and Light*. Chapter 3 reexamines *Water and Light* from the perspective of Webb's formal interventions. I suggest that Webb's precise attention to prosodic structures is integral to her process of seeing in the dark in that it allows her to be simultaneously active and receptive: while the conscious mind works actively with the formal ingredients in the poem, the rest of the psyche remains open to associative processes and intuitive leaps. I also argue that the formal changes in Webb's "Anti Ghazals" contribute to her feminist critique of the ghazal tradition by foregrounding renegade lines and anti-romantic tropes.

In chapter 4, I consider the changes in pronoun configurations from Webb's early work, through *Wilson's Bowl*, to *Hanging Fire*. In tracing Webb's shift from the "I/you" configuration of the traditional lyric to an "I/we" configuration which empowers the "I" by association with a community, I expand the discussion of polyvocal subjectivity that I began in chapter 1 into an analysis of how shifting pronoun relations construct different subjectivities and relationships. Chapter 5 examines intertextuality in *Wilson's Bowl* and *Water and Light* and circles back over Webb's strategies of resistance, arguing that Webb rewrites received cultural scripts to open up alternative meanings. Drawing on Jessica Benjamin's notion of intersubjectivity in which "assertion *and* recognition become the vital moves in the dialogue between self and other" (Benjamin, 22), I suggest that Webb's intertextual dialogues (especially those with recurring father figures) enact both attraction and rejection, enact both "the erotic and violent aspects of . . . intertextual relations" (Worton and Still, 2).

Chapter 6 shifts to the topic of Webb criticism and reiterates my concern with feminist interventions by arguing for the value of situated and historicized criticism in recuperating subjectivities and "histories hitherto misrepresented or rendered invisible" (Said, 30-31). Finally, in chapter 7, I provide a chronology of Webb's life and a "bio-text" in which Webb's books are discussed in the context of life events. Throughout the book, cross-references between chapters show the network of connections that operate within the book and offer the reader access to those networks.

I have used this circular structure for the book partially to resist the evolutionary metaphor of growth and development that seems always to invade any discussion of a single writer. Webb's work is more meaningfully seen in terms of recurring concerns and diverse but intersecting writing strategies than as a progressive development. The growth and development model posits stages in a process of individuation (following Freud's notion of necessary rebellion) that lead to intellectual and artistic autonomy, whereas the spiral structure posits recurrences, intersections, and interventions within social and epistemological formations that expand the boundaries of sense or normalcy.

My title for this book—*Seeing in the Dark*—challenges the identification of women with alterity by claiming positive values for darkness and thus making "darkness" visible. As well, "seeing in the dark" metaphorizes my attempts to reconceptualize Webb's work via feminist theories which offer expanded modes of seeing and reading. In this connection—as writer/theorist Johanna Drucker suggests—theory has proved to be an "an essential aspect of claiming a place from which to write" as well as a "perspectivizing tool, that which permits the two-dimensional plane of the page to be located in the multiple dimensions of the world, of the discourses of power and politics" (Drucker, 18). In placing Webb's work in feminist contexts, I hope to make her pivotal to a politics of social change in which "new" subjectivities are garnering increased visibility and value.

Acknowledgements

This book could not have been written without the support and encouragement of my community of family, friends, and colleagues in Calgary, Edmonton, Vancouver, and the West Kootenay region of B.C.

Special thanks to Jeanne Perreault and Bryn Pinchin for their helpful comments on portions of the manuscript; to Jeff Derkson for his excellent substantive editing; to Lorna Knight for help with the Webb papers at the National Library; to Susan Rudy, Janice Williamson, Aritha van Herk, Douglas Barbour, Karen McLaughlin, and my colleagues at the Alberta College of Art and Design who, together with those named above, have provided the intellectual engagement and emotional support that have been crucial to the writing of this book.

My thanks, also, to my husband, Fred Wah, for his attentive listening to my ramblings, questions, and tentative thoughts. Many drives from Calgary to Vancouver, or to our Kootenay Lake cabin, have been spent talking about this book, as well as many breakfasts, lunches, dinners, mornings, evenings, and afternoons. And thanks to our daughters Jennifer and Erika for their sustaining love, energy, and enthusiasm.

I am grateful to the following for the opportunity to present papers that served as a basis for some of the chapters in this book: the Association of Canadian Studies in Australia and New Zealand, the Indian Association of Canadian Studies, the Association of College and University Teachers of English, the organizers of "Interventing the Text" (University of Calgary, 1991), and the organizers of the "Poetry and History Conference" at the University of Stirling, Scotland (1996). As well, I thank editors Smaro Kamboureli, Shirley Neuman, and George Bowering for publishing my essays on Webb, and Roy Miki, general editor of *West Coast Line*, for inviting me to guest edit a special issue on Webb.

To the Humanities Institute at the University of Calgary I owe a special thanks for a post-doctoral fellowship in 1989-90, and for the support provided by the excellent staff (Gerry Dyer and Cindy Atkinson) and by my Institute "fellows."

The genesis of this book goes back even further, to a grey day in January 1984 when the B.C. government announced the closure of David Thompson University Centre in Nelson, B.C. That event prompted me to complete (with some welcome encouragement from the State University of New York at Buffalo) a long-abandoned PhD dissertation, which would eventually include a chapter on Phyllis Webb. Thanks to SSHRCC for providing a doctoral fellowship in 1985-86 and to Professors William Sylvestre and the late Jack Clarke at SUNYAB for their help as thesis advisors and facilitators.

I am grateful to Coach House Press for permission to reproduce poems from *Wilson's Bowl, Water and Light: Ghazals and Anti Ghazals*, and *Hanging Fire*; to Talonbooks for permissions from *Selected Poems* and *The Vision Tree*; to NeWest Press for permissions from *Nothing But Brush Strokes*; to Quadrant Editions for permissions from *Talking*; and to Louis Dudek and Robert Weaver for excerpts from their letters to Phyllis Webb, which are in the archives of the National Library.

Joe Plaskett generously gave permission to reproduce his painting of Phyllis Webb.

Finally, thanks to Phyllis Webb, for writing all those poems, for her permission to reproduce her writings, and for responding so willingly to my many questions.

List of Abbreviations

All abbreviations refer to works by Phyllis Webb unless noted other-wise.

DL	*Desire in Language* (Kristeva)
EYRE	*Even Your Right Eye*
HF	*Hanging Fire*
KR	*The Kristeva Reader* (Kristeva)
LIHE	*Language in Her Eye* (Scheier, Sheard, and Wachtel, eds.)
M	*the martyrology Books 1 & 2* (bp Nichol)
MM	"Message Machine"
NBBS	*Nothing But Brush Strokes*
NL	National Library (reference)
NP	*Naked Poems*
PT	*The Pleasures of the Text* (Barthes)
PW	*Phyllis Webb and Her Works* (ECW)
"PW"	"Phyllis Webb" (Hulcoop, *Dictionary of Literary Biography*)
RPL	*Revolution in Poetic Language* (Kristeva)
SIAG	*The Sea Is Also a Garden*
SP	*Selected Poems*
SW	*Sunday Water: Thirteen Anti Ghazals*
T	*Talking*
TCEP	*The Collected Earlier Poems* (of William Carlos Williams)
VT	*The Vision Tree*
WB	*Wilson's Bowl*
WCL	*West Coast Line* (periodical)
WL	*Water and Light*

1

Webb's Poetics of Resistance

You may read my signs
but I cross my path
and show you nothing
on your way. ("Wilson's Bowl," *WB*, 61)

The process of seeing in the dark begins, paradoxically, with temporary blindness during which you are in a state of apprehension and heightened sensitivity: you proceed by touching objects, by listening attentively, or you stand still and wait for the eye to expand until, gradually, you are able to discern shapes within the darkness. The most common form of this experience is entering a dark movie theatre and being temporarily blinded as a result of the sudden shift from a well-lit lobby to a darkened theatre. As your eyes slowly adjust to the darkness, you see the outlines of people, the rows of seats, the walls of the room, and you are able to move into the theatre, take a seat, settle in, and enjoy the movie. Entering a Phyllis Webb poem often produces an experience similar to entering the darkened theatre: at first you listen, grope, and strain to see. Only gradually, as your eye expands, are you able to move around, take a seat, and settle in to enjoy the show in Webb's darkened room(s) of meanings.

This "dark" that Webb activates in her poetry is the cultural "dark" of Western (patriarchal) thought, that negative realm supposedly inhabited by the unenlightened, imaged in Plato's cave and reinscribed in the mind/body dichotomies of Enlightenment thought. Darkness automatically confers secondary status in this paradigm; it symbolizes Otherness: the irrational, unenlightened, crude, delusional, chaotic, primitive, barbaric (and sometimes evil) place, person, or attribute as, for instance, in the "darknesses" assigned to racialized others and/or to women. Webb blurs this Enlightenment bifurcation of mind/body, reason/sensuality by initiating a seeing *within* the dark. There are no

The notes to this chapter are on p. 33-36.

handy lyric capsules of distilled meaning at the entry and exit points of her poems; instead she creates the conditions for writer and reader to enter *into* the dark and to see darkness intermingled with light rather than as a negative other. Webb's poetics thus constitute a feminist, interventionist poetics that open up some of the darkened rooms in the symbolic order.

Let me briefly demonstrate this process in the poem cited above. On first reading, I am perplexed by the paradox of "I . . . show you nothing." The word names *something*, but only in negative terms— nothing is *not* a thing, a void, an emptiness, a zero, a darkness, a blank. However "nothingness" gradually becomes meaning-full as I listen and grope my way into the poem. First, the word has materiality; indeed, it stands out as the only word of more than one syllable in the poem. Second, the dedication to Webb's friend Lilo Berliner "who walked into the sea, January, 1977" defines "nothing" as the inexplicability of Berliner's suicide, its unreadability.[1] "These poems," Webb explains in the notes at the back of the book, "are my attempt to deal with Lilo's obsessions and death" (*WB*, 88). The word becomes meaning-full within its immediate semantic surroundings.

Another ingredient of the semantic environment in this poem which expands the meaning of "nothing" is anthropologist Wilson Duff's essay titled "Nothing Comes Only in Pieces," an essay that he wrote (and Webb read) in the 1970s on the Haida creation legend. In the Haida legend, Raven is instructed to open a series of five nesting boxes. In the smallest one, he finds "nothing," out of which he then creates the world. Webb learned about this legend from Lilo Berliner, who had a correspondence with Duff about the puzzles and paradoxes in Haida art and myths. In particular, they discussed Duff's two essays, "Levels of Meaning in Haida Art" and "Nothing Comes Only in Pieces" (*NBBS*, 112-13), and the exhibition that Duff curated, titled *images stone b.c. Thirty Centuries of Northwest Coast Indian Sculpture*. Webb's connection to this material is indicated both by the book title, *Wilson's Bowl*, and by her essay on the Duff-Berliner correspondence, which includes excerpts from Duff's essays.[2]

In her essay on the Duff-Berliner correspondence, Webb offers the following excerpt from the Haida creation story as "a sample on the Nothing theme." In this section of the story, a young native man named Ray is discussing the meaning of the story with a wise old native man named Solomon Wilson.

"I was thinking about those two things in the box. One of them was that tiny little nothing that was there but was too small to have any size, so the box looked empty. You know what I think the other thing was, Sol? It was all the other things in the world that were not there, so the box still looked empty. You see, if you mixed them. . . ."

Sol's guffaw brought that line of reasoning to a halt. "You and your crazy ideas, Ray. That's sure a crazy one." They laughed together. "But you know, Ray, that old man did say that nothing comes in pieces, so at least it's something you can have a piece of, something that Raven could have a bite of. Maybe that's how it is: *you can't see nothing when it's all there, you can only recognize it when there's a little piece of it there.*" ("A Correspondence" *NBBS*, 116-17, emphasis added)

In this legend, "nothing" is not a void or a negativity; it is only "too small to have any size, so the box looked empty." But you can "recognize it when there's a little piece of it there." A similar process occurs in the above poem where Webb's poem/box at first looks empty, but then we find a little piece of "nothing" with which one makes a world of meaning.

Homi Bhabha's discussion of how a negative "in the photographic sense" is processed into a positive is helpful here in further elaborating Webb's process of resemanticizing negative terms:

discursive "transparency" is best read in the photographic sense in which a transparency is also always a negative, *processed into visibility through the technologies of reversal, enlargement, lighting, editing, projection, not a source but a re-source of light.* Such a bringing to light is never a prevision; it is always a question of the provision of visibility as a capacity, a strategy, an agency but also in the sense in which the prefix pro(vision) might indicate an elision of sight, delegation, substitution, contiguity, in place of . . . what? (My emphasis, Bhabha's ellipses; 171)

Webb similarly offers not a "prevision" but a "provision of visibility," which has the effect of processing a negative into a positive. Poetic strategies of "reversal, enlargement . . . elision of sight, delegation, substitution, contiguity" loosen meanings from their established moorings and create a "discursive transparency . . . in the photographic sense," a discursive "darkness" that can be processed into a positive.

Or, to change the metaphor, meanings crisscross in a Webb poem in a labyrinth so meandering that one has to forget about trying to find a minotaur-centre. Unlike Ariadne, Webb does not provide a thread-path leading to the bull's-eye of patriarchal thought. The "I" of Webb's poems "show[s] you nothing," refuses the role of the enlightened "I" who leads the reader to meaning. Indeed, she does the exact opposite; she continually crisscrosses and destabilizes meanings. As in the poem cited at the start of this chapter, "I" deliberately gets lost:

> You may read my signs
> but I cross my path
> and show you nothing
> on your way (*WB*, 61)

To crisscross one's path is an evasive strategy used by fugitives to confuse their trackers. The "signs" on this non-path lead nowhere, so that "you" must also crisscross and circle back. In Bhabha's terms, Webb provides only a "*provision* of visibility as a capacity, a strategy, an agency . . ." (emphasis added). Thus she engages the reader in the *processes* of seeing, thinking, finding, making meaning, of seeing within the dark.

Crucial to the success of such a process is Webb's sometimes criss-crossing, sometimes shape-shifting, sometimes disappearing I/eye. In Webb's poems, "I am one am many" to use bp Nichol's apt phrase (*M*, Book 2, "Auguries"). In the above poem, for instance, several identities inhabit the "I" and "you" of the poem: "I" can be Berliner speaking to Webb, who is the reader of Berliner's suicide, or Webb speaking to the reader reading the poem, or the poem speaking to Webb, who is reading the poem as she writes it, or Webb speaking to herself, with the reader reading over her shoulder. The pronouns are provisional and polyvocal rather than previsional.

Similarly, in a more recent poem (appropriately titled "Perform-ance") Webb self-consciously inhabits, resists, questions, conjugates, and parodies the many guises and disguises of the poetic "I":

> Who is this *I* infesting my poems? Is it I hiding behind the Trump type on the page of the book you are reading? Is it a photograph of me on the cover of *Wilson's Bowl*? Is it I? *I* said, *I* say, *I* am saying—
>
> *I am the mask, the voice, the one who begins those lyrical poems, I wandered lonely as a cloud . . . I hear the Shadowy Horses, their long manes a-shake . . . I am of Ireland/And the Hold Land of Ireland . . . I, the poet William Yeats . . . I am worn out with dreams. . . .* (Webb's ellipses, *HF*, 67)

Indeed, a provisional and polyvocal "I" is present from the start of Webb's writing. As early as "Poet" (*SP*, 14), first published in *Contem-*

porary Verse in the Winter/Spring 1951-52 issue, Webb foregrounds this provisionality: "I" moves between submission ("I am promised / I have taken the veil"), self-parody ("I have tokened the veil" or "I have punctured my fingerbase / to fill one thimble / with blood for consecration"), and frustration ("I have paced four walls / of this cell"). Thus in poems written some thirty years apart—one from 1951, one from 1984[3]—the centred, autonomous "I" is de-universalized to become contingent, performative, provisional, gendered, and multivalent.

It is important to note also that this provisional subject becomes a positive term in Webb's poetry; it, too, is "processed into visibility" in the sense of turning a negative into a positive "in the photographic sense" (Bhabha, above). In contrast to the modernist despair over "the centre [that] will not hold" (Yeats), Webb actively *cultivates* instability and provisionality as a means of seeing, being in the dark. Yeats longs for the centred, stable identity of phallocentric discourse (the collapsing centre is surely a metaphor of male impotence), while Webb actively makes "trouble," trouble in the sense suggested by Judith Butler in *Gender Trouble*, who explains that once she realized she was likely to always be "in trouble," she thought why not figure out "how best to make it, what best way to be in it" (ix).[4] Webb *makes* trouble in the poem in this active and positive way by clouding meanings, disturbing hierarchies, and continually decentring the subject. While Webb would not have named this "gender trouble"—indeed Webb refuses to "name" her poetics at all—I see gender issues from the start in Webb's refusal of a poetics of mastery, in her insistence on polyvalent subjects who provide "not a source but a re-source of light" (Bhabha), who make trouble by redirecting the light backwards to interrogate its sources in patriarchal thought and sideways or in multidirectional ways to include the female "dark."

Finally, before looking at Webb's poetics in more detail, I want to comment on the historical and theoretical "nesting boxes" that I have introduced in the preceding pages. In referring to Yeats' poem, Judith Butler's *Gender Trouble*, Lilo Berliner's suicide, bp Nichol's comments on subjectivity, and Northwest Coast native (Haida) legends, I have deliberately positioned Webb's poetics within several semantic/social fields—hegemonic, patriarchal, feminist—because I see Webb's poetics taking shape at the intersections of those various trajectories. Yeats signifies the modernist literary tradition that dominated when Webb began writing; Berliner's suicide configures the struggles of the female subject under patriarchy that Webb has investigated throughout her work;[5] the Haida creation story represents one of several non-European sources that Webb has used to find alternatives to Western models of subjectivity and creativity; and bp Nichol is one of a number of post-modern writers who helped to validate and extend Webb's interventionist practices. Webb's poetics has formed at the intersections of historical, personal, feminist, and patriarchal imperatives. It is there that she "makes trouble," there that she generates a multivalent I/eye that becomes a means of "seeing in the dark" and of resemanticizing and materializing a female "dark." Finally, Judith Butler and Homi Bhabha are two of many contemporary theorists who have provided a language and a methodology for my own "seeing in the dark."

Resistances/Reversals: "The Colour of the Light"

Webb's "troublemaking" in her early work (1955-63)[6] takes the form of subverting traditions, pluralizing rather than synthesizing meaning, disturbing the sovereign poetic self, and destabilizing the master narratives of history and myth. Webb often positions her poems in historical or mythic contexts, but then subverts, questions, and/or unravels the assumptions informing those paradigms. "The Colour of the Light," for instance, a poem from her 1954 collection in *Trio*, raises troubling questions about the colour (gender) of the light (knowledge). In each of the four sections of the poem, Webb changes the "colouring" of various stories by viewing them from a woman's perspective; she subverts established forms of knowledge (light)—ranging from mythology (the Olympian creation story), to philosophy (Jean-Paul Sartre's *Being and Nothingness*), to history, to literature (Shakespeare's *Antony and Cleopatra* and *The Tempest*). The first section recasts a creation/seduction story from the woman's point of view and emphasizes the violence, not the supposed romantic bliss of lover and beloved that prevails in patriarchal seduction narratives. The opening scene of the poem echoes the Olympian creation myth of the rape of earth by Cronos:

> On the apparent corner of two streets
> a strange man shook
> a blue cape above my head,
> I saw it as the shaking sky
> and was forthwith ravished. (*SP*, 15)

The female "I" is captured and "ravished." In section II, while passing "silently" through a park, the female "I" watches a man pause to light a cigarette. Webb's poem here resonates with Jean-Paul Sartre's scenario of the watcher in the park in *Being and Nothingness* but with significant differences.[7] In Sartre's scenario, the male subject becomes paranoid when he realizes that he himself is being watched by the person he is watching. The subject feels menaced by the possibility of becoming an object. However, as Norman Bryson points out in his critique of Sartre,[8] the existence of the watcher also serves to intensify the subject's sense of himself: "the subject can *survive* such a gaze, and survive more strongly for being exposed to this 'alterity' which may menace the subject but which does not in any sense actually dissolve or annihilate it. The subject's sense of being a subject is heightened, not undone . . ." (Bryson, 96).

In Webb's poem, however, the female subject does not enter the man's perceptual field; her "sense of being a subject" is not "heightened." Indeed "I" is a subject in grammatical form only—she is just "passing through" the park:

> A man bent to light a cigarette.
> This was in the park
> and I was passing through.
> With what succinct ease he joins
> himself to flame!
> I passed by silently noting
> how clear were the colours of pigeons
> and how mysterious the animation of children
> playing in trees. (*SP*, 15)

She admires the ease with which he enacts his desires (in lighting a [phallic] cigarette, for instance), but she herself remains invisible and silent. Then she shifts her attention away from the man to "pigeons" and "children." In contrast to Sartre's male subject whose sense of self is enhanced by the viewer, her subjectivity is enhanced by *not* being watched, by looking past the male desire, by "passing through" the park, by focussing her attention on the periphery.

Finally, section 4 problematizes the patriarchal trope of the seductive, exquisitely beautiful woman. In lines that echo, but mock, Enobarbus' famous tribute to Cleopatra's beauty—"Age cannot wither her nor custom stale / her infinite variety" (*Anthony and Cleopatra*, II, ii, 240-41)—Webb critiques the idealization of female beauty. She does so by mimicking the rhythm of Shakespeare's lines, but radically changing the content:

And the self is a grave
music will not mould
nor grief destroy;
yet this does not make refusal
somehow . . . somehow . . .
shapes fall in a torrent of design
and over the violent space
assume a convention;

Or in the white, white, quivering
instability of love
we shake a world to order:
our prismed eyes divide such light
as this world dreams on
and rarely sees. (*SP*, 16, Webb's ellipses)

In Webb's version of romance, the woman survives not by her ability to inspire great passion—with her "infinite variety"—but by closing herself off from the "music" and by inventing other definitions/visions of love based on her own passions. This is not the dream/vision of Shakespeare's *Tempest* ("We are such stuff / As dreams are made on," IV, i, 156-57), but a re-vision, a prism of her own—to echo Virginia Woolf—that refracts the light differently, that produces a different light (one that "this world . . . rarely sees").

Three of the four sections of the poem also include questions and/or comments on the conjunction of personal and social identities which, in the context of this poem, point to how women are constructed and constricted by prevailing social codes:

Knowing the apparent or the real . . .
        shaping the world in the intimate
                terms of self . . .
[. . .]
And when is the apparent not the real?
        The public and the person are inevitably
                one and the same self.
[. . .]
(and who would cleave the apparent from the real?
                (*SP*, 15-16, Webb's ellipses)[9]

"I" realizes that "the apparent" self (self-as-object) often overwhelms the experiential, "real," agenic self (self-as-subject) to the point where they become "one and the same." But the rhetorical structure of the last question—"who would cleave the apparent from the real?"—implies an impasse. Not until Webb asks *how* to break apart this subject/object fusion rather than "*who* would cleave the apparent from the real"—which shifts the focus from a dependency on individual power to an analysis of systemic oppressions—does she activate and energize a female subjectivity. Here she observes, questions, talks back, makes trouble and, in the final line of the poem, hints at alternatives to the gendered, narrative enclosures that give women object status: in saying "I thought I saw the pigeons in the trees . . ." (Webb's ellipses), the "I" glimpses the possibility of other realities, signified by the common, everyday pigeon and by the ellipses dots. As well, the conditionality of "I thought I saw" proposes an alternative to the Cartesian "I," which defines itself as autonomous ("I think, therefore I am") rather than contingent.

"Earth Descending," also from Webb's first collection in *Trio*, offers a more active female subject and takes on a more playful, comic tone. The poem tells a story of earth-woman cutting loose from her victim position in patriarchal myths and history:

> I'd squeal that this cannot, cannot
> be as good as it seems
> to be freed from old Electra
> (and even Oedipus)
> who have always hovered
> and in all and every emergency
> lowered the lid over the eye and me
> covered with night,
> (polite name for lack of sight

The tone remains playful as she continues her descent and joins the witches:

> O, how I would love
> to bet the dear old couple
> the salacious solar system
> against seven buckets of the Milky Way
> that this earthly eye
> (it is I)

> rowing wildly away
> from some universal dock
> with a leap in my heart which amounts
> to a tick-tock clocked bomb inside me
> houred for that existential arm
> of the witch below
> whose ripe, black brew,
> smouldering and mouldering
> with happy, spatted stars
> is eager to receive another.

In joining the witches, "Earth" aligns herself with an alternative tradition of empowered women, but Webb simultaneously mocks that escape route in the closing section. "Earth" declares her freedom from "that eternal circulation" in very obvious, belaboured rhymes and rhythms which continue that "eternal circulation":

> "For I, like others,
> have slipped over the solar edge
> spat and said
> 'This is the end,
> to hell with that eternal circulation
> of night, day, life, death and love all over,
> this is the end of an earth well worn
> and born to die
> and so say I
> this is the end.
> No need to belabour the point, however,
> This is the end—and right now, moreover.' " (*VT*, 25-26)

By giving Earth a personality, by making her a particular (not universal) "earth mother" figure, and by having her roam out of orbit while at the same time recognizing that we are always already constructed within the orbits of culture and history, Webb playfully resists the humanist search for coherent history and unifying myths. And while the poem participates in the existentialist debate about being and nothingness, Webb's comic tone makes a mockery of that debate. The poem brings all such debates "down-to-earth," to use the old cliché.

In "Double Entendre," also a poem from the 1950s, Webb particularizes and genders another so-called universal—the "human condition" of perpetual despair. She places the traditional *quest* narrative alongside a sensual world of pomegranates and pregnant women within which the (male) quest for abstract order seems sterile and meaningless. Many readers have taken the poem as a statement of the modernist theme of despair in the face of collapsing certainties, perhaps because the *form* of the poem is typically modernist—with its carefully balanced lines that contrast with an apparent spiritual disorder. Such readers have focussed on the lost and confused figure in the poem who searches in vain for truth and for whom neither the divine "star" nor the "human eye" prove to be reliable guides.[10]

In my view, however, there is a double-coding in the poem: the despairing figure represents not a universal truth, but rather the problems inherent in wanting a universal truth in the first place. His confusion and despair come from his expectations: "that man must / make, make // . . . a structure for his loss." It is his desire for structure, rather than the lack of structure, that renders his quest circular and meaningless:

> the fact that man must
> make, make
> bone, flesh,
> a structure for his loss
> and, like gold, take
> seeds of meaning
> pitiful
> from the dross,
> For in his strange
> peripheral orbit
> of reality and dream
> he wanders, wonders,
> through the play within the play
> knowing not
> which is the right
> the light
> the star in the cold, staring sky,
> or the star reflected in a human eye. (*VT,* 42)

This male quest yields only dried up "seeds of meaning" that are pitifully inadequate. But the poem offers a "double entendre" in the double meaning of "star" as divine or human and of "seeds" as both the dregs of abstractions and the living seeds in the pomegranate:

The seed white
    beneath the flesh
        red and diamonded
            under the skin
                rough, round,
  of the round pomegranate
      hopes in essential shape
           for a constellation of fruit
Just as the pregnant woman
    in the street
        carrying her three-year-old son
  is one and entire
      the tribe of woman
          weighted down by the race of man—
        always to be renewed (*VT,* 41)

The pomegranate—itself a sexual symbol, with its white seeds (semen) and red flesh (vulva)—and the pregnant woman are alive and growing, though the pregnant woman is also burdened with the weight of the male child in her arms. The poem offers a critique of both the enervating structures of rationality and of the "weight" of patriarchy that inhibits the generative potential of women and pomegranates.

A Balancing Act: "Chung Yung"

Webb's interest in Eastern philosophy and religion in the 1950s—especially in the Neo-Confucian notion of a world in constant flux—provides, I believe, a partial basis for her critique of rationality and abstractions. Webb's early poetry often enacts the Neo-Confucian view that history is cyclical, that everything is in motion, and that truth is a momentary instance of balance within the flux, not a transcendent form. Webb explores the Neo-Confucian concept of permanent impermanence in a poem titled "Chung Yung" from her first collection in *Trio* (1954). The two words of the title refer to the basic principle of balance in Neo-Confucianism; translated, they mean, respectively, "that which exists plumb in the middle" and "that which never wavers or wobbles" (*VT,* 155). Webb's poem enacts these balanced processes. Here are the first two stanzas:

The year has come round full circle,
All evidence, both external and internal,

Is now proven and visible;

Love has known all seasons,
Cycles within cycles have given birth
To words, patterns, moods
And placed their worth
In necessary violence
Or in absolution. (*VT*, 23)

Contradictions and oppositions are essential, not problems to be resolved.

This notion of a necessarily circular form and meaning continues through Webb's next two books (*Even Your Right Eye* and *The Sea Is Also a Garden*). "Propositions" (*SIAG*) swings back and forth between the proposition of lovers joined together as a unit and their inevitable separations. Even when the lovers join hands, their other two hands remain separate, as the half-moon contains the "hidden wholeness" of the full moon, but is still a half moon. Here is the first half of the poem:

I could divide a leaf
and give you half.

Or I could search for two leaves
sending you one.

Or I could walk to the river
and look across

and seeing you there,
or not there,

absence or presence,
would spring the balance to my day. (*VT*, 44)

The seesaw movement of thought comes to rest at various balance points, with all the contraries still in place. Also, the balanced rhythms of the couplet match the poem's pivoting semantics.

In poem after poem in *The Sea Is Also a Garden*, she maintains this balanced interplay of contraries. "Sitting," "Mad Gardener to the Sea," "Two Pears," and "Making" are some of the most striking examples. Even a poem such as "Breaking," often read as a definitive statement of

existential despair because of the last line—"What are we whole or
beautiful or good for but to be absolutely broken?"—is, in my reading,
a set of balanced contraries. From the contradictions of the first line
("Give us wholeness, for we are broken") to the question mark at the
end of the last line, which undermines its status as statement, the poem
pivots in a seesaw pattern of thought: why do we search for wholeness
when all we see is brokeness? whom do we expect to provide it when
there are only the "[s]hattered gods" and "self-iconoclasts" left?

> The crucifix has clattered to the ground,
> the living Christ has spent a year in Paris,
> travelled on the Métro, fallen in the Seine.
> We would not raise our silly gods again.
> Stigmata sting, they suddenly appear
> on every blessed person everywhere. (*VT*, 46)

Christ's stigmata, the marks of pain and suffering, are now visible on
each person. Suffering is everywhere, as the stanza-length list of figures
reminds us: "Ophelia, Hamlet, Othello, Lear,/ Kit Smart, William
Blake, John Clare, Van Gogh, Henry IV of Pirandello,/ Gerard de Ner-
val, Antonin Artaud." But then comes a contrary viewpoint, itself
stated in the contradictory form of a double negative: "There is a justice
in destruction. / It isn't 'isn't fair.'" The closing question, in the con-
text of the preceding demystification and desacrilization of both whole-
ness and "breaking," maintains the balance of contrary perspectives
rather than offering a resolution of the poem's opposing positions.
Whether held in tension, or balanced to the point of paralysis, Webb's
question/answer, thesis/antithesis structures pluralize and destabilize
truth.

However, while enacting a dialectic of contraries and paradoxes,
Webb's poems remain within the pivoting rhythms of binary opposi-
tions and thus often get stuck in a kind of paralysis or stasis of thought.
Not until *Naked Poems* does Webb successfully break up the binary
structures of patriarchal discourse (whether Confucian or Western).
The paralysis or stasis imposed by binary systems is particularly notice-
able in Webb's 1962 collection *The Sea Is Also a Garden*. In "The Glass
Castle," a poem that presents Webb's "image for the mind," for in-
stance, the poet pivots between some familiar dichotomies: inaction and
action, silence and speech, private and public, light and dark. At the
centre of the poet's mind is stillness, verging on paralysis; she feels
immobilized; all she can say is "'I am here. I do not know ...'"

(Webb's ellipses); she has only "moved the symbols and polished up the view"; her "statement" is "judicious and polite." The other female figures in this space have little to offer in the way of alternatives: "the antique whores and stoned Cassandras," on the one hand, represent abused and exploited women; "Sleeping Beauty" is the other extreme—the somnambulant woman who lies around waiting for a "princely kiss." The poem ends with a view of writing, too, as a balancing act:

> I do not mean I shall not crack the pane.
> I merely make a statement, judicious and polite,
> that in this poise of crystal space
> I balance and I claim the five gods of reality
> to bless and keep me sane. (*VT*, 50)

The poem moves from word to word with precisely measured steps. Most of the words are one-syllable units occupying equal amounts of time, perhaps reminiscent of Marianne Moore's syllabic verse which Webb consciously imitated in at least one early poem (Sujir interview, 32). In any case, the poem leaves one with the feeling of the (female) writer completely contained, if not immobilized, by the binary discourse that she occupies. Without recognizing the gender bias concealed within the binary oppositions, she has no way out of the paralysis.

Buddhism: Self/No-Self

In Buddhism, Webb finds further support for her resistance to the notion of singularity and unity. Buddhism, like Neo-Confucianism, emphasizes the permanent impermanence of everything, including the self. Webb became quite involved in Buddhism in the 1950s, to the point even of seriously considering becoming a Buddhist herself,[11] and some of her poems of the 1950s refer to Buddhist practice. "Sitting" enacts the Buddhist practice of meditation:

> The degree of nothingness
> is important:
> to sit emptily
> in the sun
> receiving fire
> that is the way
> to mend
> an extraordinary world,

sitting perfectly
still
and only
remotely human. (*VT*, 52)

In "To a Zen Buddhist Who Laughs Daily," she speaks of the healing power of Zen laughter:

O laugh laugh out the butterflies and dragons
from the places of desire,
Roar out the dalliance of the poppy's core,
Laugh out the lotus and hang it on
Pools of intuition. (*Trio*, n.p.)

In a footnote to this poem, Webb explains the Zen Buddhist mistrust of rationality

The rapid question and answer method between master and novice is one of many in which intuitive insights are gained; to go beyond the intellect is essential: "Zen roars with laughter at reasoning, logic and the laws of thought." (*Trio*, n.p.)

In another Zen-like poem, Webb first observes a "long line of baby caterpillars" following their leader in an orderly march to the "Japanese Plum Tree" and then exclaims: "Take away my wisdom and my categories," reflecting the Zen critique of orderly, rational thought (*VT*, 56). Indeed, her resistance to theorizing about her writing practice is perhaps rooted in this mistrust of analytic processes. As Buddhist scholar D.T. Suzuki explains, for the Buddhist, analysis is analogous to peeling an onion—it leads to nothing: "When skin after skin is taken off, we finally come to nothing, and there is no onion . . . when we analyze it it ceases to exist" (58). In an essay called "Notes on the Creative Process," Webb gives a similar view of the creative process. To her opening question "Where do poems come from?" she replies: "That is a continuing mystery unfolding itself with each new poem but never thoroughly disclosing itself" (*NBBS*, 25). Her emphasis on the "mystery" has parallels in the Buddhist doctrine of "becoming" in which "everything changes; everything is transient . . ." (Suzuki, 59-60).

But I'm not so much interested in Buddhism as a topic in Webb's work as in the implications of Buddhist thought for her poetics. Buddhist notions of no "self" (that is of no autonomous, stable subject) are particularly relevant to Webb's poetics. The *Encyclopedia of Religion* explains:

Our incapacity to control change . . . reveals the reality of no-self—
nothing is "I" or "mine." The experience of no-self, on the other
hand, is liberating; it releases one from craving and the causes of sor-
row; it leads to peace, *nirvana*. (357)

In such a view, notions of control—whether of language or world—
simply do not apply. In Webb's poetry of the 1950s, although she
sometimes occupies the position of the centred subject—as dictated by
the form of the lyric—she seems uncomfortable in that position and
destabilizes the singular "I" in various ways. In one of her early poems,
a Cartesian subject ("the I aware") and a historical subject ("born of the
weight of eons") interact with and destabilize each other continuously:

> This our inheritance
> is our distress,
> born of the weight of eons
> it skeletons our flesh,
> bearing us on
> we wear it
> though it bares us.
>
> The eye's lid covers
> the I aware,
>
> the hand hovers
> over, then plunders
> emerging despair.
> (". . . Is Our Distress," *Trio*; *SP*, 13; Webb's ellipses)

In "Poet," the pronoun "I," which appears twelve times in twenty-two
lines, speaks in many voices—the voice of God, a trickster's voice
which tells talltales from "the tallest of mouths," a parodic voice which
mocks the woman's nun-like submission to the holy orders of the
poem:

> I am promised
> I have taken the veil
> I have made obeisances
> I have walked on words of nails
> to knock on silences
> I have tokened the veil
> to my face
> mouth covered with symbol

[. . .]
and I have paced four walls
of this cell, I have paced
for the word, and I have heard,
curiously, I have heard the tallest of mouths
call down behind my veil
to limit or enlargen me
as I or it prevails. (*Trio*; *SP*, 14)

Some of Webb's early poems have the more traditional, self-expressive lyric subject. "Lament," for instance, revolves around a typically anguished lyric "I." But even here there is also an ironic awareness of a performative and constructed subjectivity:

But I, how can I, I,
craving the resolution of my earth
take up my little gang of sweet pretence
and saunter day-dreary down the alleys, or pursue
the half-disastrous night? Where is that virtue
I would claim with tense impersonal unworth,
where does it dwell, that virtuous land
where one can die without a second birth?

It is not here, neither in the petulance
of my cries, nor in the tracers of my active fear,
not in my suicide of love, my dear.
That place of perfect animals and men
is simply the circle we would charm our children in
and why we frame our lonely poems in
the shape of a frugal sadness. (*EYRE*; *VT*, 40)

While this poem perhaps relates more to a feminist critique of the historical limitations placed on women than to the Buddhist concept of no-self, Webb's reading in Buddhism contributes to this critique in providing an alternative to the Western equation of subjectivity and mastery.

In "Marvell's Garden," Webb interrogates the tradition of an autonomous and self-expressive "I" directly. In Andrew Marvell's seventeenth-century poem "The Garden," the poet lives apart from the world as a bird in a paradisal, secluded garden. Webb's poet still inhabits the garden, but reluctantly. Caught in shifting personal and cultural directives, "I" keeps changing positions and perspectives:

Marvell's garden, that place of solitude,
is not where I'd choose to live
yet is the fixed sundial
that turns me round
unwillingly
[. . .]
That was his garden, a kind of attitude
stuck out of an earth too carefully attended,
wanting to be left alone.
And I don't blame him for that.
God knows, too many fences fence us out
and his garden closed in on Paradise.

Here "I" shares the desire/need for separation of self and world; but further on, "I" weeps because of that separation: "Oh, I have wept for some new convulsion / to tear together this world and his." Yet the "I" is still drawn to his world:

But then I saw his luminous plumèd Wings
prepared for flight,
and then I heard him singing glory
in a green tree,
and then I caught the vest he'd laid aside
all blest with fire.

And I have gone walking slowly in
his garden of necessity
leaving brothers, lovers, Christ
outside my walls
where they have wept without
and I within. (EYRE; VT, 33-34)

Although "I" puts on the traditional poet's robes ("caught the vest he'd laid aside"), the image of the poet weeping behind the walls of the enclosed garden and the lovers and brothers weeping outside is hardly an unqualified affirmation of the tradition.

Here again is "gender trouble." The poem allegorizes the woman writer's personal and social losses on entering a traditionally male space and also questions its enclosures and exclusions. Still, the poem is cast in the traditional lyric mode of an autonomous consciousness engaged in personal exploration and discovery, so it has the effect of affirming while questioning that tradition. Not surprisingly, this poem has been considered one of Webb's best and has been frequently quoted and anthologized, a case of the canon perpetuating and reinforcing itself, of patriarchy reading women's texts in ways that fit its traditions.

While subverting the sovereign self by such means as self-parody, self-questioning, multiple speakers, or a fluid "I," Webb does not directly challenge the autonomous subject until the end of *The Sea Is Also a Garden* (1962). In the final poem of that book Webb gives a poetic manifesto of sorts which she calls a "Poetics Against the Angel of Death." She observes that traditional verse forms encode and enact an oppressive ideology and she proposes to escape via non-Western poetic forms; the "Great Iambic Pentameter" has become for her an "Angel of Death" or "Hound of Heaven." In recombining the traditional metaphors of Heavenly Angel and Hound from Hell into a demonic Heavenly figure, she emphasizes the debilitating effect of the hegemonic:

> I am sorry to speak of death again
> (some say I'll have a long life)
> but last night Wordsworth's "Prelude"
> suddenly made sense—I mean the measure,
> the elevated tone, the attitude
> of private Man speaking to public men.
> Last night I thought I would not wake again
> but now with this June morning I run ragged to elude
> The Great Iambic Pentameter
> who is the Hound of Heaven in our stress
> because I want to die
> writing Haiku
> or, better,
> long lines, clean and syllabic as knotted bamboo. Yes!
>   (*SIAG; VT*, 60)

The link Webb makes here between "measure" and "attitude" is crucial to her changing poetics because it links form and ideology. She sees that the iambic pentameter lines enact an ideology of mastery; to write in those forms is to be hounded by that ideology. Even the modernist lyric, notwithstanding its aperiodic rhymes and rhythms or collaged, multivoiced, fragmented structure, is essentially monologic[12] in the sense that there is an I/you structure at the centre of the poem, the I of "private Man speaking to public men."[13] Indeed, so dominant is this particular form of poetry that all poetry is often assumed to be lyric poetry. For instance, Bakhtin's claim that all poetry is by definition monologic conflates all poetry with the self-expressive lyric. Marjorie Perloff shows how Harold Bloom and others similarly assume that poetry means lyric. She cites Bloom, for instance, saying that

> from 1744 or so to the present day the best poetry internalized its subject matter, particularly in the mode of Wordsworth after 1798. *Wordsworth had no true subject except his own subjective nature*, and very nearly all significant poetry since Wordsworth, even by American poets, has repeated Wordsworth's inward turning. (Bloom, *Agon*, 1982, cited in Perloff, *Dance* . . . , 174, Perloff's emphasis)

Perloff's subsequent analysis, like Webb's statements in "Poetics Against the Angel of Death," points to poetic forms that are indeterminate and multivalent.

Webb's declared resistance to a poetics of "private Man speaking to public men" marks a deliberate shift in her writing away from lyric monologism. Her involvement in Buddhist and Confucian philosophy, I believe, contributed to this shift by providing alternative views of self and world.

By the 1960s, there were also alternative models in North America. In particular, the writers published in *The New American Poetry* anthology (1960), whom Webb read and met in Vancouver in the early 1960s, provided models for alternative poetic practices. In the work of Robert Creeley, Robert Duncan, Charles Olson, Denise Levertov, and Allen Ginsberg, Webb found particular tools for moving into open forms and further destabilizing the sovereign, monologic poetic self— tools such as tone leading of vowels, the breath line, and field composition. In "Polishing up the View," a radio talk based on a 1964 interview of Webb by Dorothy Livesay, Webb describes what she learned from these writers: Duncan "has the most to offer me because he is a great explorer in the realm of form. . . . And because he is very interested in *sound*, especially the vowel sounds . . ." (*T*, 46); "Creeley too," she continues "has been important simply because his music is so very subtle" (*T*, 47); Ginsberg offers a very different, but also useful model of "a poem which is sustained by a tremendous energy and by a kind of intuitive sense of form" (*T*, 47). From Olson, who "has solved the problem of line-breaking with a good deal of accuracy and perception," she learned about "the logic of the breath" (*T*, 48) and, finally, in Levertov's work, she understood how Olson's principle that "one perception must follow another perception immediately" determines line-

breaks and thus helped her to feel "more secure about my line endings"
(*T*, 49).

Naked Poems: "A new alphabet / gasps for air" (*VT*, 89)

The specificity of Webb's comments shows her debt to Olson, Duncan,
Levertov and others in developing an open-form poetics in *Naked
Poems*. Begun in the spring of 1963, *Naked Poems* is a watershed book
which marks a radical shift in Webb's poetics to "field" composition.[14]
Modelled partially on particle physics and gestalt psychology, field the-
ory posits a writing process in which all the ingredients of the poem
become part of a field of possibility within which the writer works.
Everything from the breath, vowel, consonant, word, line, and page to
meanings and themes are interconnected to produce the poem as "high
energy construct" (Olson, "PV" [1950], 148). The concept is not un-
like the Buddhist notion of a world in constant flux. Field theory, how-
ever, offered specific applications to the writing process; for Webb, it
provided the ways and means by which to develop "a new alphabet."

The "new alphabet" in *Naked Poems* is both formal and concep-
tual: Webb develops a woman-to-woman language, including the lan-
guage of a lesbian erotic, to displace the discourse of "private Man
speaking to public men." The short, haiku-like lines, surrounded by
white space, foreground the materiality of words; the variable rhythmic
weights and measures resist closing cadence; the incomplete syntax dis-
locates the direct line between subject-verb-object; and the narrative
trajectory of the serial poem intersects the lyric self to produce a series
of provisional subject positions rather than a stable, monologic subjec-
tivity. Here is the first poem of the book:

> MOVING
> to establish distance
> between our houses.
>
> It seems
> I welcome you in.
>
> Your mouth blesses me
> all over.
>
> There is room. (*VT*, 65)

The poem foregrounds various physical movements that are also emotionally "moving": the movements of bodies in making love, moving from house to house, and moving from word to word. The lover's mouth moves over the body; the reader's eye moves over the page. The writer moves around in language, moves language around, to make room(s) for the women lovers. "There is room" on the page for such movements. In the original Periwinkle press edition (and even on the slightly smaller pages of the 1971 *Selected Poems* and the 1982 *Vision Tree*), the spaciousness of the page gives each poem ample room. There is just one poem per page, taking up less than half of the six-by-nine inch page. The smallness of the poems in relation to the white space makes them *liminal*; positioned on the threshold of meaning and consciousness, they are barely perceptible.

These poems create new "rooms" in the discourse of love. In Suite I and Suite II, Webb constructs two suites of language rooms for the lovers to inhabit. A series of poems for the "Sweet One" (Suite I),[15] they are both a song to the lover (as in the musical term Suite) and a space for the lovers (as in a suite of rooms).

> AND
> here
> and here and
> here
> and over   and
> over   your mouth (*VT*, 66)

"Here" is on the page, in the ear, on the lover's body, and in language. The page, the word, the left-hand margin become palpable. They become threshold points, points where meanings emerge at the edges of silence and white space.

> YOU
> took
>
> with so much
> gentleness
>
> my dark (*VT*, 71)

As new rooms in language are constructed, the lyric I disperses into shifting and provisional constructs. The speaker's physical/mental position shifts, for instance, from opening the door to "welcome you in" (65) in the first poem, to turning inward ("I am enclosed / by a

thought" [67]), to watching "two flies / on the ceiling" (69), to rear-
ranging her room as a private sanctuary ("I people / this room / with
things" [70]). The speaker's discursive position also keeps shifting:
sometimes "I" addresses "you" directly (65); sometimes the "I" is self-
reflexive (69-70, 73, 77); sometimes "you" dominates (71,74); some-
times there is no grammatical subject at all (66).

Particularly in the third section of the book—titled "Non Lin-
ear"—the possibility of a monologic self is continually undermined by
nonlinear grammatical and discursive structures. With no grammatical
subject at all in the first two poems, each line begins within a field of
meaning. The prepositions define spatial relationships of near/far,
inside/outside, but there is neither agency nor action. Here is the sec-
ond poem in the "Non Linear" section:

> near the white Tanabe
> narcissus
> near Layton's *Love*
> daffodils
> outside   falling on
> the pavement
> the plum blossoms
> of Cypress Street (*VT*, 82)

The only verb—"falling"—introduces motion in the continuous
"ing" form that has no beginning or ending. These "Non Linear"
poems enact liminal subjectivities; they investigate a threshold con-
sciousness. When a grammatical subject does appear in the third poem
in the sequence, the "I" is literally in parenthesis:

> the yellow chrysanthemums
>   (I hide my head when I sleep)
> a stillness
> in jade
>   (Your hand reaches out)
> the chrysanthemums
> are
>   (Job's moaning, is it, the dark?
> a whirlwind!
> Eros! *Agapé Agapé* (*VT*, 83).

The gesture of the hand reaching toward love is also bracketed, as in-
deed the female erotic is bracketed by linguistic and social codes that

define woman as passive sexual objects. However, "Agapé" means not only the love of God (as in Job's moaning) but also a love feast and a state of being "wide open, in a state of wonder" (*Webster's New Collegiate Dictionary*). The last meaning includes the possibility of an emergent (lesbian) love.

In the next two poems, "I" comes out of hiding, although only to enter the unspoken and unwritten dark of women's absence and to speak her fears:

>   walking in dark
>   waking in dark the presence of all
>   the absences we have known.   Oceans.
>   so we are distinguished to ourselves
>   don't want that distinction.
>   I am afraid.   I said that.   I said that
>   for you. (*VT*, 85)

Not surprisingly, she is afraid of this dark. Waking and walking in the dark of the unspoken female erotic evokes all the negative terms of woman's sexuality—from the vagina *dentata* to Medusa's head of snake hair. Although the possibility of a pleasurable darkness was introduced in "Suite One" with the lines "YOU / took / with so much / gentleness / my dark" (*VT*, 71), the long tradition of negation is not easily erased. Here again, speaker and reader are in a liminal space. The only light to read by is moonlight, which the speaker equates with the romantic view of woman: "My white skin / is not the moonlight./ If it is / tell me, who reads / by that light?" (*VT*, 86). Who indeed! Certainly not the woman poet reading/ writing lesbian love.[16] Three poems later, a new language is born:

>   Hieratic sounds emerge
>   from the Priestess of
>   Motion
>   a new alphabet
>   gasps for air.
>
>   We disappear in the musk of her coming. (*VT*, 89)

Appropriately, the birth of this new language is described in erotic as well as apocryphal terms—"coming" is both sexual and apocryphal—suggesting the intense physical pleasure as well as the psychic release in the development of a women's discourse of love. The "we" who disappear (in the last line) are the women of patriarchal discourse: the iconic moonlit figure, the figure hiding her head, the self-parodying figure, the figure who is afraid of the female dark.

But the oppressive structures do not then instantly disappear. This is not the apocryphal birth of a fully formed autonomous individual as in the case of Aphrodite springing from the head of Zeus. This is the opening of a threshold. Three poems later, "I" wryly observes that no one has noticed the change:

> I have given up
> complaining
>
> but nobody
> notices (*VT*, 92)

And in the last poem, we find the limp body "falling / . . . into the arms of the oppressor," a reminder that patriarchal systems have not disappeared. The narrative trajectory of the book—which traces a liminal woman's consciousness and voice(s)—remains "Non Linear" (that is to say, there is no resolution). Instead, social, historical, and linguistic vectors continually intersect the I/eye, producing a polyvalent and variously constellated subject. However, the speaker's various activities do reconfigure and resemanticize female subjectivity as active and participatory.

The speaker's activities also reconfigure the discourse of romance. The flowers, birds, butterflies, plum blossoms, moonlight, and assorted colours, while referencing natural objects are also shown to be *words/ signs* in a semiotic system that equates nature with woman, spring with romance, and idealizes women to the point of immobility. The discourse of romance places women on a pedestal, as the idealized object of the male gaze; she occupies a "pseudo-centre, a mystifying centre, a blind spot" (Kristeva, *DL*, 50). The colours and objects in the poems invoke the old stories. Irving Layton's collection of *Love*[17] poems on the table is one obvious example *(VT*, 82).

But the active female subject also changes the stories, resemanticizes the images. The articulation of a lesbian erotic, for instance, introduces the possibility of pleasurable darkness. Likewise, the sunlight is not the light of Plato's world of absolute truth that exists outside the sensory (female) world; it is a "gold darkening / light" (*VT*, 78) within this particular Suite of (language) rooms. This light (tuth) is changed by the lesbian coding, here signified by the purple colour of the curtains:

"The sun comes through / plum curtains" (*VT*, 74). The speaker also distances herself from white as a symbol of female purity and innocence—represented in the poem in the white rose petals, the white painting, her white skin, and the whiteness of the moonlight. She declares: "My white skin / is not the moonlight" (*VT*, 86). And when the tide is out (signifying an opening in the discursive space?) a variegated collection of objects and colours appears: "green / moss weed / kelp shells pebbles / lost orange rind / orange crab" (*VT*, 87). When the tide comes in again, it is a flood tide with waves (of language, of desire, of Event) "hounding the window." Quite different from the "Hound of Heaven" in "Poetics Against the Angel of Death," this "hound" is from the earth:

> I hear the waves
> hounding the window:
> lord, they are the root waves
> of the poem's meter
> the waves of the
> root poem's sex.
> The waves of Event
> (the major planets, the minor
> planets, the Act)
> break down at my window:
> I also hear those waves. (*VT*, 90)

Finally, and perhaps most importantly, the traditional meaning of the Fall and the fallen woman is unsettled, in the last poem of the "Non Linear" section when the body falls "limp into the arms / of the oppressor" (*VT*, 93). This fall is both physical—like the plum blossoms falling, caused by the laws of gravity—and ethical, as in the fallen woman. But the cause of the woman's "fall" is not woman's weakness, as in the biblical story, but the oppressor's touch:

> "That ye resist not
> evil" falling
> limp into the arms
> of the oppressor
> he is not undone
> by the burden
> of your righteousness
> he has touched you (*VT*, 93)

In the last section of *Naked Poems*, titled "Some Final Questions," Webb continues to explore the vulnerability and instability of female subjectivity, especially as it is framed by hegemonic discourses. Here the investigation takes the form of self-interrogation. Webb poses the standard questions asked of the female subject under patriarchy: these are the questions that women ask themselves, that women ask of each other, that therapists ask, that husbands, lovers, brothers, fathers ask. *"What are you sad about? [. . .] Why are you standing there staring? [. . .] Now you are sitting doubled up in pain. / What's that for? [. . .] What do you really want?"* (*VT*, 101-104). This last question is especially resonant in that it echoes Freud's "what do women want" and brings in the whole discourse and practice of psychoanalysis and its interrogation of the female subject.

The question/answer structure of this section enacts the female split subject who, on the one hand, internalizes the patriarchal discourse that silences her, while, on the other, struggles to reshape that discourse. The white space on the page between the questions and answers further enacts that split. But the white space also foregrounds the gaps, divisions, and tensions between question and answer and thus initiates a transformative process. At first the respondent is typically passive, detached from her own feelings: "I am watching a shadow / shadowing a shadow" (*VT*, 102) is one response. In the next, she withdraws into a protective foetal position, a posture that offers both self-protection and self-creation.

> doubled up I feel
> small like these poems
> the area of attack
> is diminished (*VT*, 103)

But when the questioner asks about desire (with Freud's question "*What do you really want?*"), the respondent becomes more assertive. She "wants" the apple from the Tree of Knowledge—symbol of female weakness and subservience in patriarchal discourse—but she "wants the apple" resemanticized as a sign/symbol of an embodied knowledge:

> want the apple on the bough in
> the hand in the mouth seed
> planted in the brain want
> to think "apple" (*VT*, 104)

She wants to get out of the Garden of Eden and enter a world where eating an apple signifies an active, sensory, thinking, feeling consciousness.

The transformation of women into an active subject is also facilitated by simply refusing to answer the questioner. When, in the next exchange, the speaker asks: *"I don't get it. Are you talking about / process and individuation. Or absolutes / whole numbers that sort of thing?* (*VT*, 104) the reply is simply the colloquial "Yeah." This defiant nose-thumbing gesture both mocks and diverts attention away from the formal discourse. The questioner's language loses some of its power and authority in the face of the defiant "Yeah." The next exchange continues the focus on language issues: "I am trying to write a poem" is the answer to *"But why don't you do something?"* (*VT*, 106) suggesting that one way to empower the female subject is through speaking/writing the self (selves). But the questioner has the last word, with the final question *"Oh?"* (*VT*, 108) which receives no response, leaving female subjectivity still in process.

By writing women's internalized questions and uncertainties, by foregrounding the various discourses and disguises that construct female subjectivity, Webb opens up possibilities for action and agency. In *Naked Poems*, Webb not only thematizes female vulnerability; she also initiates a transformative process. Her interrogation of language and subjectivity breaks open the "darknesses" associated with the female erotic and intermingles romanticized object and active subject within a "new language."

Active/Passive Processes

Following *Naked Poems*, Webb continues the process of reconfiguring female subjectivities within various discursive fields by making "trouble," to return to my opening argument. Since I discuss *Wilson's Bowl*, *Water and Light*, and *Hanging Fire* extensively in the next three chapters, I will here only briefly outline some of the features of Webb's poetics in those books. In *Wilson's Bowl*, Webb moves away from the intensely personal world of *Naked Poems* into "a study of power" in historical and social domains (*WB*, Foreword). The specific subjects include "Portraits" of historical and contemporary father figures and investigations of social issues such as war crimes, torture, and imprisonment ("Crimes"). The poems are also formally quite different, with longer lines and larger, more varied structures. Webb's poetics in *Wilson's Bowl* is initially informed by her interest in anarchist political theory, a theory that attracted her because of its opposition to centres and authorities.[18] While Webb eventually realized that anarchist theory in itself functioned as an authority structure (it was "totally unauthoritarian," she comments, "except I had my authority in Kropotkin, as a godlike or Christlike figure" [Sujir interview, 34]), it provided a useful impetus for her initial resistance to established systems. But when she read Adrienne Rich's *Of Woman Born* in the 1970s, she turned to feminist analyses of societal structures as a means to overcome her dependency on authority figures of various kinds.

Equally important, I believe, to Webb's investigations of decentred personal and poetic structures in *Wilson's Bowl* were the Haida creation stories which Webb became interested in during the 1970s via "a strange network of connections" with Lilo Berliner, Beth and Ray Hill, and Wilson Duff.[19] Webb draws on concepts from the Haida creation myths—in particular, the Haida concept of creation as intertransformation—to undermine the binary structures of Western thought which assign second-class status to women, to aboriginal people, and to any "Others" who are identified with the antirational, "primitive," "dark" side of the binary system. As with Webb's use of Confucianism and Buddhism in the 1950s, she found concepts in the Haida stories that helped her to challenge her own traditions.[20]

In the Haida creation story, Raven creates the world via a process quite unlike the Christian concept of creation as a single, individual act of "in the beginning God created the heaven and the earth." According to the Haida legend, Raven and his mother come into being simultaneously: as Raven's mother is creating him, Raven is creating his mother. Wilson Duff, writing about the Haida response to "the paradox of creation, which the mind creates by postulating an initial nothingness out of which the world emerges" explains:

> But how can something be formed out of nothing? The Haida answer was to construct another intertransformation of two opposite things into each other. Raven, in the fact of being born, brings into existence his own mother. A process, creating its own antecedents and its own consequences, both at the same time. Needless to say, in this system there is no "beginning of time," there only exists the present moment. There is no creation, there is only transformation. Opposites intertransforming into each other. (Quoted in Webb, *NBBS*, 120)

In this model, creation—whether of a world or a poem—is interactive rather than autonomous.

Webb's poem "Free Translations" (*WB*, 56-57) is based on a simi-
lar model; she offers a translation that involves interactions and inter-
transformations between Christian and Haida creation stories. First,
Webb translates the *form* of the Haida story: the five nesting boxes
described in the legend are replicated in the five-part form of the poem.
As well, Raven is "intertransformed" into a hybrid figure. The recita-
tion of Raven's daily acts in the poem echoes the Christian narrative of
a seven-day creation process, but the actions themselves (hiding, chasing
women, showing off, stealing, etc.) are typical of Raven's trickster role
in Haida legends. Raven is also modernized and Americanized—he
"sings Cole Porter songs in the shower / and thinks he's James Cagney"
(*WB*, 56) yet he also performs his traditional life-giving role: "he's
going to steal the sun. . . . / Then we can all shine" (*WB*, 57).

One of the effects of Webb's "Free Translations" is to inter-
transform the initial nothingness and emptiness described at the start of
the poem into the shining sun by the end. The poem begins with
"nothing":

> Raven did not come on Thursday.
> He sent nothing.
> Not a word. Not a sign.
> Nothing on Thursday. Nothing on Friday. Nothing
> on Saturday. Nothing on Sunday.
> Then he sent eagles. (*WB*, 56)

But by the time the reader hears nothing for the third time, it has become
something. By the fifth repetition, nothing is full of possibility. Similarly,
the pivotal third section of the poem begins with the baby raven and ends
with the mother and thus further foregrounds the intertransformative
processes that changes nothing into something. A "negative transparency"
(in the photographic sense suggested by Homi Bhabha discussed earlier in
this chapter) is converted to a positive via the semantic chemistry of repe-
tition and variation (i.e., "free translations"). In the closing image, the
poem is suffused with a collective light.

The connections to the Haida concepts of interactive creation pro-
cesses are obvious here because Webb works directly with the Haida
legend. A less obvious parallel is enacted in the various intertextual
translations and intertransformations in other poems in *Wilson's Bowl*[21]
(see chapter 5). As well, the circular, circling forms of Webb's *Ghazals
and Anti Ghazals* in *Water and Light* (1984), discussed in the next two
chapters, enact interactive and intertransformative creative process.

More recently, in *Hanging Fire* (1990), Webb cultivates a "curvilin-
ear, or else an oblique, angled, perverse method" ("MM," *LIHE*, 294)
that similarly brings together receptivity and agency in an interactive
relation. Her method in *Hanging Fire*, as she explains at the start of the
book, was to wait for " 'given' words, phrases, or sentences that arrive
unbidden in my head" (*HF*, 7). Her initial position is passive and recep-
tive, but she also has agency in the sense that she produces the phrases
(they occur in her head) and she writes the poems. She simultaneously
invents and receives, just as Raven creates his mother even as she is
creating him. Webb's passivity is intertransformative, not only in the
genesis of the poems, but also in the sense that her receptive stance
opens up communication channels between the private self and the
public, intertextual, and social contexts that are brought into the poem
by the received words and phrases. Webb explains the expansive effects
of her passivity in an interview with Smaro Kamboureli: "this passive
process of awaiting the words, listening for the words, and then writing
from them, responding to them, . . . led me so much outward. This
very inward, private process, led me more and more outside. It con-
nected me, it associated me with the outside world" (Kamboureli inter-
view, 30).

However, in an essay written shortly after *Hanging Fire* was com-
pleted, Webb questions her apparent passivity in the writing process,
asking "[d]oes it reflect more accurately than I'd care to admit the laid-
back, unwilled, apolitical position of the supine female of all those
nudes and odalisques of so many paintings from the cultural 'patri-
mony,' " ("MM," *LIHE*, 293). But later in the essay, she concludes that
her process of "intense listening" (293) is not entirely passive:

> These conscious questionings of my own passivity have, I realize now,
> been more pervasive over the last two years than I'd noticed. Take the
> most extraordinary, for me, of my given phrases, "the salt tax."
> Where did it come from, why? I heard it very clearly for the first time
> on September 8, 1988. It was followed by "paradigm shift" and "cos-
> mic rays" on September 12, "seeing is believing" on the 13th and
> 14th, and "the cedar trees" on the 15th. I knew what the salt tax was,
> and had been greatly moved when I was young by Gandhi's person
> and his philosophy of passive resistance, Satyagraha, but the phrase
> seemed unpromising as an entry into a poem. Even with all those
> other phrases beaming in, an unusual number of them, "the salt tax"
> recurred insistently and I finally wrote the poem on September
> 17th. . . . It is, I hope, not too far-fetched to suggest that the poem
> commemorating Gandhi's trek to the sea to protest the salt tax, "to

steal a handful of free-ee-ee-ee-dom" is in some subliminal way dealing with my own passivity, offering reconciliation. The hooking together of "passive" and "resistance" with such a neat paradoxical click made a supremely useful political slogan that's had a long life. It tells me again that some kinds of passive behaviour are productive of real change, social and otherwise. (295-96)

Like Gandhi's passive resistance, which successfully undermined and transformed the colonial system in India, Webb's passive/active listening provides an effective means of resisting and intertransforming established (and colonizing) knowledge systems.

Webb's compositional method in *Hanging Fire* thus gave her yet another way to undermine the autonomous self, to generate polyvocality, and to explore issues of power and control. The metaphor of holding your fire, suggested by the title *Hanging Fire*, figures a passive resistance of extreme intensity. From the "Poet" of the early 1950s who questions her various guises and disguises, to the actively passive and passively active subject positions in *Hanging Fire*, Webb offers a politically and socially committed poetry that powerfully resists controlling and limiting structures and in so doing generates ways of seeing and being in the "dark."

Notes

1 Just before Lilo Berliner committed suicide, she left her letters from Wilson Duff on Webb's doorstep, thus involving Webb fairly directly in both the event of the suicide and in the correspondence between Wilson Duff and Lilo Berliner that preceded it. See chapter 7 for more details about Webb's friendship with Berliner and Webb's publication of a selection of the Berliner/Duff letters in "A Correspondence" (*NBBS*). See also note 19 below.

2 See chapter 7 for more discussion of Webb's essay on the correspondence between Wilson Duff and Lilo Berliner and its relationship to the "Wilson's Bowl" poems.

3 "Performance" was first published in *Canadian Literature*, 100 (1984): 352-53.

4 Butler opens the book with a delightful spin on the word "trouble," a spin that turns it into a positive term: "To make trouble was, within the reigning discourse of my childhood, something one should never do precisely because that would get one *in* trouble. The rebellion and its reprimand seemed to be caught up in the same terms, a phenomenon that gave rise to my first critical insight into the subtle ruse of power: The prevailing law threatened one with trouble, even put one in trouble, all to keep one out of

trouble. Hence, I concluded that trouble is inevitable and the task, how best to make it, what best way to be in it" (Butler, *Gender Trouble*, ix).

5 See Janice Williamson's essay "The Feminine Suicide Narratives of Phyllis Webb," *West Coast Line* Number Six, 25, 3 (1991-92): 155-74.

6 I am referring to "Falling Glass" (Webb's section of *Trio*), *Even Your Right Eye*, and *The Sea Is Also a Garden*.

7 I am not sure whether Webb had read Sartre's *Being and Nothingness* (first published in France in 1943) when she wrote this poem in the early 1950s. The English translation did not appear until 1955. However, I am assuming Webb would have been familiar with earlier works of Sartre's which form the basis of *Being and Nothingness* from her studies in philosophy at the University of British Columbia (1945-49). In any case, I find striking parallels between the scene described by Sartre and Webb's poem. In *Being and Nothingness*, Sartre writes: "I am in a public park. Not far away there is a lawn and along the edge of that lawn there are benches. A man passes by those benches. I see this man; I apprehend him as an object and at the same time as a man. What does this signify? What do I mean when I assert that this object is a man?" (254). Further on, he explains the effects of the man's presence on his own being: "The Other is first the permanent flight of things toward a goal which I apprehend as an object at a certain distance from me but which escapes me inasmuch as it unfolds about itself its own distances. . . . Thus suddenly an object has appeared which has stolen the world from me. Everything is in place; everything still exists for me; but everything is traversed by an invisible flight and fixed in the direction of a new object. The appearance of the Other in the world corresponds therefore to a fixed sliding of the whole universe, to a decentralization of the world which undermines the centralization which I am simultaneously effecting" (255).

8 Bryson's comments are made in the context of explaining a critique of Sartre in Japanese philosophy by "the most influential Japanese philosopher of the twentieth century, Nishida" whose ideas are explained in Keiji Nishitani's *Religion and Nothingness*. "Nishitani's critique of Sartre," Bryson explains, which "occupies a crucial section of Nishitani's book *Religion and Nothingness*, is based on "the observation that with Sartre there is no radical overturning of the enclosure of thought which treats the questions of ontology, of subject and object, from *within the standpoint of the subject*. Nishitani argues that the Sartrean *je* is capable of reaching a level of nihility in which everything that exists is cast into doubt, except the fundamental irreducibility of the *je* which does the doubting" (94-95).

9 Curiously, Webb agreed with Sharon Thesen's suggestion that these lines be omitted when the poem was republished in *The Vision Tree* in 1982, perhaps because of the extreme passivity implied by the ironic, distancing tone ("That [revision] was very much Sharon's insistence," Webb explains to Stephen Scobie, "and I agreed with her, but now when I read it over I

still hear the old rhythm, and think 'Oh, there's something missing'" [Scobie interview, 4]).

10 See, for instance, Helen Sonthoff's article "Structure of Loss: The Poetry of Phyllis Webb," *Canadian Literature*, 9 (1961): 15-22, and John Hulcoop's introduction to the 1971 edition of *Selected Poems* (Vancouver: Talonbooks, 1971), 9-41. Hulcoop, however, offers a somewhat different reading of the poem some twenty years later in his ECW monograph *Phyllis Webb*. Referring to "Old Woman" and "Double Entendre," Hulcoop comments: "In these two poems, we hear the voice of the feminist poet struggling to express itself in / in spite of / against a world of man-made, man-measured time" (31).

11 Webb explains to Eleanor Wachtel that "I actually made this real decision about whether or not to become a Buddhist. I was living on University Avenue [in Montreal], in an awful, beastly room. I read Mann's *The Magic Mountain*, which produced the need for a decision. I concluded that I was too much a North American, that I really believed in conflict and suffering for growth. I was too much of a materialist—the rational, socialist world brought me back" (quoted in Watchtel, 11).

12 I use this term as defined by M.M. Bakhtin in *The Problem of Dostoevsky's Poetics* to refer to a structure that constructs a single consciousness and worldview or ideology, although there may be many different voices (79-80).

13 Antony Easthope explains with regard to Eliot's "The Wasteland": "Subject and object are no longer represented as reciprocally held in place, and the referential effect is not achieved. Yet the poem still represents a speaker, an 'I' aware of itself and its feelings . . ." (*Poetry as Discourse*, 137-38). While Webb's "I"/eye(s) is certainly "aware of itself and its feeling," I don't think it occupies as central a position in the poem as Eliot's does.

14 See Charles Olson's discussion of "composition by field" in his essay "Projective Verse" and Robert Duncan's essay "Ideas of the Meaning of Form" as well as his poetry collection *The Opening of the Field*.

15 Resonating with Susan Rudy Dorscht's essay (see note 16).

16 For further discussion of the problems in writing the lesbian erotic see Susan Rudy Dorscht's analysis of "the discourses of compulsory heterosexuality" in "poems dressed in a dress and naked: sweet lines from phyllis" (*West Coast Line* Number Six, 25, 3 [1991/92]: 54-63).

17 Probably a reference to the anthology *Love Where the Nights Are Long: Canadian Love Poems*, selected by Irving Layton and published by McClelland and Stewart in 1962.

18 Webb explains in the "Notes to the Poems" at the back of *Wilson's Bowl* that her interest in anarchism began with Paul Goodman's novel *The Empire City* and continued with her study of the Russian anarchist Prince Kropotkin. She also notes that "[t]wo basic works on the life of Kropotkin are *Memoirs of a Revolutionalist*, by Peter Kropotkin, ed. James Allen Rogers

(Gloucester, Mass.: Peter Smith, 1967), and *The Anarchist Prince* by George Woodcock and Ivan Avakumovic (London: T.V. Boardman & Co., Ltd., 1950)" (*WB*, 87).

19 Webb explains this "strange network of connections" as follows: "Early in 1973, Lilo Berliner, a reference librarian at the University of Victoria, wrote to Wilson Duff, a well-known anthropologist and professor at the University of British Columbia, requesting permission to xerox one of his papers, 'Levels of Meaning in Haida Art.' Lilo was passionately interested in Northwest Coast Indian art, particularly petroglyphs—Indian rock carvings. It was because of my own new discovery of petroglyphs in 1970 that I was introduced first to Lilo Berliner and then to Beth Hill, who was working on her book *Indian Petroglyphs of the Pacific Northwest*. Duff had sent Beth Hill his 'Levels of Meaning' and she had shown it to Lilo. This strange network of connections was to affect all our lives in ways we could not foresee" ("A Correspondence," *NBBS*, 111). See also notes 2 and 3 above.

20 Because Webb uses the Haida legends as a way of seeing her own culture differently, as a basis for critiquing Western traditions, I would argue that hers is not an appropriation of native material. In my view, appropriation involves using native legends for their exotic and/or entertainment value and/or assuming unquestioned ownership of them.

21 For further discussion of intertextuality in *Wilson's Bowl*, see chapter 5.

2

Reading *Water and Light*

Water and Light, Webb's collection of *Ghazals and Anti Ghazals* published in 1984, dazzles the reader with poems that shimmer and shine like the water and light of the title, but it is also a difficult book to read because the reader finds herself, as in Webb's previous books, drawn into clusters of meaning particles rather than offered narrative paths or epiphanic lyric moments. She finds herself in the "grand dark," as in the title poem:

> WATER AND LIGHT   WATER AND LIGHT
> and the grand dark attending (*WL*, [6])

The reader's field of sensibility and meaning is complicated by this attendant "grand dark." As well, the ghazal form itself—a form of Urdu poetry in which "each couplet [is] wholly independent of any other in meaning" (Ahmad, 1971, xvi)—fractures meaning into discrete units and adds a formal disjunctiveness.[1]

Water and Light thus invites a participatory reader who is willing to construct, dissolve, and reconstruct meanings as she reads; who recognizes that reading involves a "convergence of text and reader" (Iser, 1988, 212) rather than a direct transfer of information; and who recognizes her complicity in defining meaning and value. Such a reader is neither innocent nor neutral. She recognizes the engagement of the text with a body and the engagement of that body with history. In the process, as Patrocinio Schweickart explains, "[r]eading induces a doubling of the reader's subjectivity, so that one can be placed at the disposal of the text while the other remains with the reader" (Schweickart, 31). As clear as this may sound "in theory," as they say, I have found this difficult to do in practice. Old reading and writing habits are hard to break. At a particularly frustrating point in my process, I shifted to a journal as a means of working though some of the problems.

The notes to this chapter are on p. 57-58.

March 13. *How to position myself as reader/critic. Why say anything about a poem. Don't want to be the connoisseur who speaks from a position of superior sensibility. Why not? Because that reader stays in the armchair comfort zone, in the light, never considering or questioning his (yes usually male) assumptions. I want to move in/with the text, want to be aware of my movements. How does a reader see in the dark? Enough delaying tactics Pauline. Time to start writing.*

March 15. *What glasses shall I put on today—always struggling to find a workable frame, lens, position. Yesterday, I got excited about Webb's play with the ghazal form. I saw all the language structures that she works with—sound patterns, line balances and imbalances, rhythmic play, cadence—a merry-go-round. How to talk about my pleasure? What is an embodied pleasure? I want an experiential approach in this chapter . . . yet just "reading" the poems seems boring boring.*

March 25. *Coming back to this chapter after a break I think I see the problem. As a reader/listener, I like being "inside" the poem, experiencing, drifting here and there. But as a feminist critic, teacher, writer, I want to look at political questions, see the poem in social and theoretical contexts. That puts me "outside" the poem (sort of) . . . a mind/body split? . . . No, it's more that "doubling of the reader's subjectivity" that Schweickart speaks of. On rereading the chapter, I find it doesn't occupy this middle ground. . . . It's an amorphous blur.*

April 2. *Talking with J. to-day, I realized it's the erotic, sensual activity that I like so much in Webb's work. Words have a kind of sexual energy, they attract each other . . . or move away. But I don't have a language to talk about that. What is an embodied criticism? Even though I've learned most of what I know about poetry from talking with people at my dining room table, when it comes to writing, I lose touch with that embodied experience. How to get the sensual/experiential into critical writing? Yikes, too much risk!*

April 4. *So you think you're an innocent reader do you. Ha. You want to just write your spontaneous responses to the poems, but you don't like what you write. Of course not because it proposes a fake innocence. Being in the dark does not mean you are innocent, or passive. You have to be even* more *active, more aware of context, more aware of how seeing is ideological.*

April 16. *To-day Webb's title "Middle Distance" makes sense as a metaphor for the different places/spaces of writing, a point of many convergences. I like the metaphor of being in the midst, with a moveable centre. Truth as a variable, moving point. As a mobile unit. Always relational. I don't have to compartmentalize. This allows me* inside *the poem, gets the personal* inside *the political or social context.*

Clustering

Clustering, a term widely used in recent studies of brain processes to describe the right-brain intuitive leaps that connect seemingly random particles (Rico, 5-20), provides one model for reading Webb's *Water and Light*. The words, sounds, sights in the poems coalesce into temporary clusters of meaning, formed along associative trajectories. Clustering is also the term Webb used to describe how she wrote and then later organized these poems: "The book got structured after the poems got written," she comments, "and I began to see the clustering that had already happened" (Butling interview). Webb explains that she then added the Section titles to reflect the clusters that had occurred. This chapter likewise is structured in several clusters based on the diverse but overlapping directions that my reading of the poems has taken me.

In the following reading of one ghazal (or is it an anti ghazal?), the clustering processes initiate, for me, a complex "seeing":

> My loves are dying. Or is it that my love
> is dying, day by day, brief life, brief candle,
>
> a flame, *flambeau*, torch, alive, singing
> somewhere in the shadow: Here, this way, here.
>
> Hear the atoms ambling, the genes a-tick
> in grandfather's clock, in the old bones of beach.
>
> Sun on the Sunday water in November.
> Dead leaves on wet ground. The ferry leaves on time.
>
> Time in your flight—O—a wristwatch strapped
> to my heart, ticking erratically, winding down. (*WL*, 17)

Love, loves, dying, dying, brief, brief at the start of this poem, I am drawn into the litany of repeating sounds in a single beat rhythm. A sensory pleasure. But what about all the dying? Are her lovers dying? Or is she losing the ability to love? Or is it love in general that is dying? Probably all of the above and more. I recognize the familiar lyric romantic angst about transience and decay. The echo of Shakespeare's lines "out, out brief candle / life's but a walking shadow" (*Macbeth*) sets off a string of associations about the meaning (or meaninglessness) of life. Dying, dying, day by day—a literary litany. But the next couplet shifts to the light/life, heat/passion of "a flame, flambeau, torch, alive, singing / somewhere in the shadow: Here, this way, here." The associative process leads from Shakespeare's "brief candle" in the first couplet to "a flame" at the start of the second. No more romantic angst. The lines pick up energy, speed. But "Here" stops me, especially the second time it appears ("Here, this way, here"). I stop, feel, see, hear the words as material. As ignition point. Also as affirmation: the homonym "hear hear" is a statement of agreement and approval. Yes, indeed.

In the next (and last) three couplets, I follow several diverse trajectories, formed through clustering processes. In some cases, words are linked by assonance "atoms ambling," "old bones of beach." Indeed, sounds often lead the poem: "Sun" leads to "Sunday water"; "dead leaves" to "The ferry leaves"; "time // Time" to "flight" to "winding" (which echoes the opening sounds in dying dying). With each couplet, I see particles of language clustering into different arrangements of rhythm, tone, sound, and meaning.

Clustering also offers me a way to talk about thematic structures without using the discourse of universalism. In the above poem, for instance, on a second or third reading, I begin to see thematic links. A motif of death and dying runs throughout, for instance, in the "shadow" on the edges of the candlelight, in the "old bones," the "dead leaves," and the "heart winding down." As well, life continues in the genetic networks ("genes a-tick") and in the sub-atomic world ("atoms ambling"), but life is also being damaged or destroyed by these same processes—via genetic engineering and atomic bombs. Growth and decay again intermingle in the fourth couplet where "leaves" functions as both noun and verb. The leaves on the ground and the ferry leaving enact the passages of time which produce both growth and decay. Yet, while the poem addresses current concerns with ecological imbalances in genetic and biological systems, any impulse to generalize or universalize is intercepted by the presence of other semantic/phonic clustering processes that move in other directions.

Indeed, in another ghazal from the first section, the process of clustering is thematized as a push/pull of centripetal and centrifugal movements. Centripetal movements are metaphorized as the "pull / . . . of the pen across the page" which pulls the poem toward the normative while the centripetal, "the forward memory / of hand beyond the grasp," moves toward excess and disarray, away from the "grasp" of the centre. Centripetal and centrifugal trajectories are also enacted in the movement of lines toward and away from the ghazal norm of balanced couplets. Notice the varying line lengths:

> The pull, this way and that, ultimately the pull
> of the pen across the page.
>
> Sniffing for poems, the forward memory
> of hand beyond the grasp.
>
> Not grasping, not at all. *Reaching* is
> different—can't touch that sun.
>
> Too hot. That star. This cross-eyed
> vision. Days and nights, sun, moon—the up-there claptrap.
>
> And down here, trappings of "as above"—crosswalks,
> traffic lights, sirens, this alexandrite burning on this hand.
>
> (*WL*, 18)

"Grasping" is the centrifugal, generalizing, and deadening "up-there claptrap"—which holds meanings in place; "reaching" is the "forward memory / of hand," the centripetal pen sniffing out possibilities. Webb's "cross-eyed / vision" intermingles the two, collapsing the old binaries of "up-there" and "down-here," heaven and earth, mind and body, general and particular, intellectual and sexual, male and female. Words cluster at various "crosswalks" in the poem where the red and green traffic lights enact centrifugal and centripetal trajectories. Similarly, the alexandrite stone changes colour from grass-green to red when the light changes to artificial or transmitted light (as the discourse of universalism stops the traffic flow?). The reader remains at the crosswalk where both red and green traffic lights operate, aware of the attendant "grand dark."

Thematic clusters are also generated by the quotations from the ghazals of the Urdu writer Ghalib, which serve as epigraphs for each of the five sections of the book. The first epigraph, for instance, Ghalib's self-reflexive comment that "*I'm too old for an inner wildness, Ghalib, / when the violence of the world is all around me,*" generates clusters of words, images, meanings around themes of aging and violence. Throughout section one, death appears in many forms: in the beheading of women in the first poem, the black death on the rose bush or the sheep going to slaughter in the second, the crash of the dead tree in the third, the "morning poem destroyed" in the fifth, the giant bird Yahweh crushing his eggs in the nest in the sixth, the darkness that comes as "Evening Autumn closes in" in the seventh, the violent storm in the eighth, and the litany of dying in the ninth:

> My loves are dying. Or is it that my love
> is dying, day by day, brief life, brief candle, (WL, 17)

On the other hand, the phrase "inner wildness" generates a contrapuntal cluster of regenerative images that intervene in the "violence all around us." Several poems end with images of growth or birth, for instance. At the end of the fifth poem, "All the big animals turn toward the Great Wall of China" (WL, 13), certainly a new direction if not a new beginning. In the next, although the "eggs of Yahweh" are destroyed, the last words of the poem offer the nurturing image of "his warm breast" (WL, 14). The seventh ends with the word "*Seeds*" and the image of the poet "flying East" on the wings of Japanese poetic forms which, like the wing-shaped maple tree seed-pods, carry the seeds for new growth (WL, 15). Also, the title of the section—"Sunday Water"—points to the transformative process of baptism which imbues the body with spirituality as well as to the restorative effects of writing: Webb describes the writing process as itself a kind of Sunday water, the last six poems being a "quiet storm of six" written "on Sunday, November 29" (Preface, SW).

As the term clustering denotes, however, these meanings only temporarily cohere in different formations within dynamic fields. In the closing ghazal of section one, the visionary third eye (that "all-seeing" inner eye) proves intimidating rather than transformative, which undermines any possibility of a metanarrative of resolution. As well, the disjunctive form of the ghazal (which I examine closely in the next chapter)—where rhyme rather than reason is the organizing principle—continually interrupts or destabilizes settled meanings. I quote the entire poem:

> The card is dealt, out of the blank pack,
> preordained, imprinted on hidden lines.
>
> Now for the Third Eye to read the grown signs:
> flickers of doubt tic mouth, twitch eye's lid.
>
> But it's open—always—the third one,
> guardian of splendours, crimes.

Seeing all, all-seeing, even in sleep knows
space (outer, inner, around), tracks freak snows,

slumbering ponies. Love, I am timid
before this oracular seer, opal, apple of my eye. (*WL*, 21)

Here both ideological and formal "preordained" patterns assert them-
selves: the poem returns to the prescribed pattern of five couplets
(which Webb had departed from in the preceding two ghazals); it has
the prescribed rhyme pattern ("lines . . . signs . . . eye's . . . crimes . . .
I . . . eye"); and the speaker is structured by prescribed social conven-
tions "imprinted on hidden lines" which predetermine her response to
Love. Love with a capital "L" proposes a perfection, an oppressive
idealization ("apple of my eye") which she cannot possibly live up to.
The violence here is ideological. However, regenerative possibilities
have not disappeared altogether; they float as particles, as individual
word/sounds/images which could recombine to form different clusters
of rhyme, alternative structures of meaning.

Double(d) Agent: "I Daniel"

In "I Daniel"—the third section of *Water and Light*—the notion of
clustering applies not only to thematic structures but also to the speak-
ing subject. The polymorphous personae of this section—figured in
the grammatical blend of subject and object in "I Daniel"—is inhab-
ited by several subject positions: "I Daniel" includes action and agency,
messenger and message, male and female (on hearing Webb read the
poem out loud, for instance, the historical male voice of the biblical
Daniel is noticeably "contaminated" by being spoken in the female reg-
ister). The reader too inhabits the cluster; as Stephen Scobie summar-
izes: "Daniel is both messenger and source, critic and author, reader
and writer" (Scobie, "I and I," 67).

The first poem of the sequence introduces this multivoiced, con-
stellated subject, intertwined with linguistic, social, and historical reali-
ties:

But I Daniel was grieved
and the vision of my head troubled me,

and I do not want to keep
the matter in my heart

for the heart of the matter
is something different.

Neither do I want happiness
without vision.

I am apocryphal and received.
I live now and in time past

among all kinds of musick—sackbut,
cornet, flute, psaltery, harp, and dulcimer.

You come bearing jobs and treachery and money,

but I Daniel, servant to powers
that pass all understanding,

grieve into time, times, and the dividing of time. (*WL*, 35)

"I Daniel" is not an individual, autonomous consciousness, nor a nar-
cissistic subject that speaks the self; the "I" in the above poem is a
clustered subjectivity formed at the intersections of time, history, lan-
guage, music, money, happiness, grief, and individual/social reality. It is
shaped by the spiritual, the material, and the historical ("time, times
and the dividing of time"). In subsequent poems, "I" is variously self-
serving: "I . . . pocket the coin" (*WL*, 37), narcissistic: "my own name
fascinates me" (*WL*, 36), and altruistic: "I also serve the kings" (*WL*,
36). He is also confused (*WL*, 39), duplicitous ("I play and trick my
way" [*WL*, 42]), sorrowful and sick (*WL*, 40-41). The requirements for
the position of speaking subject include a mixture of receptivity, acuity,
ignorance, blindness, narcissism, materialism, humility, selfishness, and
altruism:

Listen, I dream the dream,
I deliver its coded message

and pocket the coin.
Keep your jobs and dollars.

I go into the dark on the King's business
and spend my time thanking him

for the privilege of my servitude. (*WL*, 37)

One of the most striking features of Webb's polymorphous "I Daniel" is his loss of individuality and originality, those mainstays of the Cartesian I. Daniel's vision derives from re-membering rather than from inspiration: for instance, when King Nebuchadnezzar announces that he had a prophetic dream but he can't remember it, and commands Daniel to "remember" it for him, Daniel does so by plugging into a textual field, so to speak, and producing a "printout of the King's text":

> here, now, in my own hand
> the printout of the King's text
>
> which he has forgotten
> and I remember. (*WL*, 37)

The metaphor of a "printout" locates the source of vision within a textual field rather than in a transcendent realm, and reconfigures the writer as one who re-members rather than invents, who often does not understand the message, who speaks from within the dark. Sometimes Daniel simply listens to "a silver bird / flying about my ears"; sometimes he turns inward: "I closed my eyes and sealed them" (*WL*, 38). Then he can hear "the bird / song in the apparatus" (*WL*, 38); sometimes he is as much reader as writer: "The hand moved along the wall. / I was able to read, that's all" (*WL*, 39).

Similarly, the reader too re-members the poem in the sense that she puts the pieces together. The reader's active role is emphasized in the epigraph to the "I Daniel" section:

> *No wonder you came looking for me, you*
> *who care for the grieving, and I the sound of grief.* ([5])

"You" participate through your desire, concern, or need (to "care for" implies all three) for "the grieving." As in the biblical story, Daniel's "visions" were produced at King Nebuchadnezzar's request, so also in the writer-reader exchange, meaning is partially produced by the reader's active engagement:

> Confusion of faces, yours among them,
> the poetry tangled, no vision of my own to speak of.
>
> The hand moved along the wall.
> I was able to read, that's all. (*WL*, 39)

Webb's clustering of various subject positions in the figure of "I Daniel" thus re-locates reader and writer within textual fields where they participate together in the production of meanings.

"toward the particular, the local, the dialectical and private" (*SW*)

The concept of clustering is helpful in suggesting reading methods that allow one to attend to the "grand dark," to name thematic clusters without universalizing them, and to be aware of one's active engagement in the process. However it does not provide a methodology for analyzing the implications of a reconfigured dark because it implies a pluralistic and hence neutral social space in which all parts have equal weight and value. For a more politicized reading of *Water and Light*, I will consider the social and epistemological issues raised by Webb's re-writing of the ghazal tradition. In my view, Webb's "Ghazals and Anti Ghazals" enact a feminist critique of the tradition of romance, a tradition that has silenced women by idealizing them.

The subject of the traditional ghazal is love—both human and divine. Aijaz Ahmad, editor of *The Ghazals of Ghalib* (one of the collections that Webb used as a model for *Water and Light*), explains: "This is a poetry . . . of love—not about love but of love. Love is the great, over-arching metaphor because love is conceived as the basic human relation and all life is lived in terms of this relation" (xxiii-xxiv). Within this tradition, as Webb explains in the Preface to the chapbook *Sunday Water: Thirteen Anti Ghazals*, "the Beloved represent[s] . . . not a particular woman but an idealized and universal image of Love." But Webb's ghazals resist the idealization of woman and instead "tend toward the particular, the local, the dialectical and private. . . . Hence 'anti Ghazals.'" However, in so doing, Webb does not simply set up a contrary and equally predetermined subject. Rather, she intersects the ideal with a contrary movement toward the particular so that the two inhabit and "contaminate" each other. The idealized figure of the Beloved does not disappear—"in the end . . . Love returns to sit on her 'throne of *accidie*,' a mystical power intrudes, birds sing, a Sitar is plucked, and the Third Eye, opal, opens" (Webb, Preface, *SW*). But at the same time Webb's insistence on the "particular, the local, the dialectical, and private" undermines the power of the ideal to dictate the terms of particular women's lives.

Several critics have already discussed the liberating effect of these poems for the female subject. John Hulcoop describes Webb's "adoption/adaptation of the [ghazal] form [as]. . . . an act of liberation a liberation of self-as-woman from male socio-sexual, political, and poetic conventions" (Hulcoop, "Webb's 'Water and Light,'" 157). Similarly, Cecelia Frey argues that "[f]emale as object is supplanted by female as writing subject intoxicated with the possibilities of poetry and language, possibilities which, ultimately, are those of the self" (37). Susan Glickman proposes that "Webb discovered in the ghazal a way of liberating herself from the patriarchal tradition of English literature and presenting more accurately her modern, female experience" (59). However, all three focus on individual liberation rather than social change. I see the poems as interventions in restrictive social and epistemological systems as well as acts of individual liberation.

Crucial to the success of this intervention is the fact that Webb's critique is from a complicit position. Working in the midst of divergent and sometimes competing semantic trajectories, she intersects and de-stabilizes the generalizing tropes of romance with "the particular, the local, the dialectical, and private." While individual liberation is based on self-action as the basis of change, Webb's anti ghazals include interventions in the discursive and social contexts that construct the individual subject.

In the last poem of the book, while chiding Ghalib for romanticizing the subject, yet using romantic images of moonlight and cherry blossoms herself, Webb admits her attraction to and complicity with the discourse of romance. I quote the entire poem:

> Ah Ghalib, you are drinking too much,
> your lines are becoming maudlin.
>
> Here, take this tea and sober up. The moon
> is full tonight, and I can't sleep.
>
> And look—this small branch of cherry
> blossoms, picked today, and it's only February.
>
> You could use a few cool Japanese images
> to put you on the straight and narrow.

Still, I love to study your graceful script,
Urdu amorous, flowing across the page.

There were nights I watched you dip your pen
into the old Persian too, inscribe 'Asad'

with a youthful flourish. Remember Asad,
Ghalib?

Mirza Asadullah Beg Khan, who are you really?
Born in Agra, of Turkish ancestry,

fond of women, politics, money, wine.
'Losses and consequent grief' a recurring

theme, also 'a poetry . . . of what was,
what could have been possible.'

Ah Ghalib, you are almost asleep,
head on the table, hand flung out,

upturned. In the blue and white jar
a cherry branch, dark pink in moonlight—

from the land of
only what is. (WL, 60-61)

Webb's particularizing changes (but does not erase) Ghalib's generalizing. Webb does end with the local and particular, but throughout the poem she recognizes her own participation in the traditions and tropes of romantic love. The poem offers not a pluralistic vision of equal and opposite differences that remain stable, but an expanded conceptual space that intermingles and thus changes both. She expands the epistemic field to produce a hybrid or mottled subject.

Section two—"The Birds"—offers all manner of female figures who are variously generalized and particularized. There is the very public figure of Yoko Ono (WL, 25), the domestic "My dear ladies, birds of a feather" (WL, 26), the literary "eye-sad dryad" collapsed on the page in the fourth poem (WL, 28), or the tenacious "green canary" of the final one (WL, 32). Birds are calling, nesting, singing, phlupping, chirping, clawing, soaring, collapsing; women are talking, protesting, acting, loving, and living in particular, individual ways throughout the book. In section one, "Mrs. Olsson, organic gardener, lectures me on the good life" (*WL*, 13); in another, the same "slim and sprightly" Mrs. Olsson (who is 91!) swims in the bay. In the same poem, a woman named "Robin" hangs sheets on the line in order to conceal her house renovations from the building inspector. This domestic and practical gesture is also a metaphor for the self-protective strategy of "hiding" her social and epistemological "renovations" from the patriarchal order represented by the "building inspector" who will likely not approve of her feminist reconstructions. In the next couplet, the "I" complains about the pressure to live up to ideals of femininity. Here is the entire poem:

> Mrs. Olsson at 91 is slim and sprightly.
> She still swims in the clamshell bay.
>
> Around the corner, Robin hangs out big sheets
> to hide her new added on kitchen from the building inspector.
>
> I fly from the wide-open mouth of the seraphim.
> Something or somebody always wants to improve me.
>
> Come down, eagle, from your nifty height.
> Let me look you in the eye, Mr. America.
>
> Crash—in the woods at night.
> Only a dead tree falling. (*WL*, 11)

The building inspector who imposes higher taxes, the seraphim who enacts God's commands, the eagle, and Mr. America are all authority figures who represent the law of the father and its oppressive ideals. But the three women in this poem—Mrs. Olsson, Robin, and "I"—resist in particular ways. The crash in the last couplet brings the momentary hope that the symbols and codes have collapsed. But no, it's "[o]nly a dead tree falling." When a tree becomes old and decayed, it falls down; authority symbols and patriarchal systems are not so easily undermined. Still, the three women do succeed in circumventing, evading, or defying the imposed Law by their "particular, . . . local, . . . dialectic, and private" actions.

Their actions also contrast with the inaction of the Beloved, that idealized female figure to whom the ghazal was traditionally addressed. Webb's presentation of the Beloved is ironic:

Drunken and amatory, illogical, stoned, mellifluous
journey of the ten lines.

The singer sings one couplet or two

over and over to the Beloved who reigns

on the throne of *accidie*, distant, alone,
hearing, as if from a distance, a bell

and not this stringy instrument scraping away,
whining about love's ultimate perfection.

Wait! Everything is waiting for a condition of grace:
the string of the Sitar, this Gat, a distant bell,

even the Beloved in her bored flesh. (*WL*, 20)

Gone is the male fantasy of a pleasure-filled love paradise. Instead, the
Beloved is bored and listless, tired of listening to the endless "whining
about love's ultimate perfection."

Webb also inserts a female writing subject into the ghazal tradition
and in so doing further "contaminates" the male-dominated tradition.
Again, she does not simply insert an equal but opposite and equally pre-
determined subject. Hers is a subject-in-process, a "moving line" as
Sharon Thesen puts it (*VT*, 13). Traditionally, the ghazal writer would
use a nom de plume, which represents an idealized (and unchanging)
self. But Webb's nom de plume, "Fishstar," is a friendly companion,
not an idealized alter ego, sometimes a confidante—"Words fail me, /
Fishstar," the speaker confides in one poem—or someone to argue
with: "But I tell you, / *Fishstar*, the colour of chaos was not // peacock
blue" (*WL*, 30). While the name Fishstar echoes Ishtar, the Babylonian
goddess of love and fertility who enacts the twin ideals of woman as
object of desire and *agency* of fertility, the name has "immediate, particu-
lar, . . . and private" resonances in the epigraph to Webb's *Naked Poems:*
"Star fish / fish star" (*VT*, 63). Also, while the images of fish and star
could symbolize the dual roles of Ishtar—one is of the earth, the other
celestial—they are also particular objects in Webb's local Salt Spring
Island landscape. As a blend of general and personal, idealized and par-
ticular, Fishstar—like the other female figures in the book—changes

the epistemic field. The semiotic field of "woman" is activated, ener-
gized, particularized, and thereby expanded.

Finally, in undermining the idealized tropes of the ghazal, these
poems also undermine the binary underpinnings of the romance tradi-
tion. The local, particular, bottom-up processes from "the land of /
only what is" (*WL*, 61) intersect top-down formations (of "universal"
knowledge and truth) to produce a continuum where culture and
nature, light and dark, mind and body, individual and social oppositions
dissolve. The water and light of the title, like the nom de plume Fish-
star, and the ironized figure of the Beloved, enact this intermingling of
general and particular. As also, throughout the book, the poems push
against the generalizing discourse of water as source of life and light as
source of vision, to insist on the specificity in the Pacific Coast rain-
forest. Water is ocean, rain, streams, pools, mist, as well as symbol of the
life source, the unconscious, that which cleanses, baptizes. Light, too, is
a symbol (of knowledge, truth, inspiration, or vision), but is also sun-
light, lamplight, moonlight, starlight, the play of light in the landscape.
In the title poem, eight repetitions of the word "light" enact an insis-
tent particularity:

LIGHT   LIGHT   LIGHT   LIGHT
LIGHT   LIGHT   LIGHT   LIGHT

Old doom pining away
in forest's mossy undergrowth

WEARY   WEARY   WEARY   WEARY
Oh Lord Krishna DANCE

Shiva DANCE, your anklet bells
waking the waterlilies in the pool

WATER AND LIGHT   WATER AND LIGHT
and the grand dark attending (*WL* [6])

The old gods intermingle with new growth on the forest floor in a
delightful image of a composting process that breaks culture/nature
binaries. A four-times weary Lord Krishna barely manages to dance.
Krishna, the human form of Vishnu (the preserver God of the Hindu
triad), is old and tired. Appropriately, it is Shiva, the hermaphroditic
God of both destruction and reproduction in the Hindu triad (the god

of process?) who activates this dance, who awakens the "waterlilies in the pool." The image of the "pool" (life/psyche/poem/womb), activated by the *movement* and *sound* of Shiva's ankle bells, emphasizes processual rather than predetermined meaning. Appropriately, the water lilies are *in* the pool, an image that metaphorizes the writer and reader's complicit positions.

In this reconfigured semantic and social space, the "dark" ceases to be an alterity, defined in opposition to the light; it attends (meaning literally "to be present with"). To be present with something—rather than in opposition to—initially decreases visibility. There is a mottling or camouflage effect from the mixture of light and dark. But mottling in this instance provides a useful camouflage, a useful invisibility; it offers a protective covering that prevents the figure from being "seen" and inscribed by the prevailing social codes. Webb's various interminglings within the "grand dark" allow female subjectivities to avoid this kind of erasure while also finding the room to develop agency and visibility within reconfigured semantic and social fields.

"Middle Distance"

Truth, too, becomes mottled in this intermingling of general and particular. Just as splitting the atom disclosed a subatomic flux, so also contextualizing truth discloses fluid and intersecting rather than autonomous and universal truths. Along with all those other previously autonomous entities (subject, agency, message), truth becomes localized and interactive.

Webb's title for the last section of *Water and Light*—"Middle Distance"—points to a such a processual model of truth. She argues against a transcendent light and truth imaged in the epigraph for the section:

> Sun of the World! shed your illumination on us here;
> a strange time, like a shadow, has fallen on us.

Webb's poems explore both positive and negative dimensions of the "shadow"; they posit mottled truths located in the "[m]iddle distance." Truth is a moveable point *within* a continuum, a point of convergence, as in the second ghazal of this section:

> Oh You who keep disappearing
> behind a black cloud like a woman

behind her veil, how do you feel
shut off like that from the perfect

obedience of your worshippers?
There is this Mirror, clear and unchanging?

there is this Poet counting his syllables;
he is planting lilies and roses

in cracks of the universe. He tells how
the Mirror clouds up in the heat

of his rhymes, how he goes
crazy in your black weather. (*WL*, 56)

The image of the sun (as light, illumination, inspiration) disappearing behind a black cloud reverses the conventional image of the writer losing his/her inspiration. Here the sun (as symbol of Apollo, the God of Truth) is losing its followers. But despite the black cloud (of doubt, uncertainty etc.), the poet plants "lilies and roses." The cracks in the ideological system become, not the modernist's *mise-en-abyme*, but fertile ground for new growth. In the absence of the transcendent, the poet generates a local "heat" ("the mirror clouds up in the heat // of his rhymes"). Blackness no longer signifies doubt or lack of vision, but intense activity. In yet another reconfiguration of darkness, Webb posits the experience of being without a God or muse as a positive condition rather than a state of loss. The poet's rhymes generate a creative "heat," a productive energy that comes from the interactions of body/heart/ language. However, again Webb refuses to settle into a single position in a dualistic symbolic system: along with the creative energy generated in the "cracks," there is the possibility of insanity and hysteria in the image of going "crazy in your black weather." Loss, betrayal, and paranoia intermingle with the "heat" of self-action. This is a mottled truth that comprises intersecting variables.

I find ethnographer James Clifford's explanation of the necessary interconnectedness between "local particularism" and "a single progressive or entropic metanarrative" useful here both in relation to the tensions felt in the "Middle Distance" in this poem and as a general observation about the general/particular interface in any truth claims. In *The Predicament of Culture*, Clifford writes:

> To reject a single progressive or entropic metanarrative is not to deny
> the existence of pervasive global processes unevenly at work. The
> world is increasingly connected, though not unified, economically
> and culturally. Local particularism offers no escape from these in-
> volvements. Indeed, modern ethnographic histories are perhaps con-
> demned to oscillate between two metanarratives: one of homogeniza-
> tion, the other of emergence; one of loss, the other of invention. In
> most specific conjunctures both narratives are relevant, each under-
> mining the other's claim to tell "the whole story," each denying to
> the other a privileged, Hegelian vision. (17)

Webb's poem also "oscillate[s] between two metanarratives: one of
homogenization, the other of emergence; one of loss, the other of
invention." Webb aptly names that interface "Middle Distance": the
poet writes at the interstices of loss and invention, of subjugation and
emergence. That the homogenizing narratives of the global or "univer-
sal" coexist and intermingle with the emergent energy of the local is
the truth of Webb's poem.

"Leaning," the culminating poem of both the "Middle Distance"
section and of the whole book offers a particularly acute rendering of
the tensions and resonances that inhabit the subject who is "heading
into the middle distance."[2] I quote the first half of the poem:

> I am half-way up the stairs
> of the Leaning Tower of Pisa.
>
> Don't go down. You are in this
> with me too.
>
> I am leaning out of the Leaning
> Tower heading into the middle distance
>
> where a fur-blue star contracts, becomes
> the ice-pond Brueghel's figures are skating on.
>
> North Magnetic pulls me like a flower
> out of the perpendicular
>
> angles me into outer space
> an inch at a time, the slouch

of the ground, do you hear that?
the hiccup of the sludge about the stone.

(Rodin in Paris, his amanuensis, a torso . . .)
I must change my life or crunch

over in vertigo, hands
bloodying the inside tower walls

lichen and dirt under the fingernails
Parsifal vocalizing in the crazy night

my sick head on the table where I write
slumped one degree from the horizontal

the whole culture leaning . . . (*WL*, 58, Webb's ellipses)

The tower, the speaker, and "the whole culture" are leaning on the same axis, tilted by the push/pull of various forces. The pull of "North Magnetic," of "the sludge about the stone," of the "lichen and dirt under the fingernails" enact diverse local and material vectors. The action of leaning "into the middle distance" destabilizes the earth/sky, art/nature, vertical/horizontal, male/female binaries. In this instance, the emergent narrative is one of feminist resistance to the entropic patriarchal institutions and phallic towers exemplified in the tower itself, in "Parsifal vocalizing" from Wagner's opera, or in "the phalloi of Mies"—those strikingly phallic buildings designed by American architect Mies Van Der Rohe. As Webb explains in a letter to Daphne Marlatt, "[a]ll those cultural allusions . . . [are] the dying voices of an old style of poetry . . . the death of the patriarchal culture" (Webb to Marlatt, December 30, 1982; 92).

But again, Webb offers, not a neutral observation of inevitable oscillations in a pluralistic world, but an incisive feminist "leaning" toward both individual and social change. Feeling sick from the vertigo, imprisoned in the tower, the speaker is up against the wall, her life at the "crunch." The urgency of personal imperatives compels her to act: "I must change my life or crunch // over in vertigo." However, her self-liberation takes place within the tower; it is necessarily intertwined with "pervasive global processes unevenly at work," to use Clifford's terms. The "pervasive global processes . . . at work" in this poem include the breakdown of phallocentric thought, the ecological instabilities resulting from the development of the atomic bomb (Einstein and Bohr), and the collapse of the modernist ivory tower where "high culture" was sealed off from the "smelly tourists." In this connection, the poem resonates with Virginia Woolf's 1940 essay "The Leaning Tower," where Woolf describes what she calls "Leaning Tower writers" who have become conscious of their untenable position in the face of 1930s social and political realities.[3]

Tensions between local and global are also enacted in the I/you relationship in the poem. At the start, "I" and "You" are drawn together by shared paranoia:

> Don't go down. You are in this
> with me too. (*WL*, 58)

Because "you" can be lover, friend, reader, or community, the I/you configuration in the poem also connects the singular "I" to a variety of social contexts. When "I" calls to "you" again at the end of the poem—"And you, are you still here"—the poem gestures toward a more expansive social relation than the paranoid huddling together in the tower of the opening lines. The reference to the ark in the closing couplet serves as a reminder of a global collectivity:

> And you, are you still here
>
> tilting in this stranded ark
> blind and seeing in the dark. (*WL*, 59)

The final lines also enact other conjunctions that constitute the "Middle Distance" of this poem: a "tilting" of the stationary ("stranded") ark by feminist interventions and a "seeing" into the dark that disturbs the "entropic metanarratives" (as described in Clifford, above).

In the above poem, the feminist tilt helps to destabilize the tower. In the companion poem to "Leaning" (called "Following"),[4] the feminist intervention becomes even stronger with the emergence of a group of women who collectively challenge the classic, Botticellian image of beauty:

> That which is beautiful in Botticelli
> disintegrates,
> gathers again in women. ("Following," *Canadian Literature*, 351)

Here, as Daphne Marlatt aptly puts it in a letter to Webb, is "the new spring gathering in women who speak, who get in touch, who greet each other, who move off the canvas where they've been pictured and into the world where they make their magic acts of connection" (Marlatt to Webb, November 22, 1982; 93). Indeed, while a potentially entropic metanarrative of homogeneity begins to override the narrative of "local" emergence and intervention, the poem ends at the conjunction of individual and social, enacting the intersections of emergent and entropic:

> A woman in light
> leans out
> and over me,
> waving a wand
> of old language
> unspoken beyond
> these words,
> [. . .]
> *Her white sails crossing the water—*
>
> I follow:
> a flower is held out
> and placed in the shell of Venus
> who rises, wet,
> to greet her. ("Following," *Canadian Literature*, 351-52)

As Venus greets the emerging woman, the woman also steps out of her "shell" into a sexualized body. There is no mistaking the sexualized body that "rises, wet / to greet her." The emergent and entropic narratives meet in the "Middle Distance"—that in-between space where narrative trajectories and ideological constructs intersect the "local," where the individual and social intertransform each other, and where the reader constructs mottled truths.

Notes

1 Urdu scholar Aijaz Ahmad provides the following description of the Ghazal in his introduction to the *Ghazals of Ghalib*: "At the centre of these [Urdu] poetics is the form of the ghazal, the basic poetic form in Urdu from the beginnings of the language to the middle of this century. The ghazal is a poem made up of couplets, each couplet wholly independent of any other in meaning and complete in itself as a unit of thought, emotion and commu-

nication. No two couplets have to be related to each other in any way what-
ever except formally (one may be about love, the next about the coming of a
season; one about politics, the next about spring), and yet they can be parts
of a single poem. The *only* link is in terms of prosodic structure and rhyme"
(xvi).

2 Timothy Findley has said that he found this poem so compelling that it led
   him to write an entire novel—*Not Wanted on the Voyage*. He quotes the last
   section of "Leaning" as the epigraph for the novel.

3 "The Leaning Tower" was a paper that Woolf presented to the Workers'
   Educational Association, Brighton, May 1940. She describes the privileged
   socio-economic position of contemporary British writers as a leaning tower:
   "trapped by their education, pinned down by their capital, they remained on
   top of their leaning tower, and their state of mind as we see it reflected in
   their poems and plays and novels is full of discord and bitterness, full of con-
   fusion and of compromise" (116). And further that "they are trapped on a
   leaning tower from which they cannot descend" (118).

4 In an interview with Ann Munton, Webb explains the link between "Lean-
   ing" and "Following": "The Leaning Tower is a phallic image, and once I
   wrote that poem, a similar image kept flashing and that was . . . a woman
   from Botticelli. . . . I then wrote a poem called 'Following' dealing with
   Botticelli and the women." However, Webb adds that "It's not a very good
   poem. It doesn't have the weight. It may be fatal for me to give up this male
   oppression in my psyche!" (Munton interview, 85). "Following" was pub-
   lished in *Canadian Literature*, 100 (1984): 351-52, but not included in *Water
   and Light*, presumably because Webb thought it was "not a very good
   poem."

3

Form as Process—Form in Process

Syntactivity. Under the electron microscope. Oh look and see. Against this, an image pushes through of splicing tape. Janet in the listening room late at night at CBC. Listening room. The poem as listening room. (Webb, *NBBS*, 21)

I think everything on the page affects the reader, though the reader does not have to be conscious of it. It's the poet who has to be conscious of it, because each element is part of the mysterium of the poem. (Webb, "Talking the Line," 24)

That is what I am coming to, the physics of the poem. Energy/Mass. Waxy splendour, the massive quiet of the fallen tulip petals. So much depends upon: the wit of the syntax, the rhythm and speed of the fall, the drop, the assumption of a specific light, curved. (Webb, *NBBS*, 20)

Webb has worked with structures as diverse as the sonnet, the haiku, the prose poem, the lyric, the sestina, the ghazal, William Carlos Williams's triadic line, Marianne Moore's syllabic verse, Robert Creeley's short line, Charles Olson's breath line, and Sappho's minimalist lyric forms. But Webb invariably re-forms and transforms these prosodic structures as she works with them. In my view her various adaptations of poetic forms are integral to her process of seeing in the dark; that is, Webb's active engagement with the poem's formal structures gives her a way of moving within the dark. She proceeds by engaging with what is at hand—the specifics of sound, rhythm, and syntax. This precise attention to formal processes diverts or subverts the impulse to "turn on the light" in order to see the whole room, or the impulse to stand still and speak from a narcissistic, confessional, or other "stable" position; it gives her a way of paying attention to "the mysterium of the poem" (cited above). Like the radio producer working in

The notes to this chapter are on p. 73.

59

the listening room (an experience familiar to Webb from her work at CBC radio), Webb composes by listening, layering, pacing, linking, arranging. Webb's phrase "syntactivity" (cited above) aptly configures this writing process as an activity within the syntagmatic axes of the poem. To focus on form and prosodic structure is to focus on the choices available on the horizontal rather than vertical (paradigmatic) plane. Webb proceeds by "listening" to and working with "everything on the page," as she insists in the passage cited above.

Water and Light: Ghazals and Anti Ghazals

I have chosen first to examine Webb's engagement with the formal structures in *Water and Light* because the complexities of the ghazal allow us to clearly see Webb's working methods. The ghazal conventions, as outlined by Aijaz Ahmad in the Introduction to *The Ghazals of Ghalib*, include the following:

> All the lines in a ghazal have to be of equal metrical length. The first is a rhymed couplet, and the second line of each succeeding couplet must rhyme with the opening couplet. The unit of rhyme repeated at the end of each couplet may be as short as a single syllable or as long as a phrase of half a line. (Ahmad, xvi-xvii)

How does Webb work with these conventions? In the first section of *Water and Light*, she follows them fairly closely. All but two of the ghazals have the requisite five couplets. Of the two variants, one has six couplets (*WL*, 19), the other five and a half (*WL*, 20). But once she has "learned" the form, Webb then begins to play with it.[1] In the second section of the book, I count only three out of eight ghazals in the five couplet form; in section three, two out of eight; and none at all in sections four and five. Increasingly, she varies the form: the variations include breaking the couplet pattern with single lines here and there, introducing half lines, or simply varying the total number of couplets—from two and a bit (*WL*, 29) to eighteen (*WL*, 58). Nor does she necessarily follow the prescribed rhythmic pattern of balanced lines, or the intricate end-rhyme pattern in which "the first is a rhymed couplet, and the second line of each successive couplet must rhyme with the opening couplet" (Ahmad, xvi-xvii). As the subtitle *Ghazals and Anti Ghazals* suggests, Webb works both with and against the ghazal formal conventions.

While not necessarily following all the specific rules, Webb usually follows the structural principle of the ghazal, the principle of linking otherwise discrete couplets by sound patterns. As Aijiz Ahmad explains:

> The ghazal is a poem made up of couplets, each couplet wholly inde-
> pendent of any other in meaning and complete in itself as a unit of
> thought, emotion, and communication. No two couplets have to be
> related to each other in any way whatever except formally. . . . The
> *only* link is in terms of prosodic structure and rhymes. (xvi)

At the level of form, couplets are intricately woven together; at the level
of content, they resonate against each other. Typically, the ghazal moves
by associative leaps and a "free flow of images" (Webb, quoted in
Wachtel, 14). Thus, while the ghazal form posits discontinuity on a
number of levels, the rhyme pattern facilitates an associative, image-
making process that often leads to surprising semantic and thematic res-
onances. In the "Peacock blue" ghazal, for instance, the vowels in "Pea-
cock blue" generate a sequence of words linked by rhyme: "Peacock,"
"me," "green scream," "creation," and "Peacock" form one pattern;
"blue," "you," and "blue" another; "peacock" to "cock of his head"
to "not" is yet another. Here is the complete poem:

> Peacock blue. Words fail me,
> *Fishstar*, for the packed, inbred
>
> splendour of this bird. His strut,
> the cock of his head, a royal courtier
>
> in the barnyard. Essex. See how the
> Fabulous points into the spectrum, pecks out
>
> accurately a blue-green scream for Elizabeth.
> It is morning. It is the first morning
>
> of creation, an absurd idea, but I tell you,
> *Fishstar*, the colour of chaos was not
>
> Peacock blue. (*WL*, 30)

Daphne Marlatt describes this connection between rhyme and reason as
one based on an erotic attraction:

> sound will initiate thought by a process of association. words call each
> other up, evoke each other, provoke each other, nudge each other in-
> to utterance. We know from dreams and schizophrenic speech how
> deeply association works in our psyches, a form of thought that is not

rational but erotic because it works by attractions. a drawing, a pulling toward, a "liking." (Marlatt, 45)

In Webb's poems, the sound patterns similarly connect words on many levels. The rhyming words "green scream" and "peacock," for instance, enact male sexual aggression and narcissism (me, me, me). The contrasting sequence "blue . . . you . . . blue" thematizes the receptive "you" of the sexual act. Also, the phonic circle, produced by the repetition of sounds in "Peacock blue" at the beginning and end of the poem, resonates with the procreative cycle thematized in the "Peacock blue . . . blue-green scream."

To take another example of "sound . . . initiat[ing] thought by a process of association": in the "Yoko Ono" ghazal, the long "O" in Yoko appears in every couplet except the middle one (in keeping with the convention of the second line of each couplet rhyming with the opening couplet):

> **Yo ko Ono** was seen in the Empress Hotel today.
> She can never be seen for herself alone again.
>
> Shots ring out in Iran, Afghanistan,
> El Salvador.
>
> At night here pitlampers
> kill deer.
>
> Everywhere the killings go on.
> In my own hand a flea died only yesterday.
>
> I sit in my quilted jacket calling the birds
> whose warning cries strike just beyond the window. (WL, 25)

The poem's seemingly random events, presented in a sequence of self-sufficient couplets, are linked only by rhyme, and the only "conclusion" is a phonic one, in the final repeat of the "o" sound in "window," which also links the end to the beginning in a circular or round formation similar to the "Peacock blue" ending/beginning above. Again, however, the "free flow of images" generated by the rhyme pattern leads to thematic resonances. The rhymes link a series of killings, for instance, from the perplexing murder of John Lennon (which made his wife Yoko Ono an iconic widow), to multiple deaths in El Salvador,

to illegal hunting of deer on Salt Spring Island, to the idle killing of a
flea by the poet, to birds killing themselves as they fly into the invisible
window glass. The speaker's sheltered position—she can hear the
"warning cries" but the sound is muffled by her quilted jacket and the
window glass—is also emphasized by the phonic foregrounding of the
word "window." She sits, watching, while the window protects her
from direct contact. The window thematizes the many protective bar-
riers we erect between self and world. Such meanings, however, are not
the result of the poet's conscious "intention"; the conscious mind
focusses on dealing with the formal requirements, a process which, in
turn, frees up Webb's associative thought and image processes.[2] While
the poems enact, as Doug Beardsley so aptly puts it, "the personal asso-
ciative leaps of her singing mind" (*WL*, dustjacket), they are also very
carefully constructed. As John Thompson writes in his preface to
STILT JACK (the book that introduced Webb to the ghazals), while
the ghazal "is the poem of contrasts, dreams, astonishing leaps" and
offers a "chart of the disorderly," it is not a surrealist form. On the con-
trary, ghazals "are poems of careful construction" (Thompson, "Gha-
zals"),[3] but the "careful construction" takes place at the formal rather
than semantic or thematic level, in the "syntactivity" rather than the
paradigmatic activity, so that the poem remains an intricately woven
"chart of the disorderly."

Form as Critique and Intervention

Water and Light may have begun, as Webb explains in the preface to the
chapbook *Sunday Water*, as "an exercise in the ghazal form," but in-
creasingly the poems become "Anti Ghazals." Webb's changes to the
ghazal form disrupt romantic tropes. For instance, a renegade single line
such as "even the Beloved in her bored flesh" (*WL*, 20) (which breaks
the couplet pattern by standing alone after the requisite five couplets)
detaches the Beloved structurally as well as thematically from the dis-
course of romance. Or, the gradual reduction in line length in the fol-
lowing example, which breaks the rhythmic balance, is in itself an anti-
romantic gesture: as the multisyllabic lines shrink to the single
beat/word/line of "heart," the excesses of romantic discourse are
excised from the discourse:

> The varied thrush, the orchard oriole,
> the crying dove, the skin-smooth olive

green, olive-green, with a red
pimiento

heart. (*WL*, 29)

Similarly, in the "grey-eyed dryad" poem, Webb's foregrounding of clichéd phonic and rhythmic structures and romantic epithets combines formal and thematic critique. I quote the entire poem:

Grey-eyed dryad, have you seen one
if only for the sound of

grey-eyed dryad. Or gull gone
into blue empyrion, the lift

of wind fabulous, flowing, free-for-all.
Nothing is pure praxis,

axis of this globe sends
degree by degree us into curved

path of portent, accident, perishable
eye-sad dryad. Look at her. Here. (*WL*, 28)

Romantic epithets flood the poem: like Shelley's "Prometheus Bound," the soaring freedom of the gull is intersected, inevitably, by accident or fate; the gull proves to be mortal and "perishable." But, at the end of the poem, it is the mellifluous sound pattern of "grey-eyed dryad" that collapses, as much as the romantic stereotypes, into the awkward sounding "eye-sad dryad."

Another of Webb's formal strategies is to adapt the ghazal's disjunctive structure to her interventionist purposes. Traditionally, the ghazal's disjunctiveness was a means of increasing the resonances between couplets by "setting image against image, thought against thought, discontinuously" (Glickman, 50). Webb uses it also to "liberate her psyche" from the Western lyric tradition of synthesis and unity. As Webb explains to Eleanor Wachtel, the ghazal offered a way "to subvert my own rational mind, to get more free flow of images and a little wilder in content, to liberate my psyche a bit" (14). Adrienne Rich (who worked on the translations in *The Ghazals of Ghalib*), also found the disjunctive form liberating:

The marvellous thing about these ghazals is precisely (for me) their capacity for both concentration and a gathering, cumulative effect. . . . I needed a way of dealing with very complex and scattered material which was demanding a different kind of unity from that imposed on it by the isolated, single poem in which certain experiences needed to find both their intensest rendering and to join with other experiences not logically or chronologically connected in any obvious way. [. . .] what I'm trying for, not always successfully, is a clear image or articulation behind which there are shadows, reverberations, reflections of reflections. (Quoted in Ahmad, xxv-xxvi)

In translating the form into English, Webb and Rich both found freedom from oppressive discursive patterns. Just as the haiku-like form of *Naked Poems* released Webb from the English lyric tradition of a single, autonomous subject and facilitated the development of the subject-in-process of *Naked Poems*, the disjunctive ghazal structure facilitated Webb's interventions in the "dark" of the romance tradition. While Urdu literature is no less patriarchal than English literature, Webb's outsider position in relation to Urdu culture enables her to translate the form into English without all of its ideological baggage. She can use the disjunctive form as a way of creating gaps in Western thought.

However, the first poem in *Water and Light* also shows Webb's concern with the politics of cross-cultural translation, shows "Webb's ironic awareness of the impropriety of her borrowing a middle-eastern lyrical form to speak of her 'predicament' as a poet in the West, in the light of what is going on simultaneously in the Middle East" (Glickman, 57). The last two couplets of the opening poem emphasize the violence against women in contemporary Iran (formerly Persia).

> Four or five couplets trying to dance
> into Persia. Who dances in Persia now?
>
> A magic carpet, a prayer mat, red.
> A knocked off head of somebody on her broken knees. (*WL*, 9)

Thus Webb's translation of the form into English is not without an awareness of the ghazal's role in a culture that often violently oppresses women. Her adaptations of the form pivot around this conundrum of the poet "trying to dance / into Persia," but always asking "Who dances in Persia now?" These social and political questions hover throughout the book, even as Webb does find ways to "dance" in the

ghazal form and simultaneously use it to interrogate patriarchal ideolo-
gies in the English literary tradition.

One of the ways Webb uses the ghazal form to open alternative
meanings is by activating the spaces between couplets. In the first half of
the book, where Webb more or less follows the ghazal convention of
self-contained couplets linked to each other only by rhyme patterns, the
space between couplets, as I noted above, becomes an energized silence
where intuitive leaps can take place, becomes an active space consisting
of those "shadows, reverberations, reflections of reflections" (Rich,
quoted in Ahmad, above) that have traditionally been located on the
margins of Western thought. However, in the last half of the book,
Webb increasingly intersects the autonomy of the couplet with forward
moving narrative trajectories and/or grammatical linkages (another ver-
sion of an anti ghazal) which change the activity in the white space, as
in the following example:

> Oh You who keep disappearing
> behind a black cloud like a woman
>
> behind her veil, how do you feel
> shut off like that from the perfect
>
> obedience of your worshippers?
> There is this Mirror, clear and unchanging? (*WL*, 56)

The enjambment here links abstract terms to particular (and noticeably
oppressive) actions and thus "contaminates" the ideal of "perfect
woman." The syntax yokes together the ideal and the reality while the
line breaks maintain some separation; the two are held, suspended, in a
constructive tension.

Alternatively, in "The Authors are In Eternity" a forward-moving
narrative trajectory is slowed by the grammatical autonomy of each cou-
plet:

> The Authors are in Eternity,
> or so Blake said,
>
> but I am here, feet planted
> on the ground;

I am listening to the song
of the underground river.

I go down to the same river twice,
remembering, always remembering.

I am you in your jewel-domed reading room,
I am you in your kayak skimming.

I stand in one place risking almost everything.
I weep for the last notes.

The river-stones are polished
by the blue-veined hands of Ishtar.

Poor Fishstar! Yet—all is not lost. (*WL*, 57)

Webb's "syntactivity" in this ghazal again produces a constructive tension, this time between stable form and unstable meaning. The poem follows a narrative of an emergent earth-bound, ear-to-the-ground aesthetic that interrogates "philosophy and religion, literature, and the whole Romantic quest" (Barbour, "Late Work...," 114), while the form remains in the traditional mode.

Susan Glickman theorizes that Webb's attention to the white space between couplets also relates to her investigation of gendered poetic forms that preoccupied Webb when she was writing *Naked Poems* (see chapter 7). In her essay "On the Line," Webb writes "that the long line (in English) is aggressive, with much "voice." Assertive, at least. It comes from assurance (or hysteria), high tide, full moon, open mouth, big-mouthed Whitman, yawp, yawp, and Ginsberg—howling. Male" (Webb, *NBBS*, 21). The short line, on the other hand, she describes as "private palmistry, heart line, cut to the quick" (*NBBS*, 22), a female line:

> —Emily—those gasps, those inarticulate dashes—those incitements—hiding what unspeakable—foul breath? But not revolting; *subversive*. Female. Hiding yourself—Emily—no, compressing yourself, even singing yourself—tinily—with compacted passion—a violent storm—(*NBBS*, 22)

Glickman argues that "writing in couplets gives her [Webb] units of expression which are the rhetorical equivalent of long lines," while

"the white spaces between the couplets resemble 'those gasps, those in-
articulate dashes' of Emily Dickinson's which she [Webb] cites as a '*sub-
versive* Female' alternative." Glickman concludes that Webb discovers an
"aesthetic androgyny in the ghazal" of long and short lines combined
(Glickman, 56).[4]

I would extend Glickman's argument to further emphasize Webb's
use of the "*subversive. Female*" potential of the white space. Webb's
energized white spaces open up gaps and absences in knowledge and
thus, like Emily Dickinson's cryptic dashes, they sing "with compacted
passion—a violent storm" that both disturbs and expands the poem's
semiotic field:

> Four swans in Fulford Harbour
> thirty on Somenos Lake.
>
> Wings, uprush of inspiration, brush
> past the broken shell of my ear.
>
> In bodies of water and air
> ructions, lacunae.
>
> A green canary breasts round her nest
> claws footholding the world.
>
> Sweep this away. The clean sweep.
> Angelus ringing, spare-hearted gong. (*WL*, 32)

Webb creates "ructions, lacunae" in the literary landscape; the literary
swans (perhaps in Yeats' idyllic scenes) are on the move, the literary
voice muted because of "the broken shell of my ear" (breaks in tradi-
tion). In its place, she hears the anti-lyrical, "spare-hearted gong" of the
Port Angeles (local) foghorn. Similarly, the spaces between the couplets
create "ructions, lacunae" that interrupt the literary discourse of ideal-
ized beauty.

Julia Kristeva's theory of how disruptive poetic strategies rupture
the symbolic order offers one way of understanding the subversive ef-
fects of Webb's various formal interventions.[5] "Poetry," Kristeva
writes, "confronts *order* at its most fundamental level: the logic of lan-
guage and the principle of the State" and "introduce[s] through the
symbolic that which works on, moves through, and threatens it" (*RPL*,
81). That is to say, in destabilizing linguistic structures, poetry also des-

tabilizes the ideology inscribed in those structures. Such actions release the repressed pleasures and drives of the body and of the unconscious into language:

> In cracking the socio-symbolic order, splitting it open, changing vocabulary, syntax, the word itself, and releasing from beneath them the drives borne by vocalic or kinetic differences, jouissance works its way into the social and symbolic (*RPL*, 79-80).

The disruptive effects of Webb's Anti Ghazals can be at least partially explained on the basis of Kristeva's analysis of these ruptures in the "socio-symbolic order."

The Pleasure of the Text: "Frivolities"

Any discussion of form should also include a discussion of what Roland Barthes calls *The Pleasure of the Text* (1975)—the sensory and erotic pleasures of language. I have chosen the "Frivolities" section of *Water and Light* for this discussion because these poems noticeably foreground the sound, sight, textures, and movements of words. I like Barthes' description of such writing as "language lined with flesh, a text where we can hear the grain of the throat, the patina of consonants, the voluptuousness of vowels, . . . the articulation of the body, of the tongue . . ." (*PT*, 66-67).

Repetition of sounds and rhythms, as Barthes comments, in itself "creates bliss. There are many ethnographic examples: obsessive rhythms, incantatory music, litanies, rites, and Buddhist nembutsu, etc." (*PT*, 41). In the following ghazal, the repeating words and/or core vowels offer this kind of pleasure:

> My soul, my soul, who said that?
> as the rain stumbles over my mental horizon
>
> horizon which wavers, creates the mirage
> of a café in Milano where
>
> Mary, he says, what shall we do tonight?
>
> Tonight, tonight, love, what shall we do tonight? (*WL*, 46)

In another poem, "these lines" are biting the paper, the cabbage moth eats the cabbage leaf. Kissing. Biting. Eating.

The cabbage moth looks innocent
on the green leaf. Kiss, kiss.

These lines are also hungry
biting a hole in the yellow paper

on which Fishstar writes. (*WL*, 47)

In another, the words caress the tongue:

Dentelle, she-teeth, milk-tooth,
a mouthful of lace.

Cobwebs with the devil's ace,
cut tooth, cuttle fish, scrimshaw. (*WL*, 49)

These words are delicious, tasty, palpable. Another poem is a pure
sound treat—"a candy poem":

A lozenge of dream
sticks on my tongue

Soulange, Stonehenge
sugar-mite, maple—

a candy poem
slips down my throat

a green droplet
a sweet mantra   (*WL*, 48)

The "z" sound of lozenge sticks to the tongue, along with the "s" and
"ge" of Soulange, Stonehenge. The words are palpable. This is Barthes'
"carnal stereophony" (*PT*, 66).

Indeed, these poems engage the reader with their "carnal stereo-
phony" so much so that one reviewer assumed that, like *Naked Poems,
Water and Light* was written to a lover (Estok, 12). But these are poems
of "interstellar longings"; they "are very lush with a different kind of
desire" (Williamson interview, 331). The objects of desire are words
and things, the erotic pleasure is in the language play, the lovers' union
in the act of naming.

Mulberry tree with innocent eyes,
Catalpa with your huge hands,

I am looking at you
so why can't you look back?

Seduce me, Mulberry, with your silk-spun eyelashes,
applaud, Catalpa, with leafy ambuscades.

I am a patient person from time to time,
willingly would I fall into your entrapments

of silk stockings and flowery candelabra.
Or should I save myself with long voyages

interstellar longings
where we might meet as pure event

and I would say Mulberry tree, Catalpa,
and you would say, simply, Phyllis. (*WL*, 45)

In the next poem, the "mental horizon" of memory is activated via words laden with past history ("*Mère*"), words that "pounce out of the thunder"; words that startle: the "rain stumbles," the "horizon . . . wavers," the rain is "feeding the heat of dry September" (46). The words take on an electrical charge through language/body/memory connections.

The section title "Frivolities" suggests another kind of pleasure, the writer's pleasure in play. Certainly serious issues are addressed in these poems: "the curse of mere matter, *Mère* / matter, the subject family" (*WL*, 46) suggests troubling family tensions; the "stick-pin doll, that's me, needled" (*WL*, 50) echoes a recurring theme of possession and torture in Webb's poetry; the self-destructive passivity of the nameless "she" in the last poem of the section resonates with other Webb poems which critique male dominance: "she" is "yielding sweetly / to shy, succulent (tenured) Professor Death" (*WL*, 52). But the tone throughout this section is playful and lighthearted. Indeed Webb "was sort of embarrassed by" these poems; she "thought they were kind of fluffy and light" (Butling interview). In a letter written in response to the reviewer who mistakenly assumed they were addressed to a lover

(Estok, 12), she seems almost to disclaim the poems altogether. Webb explains: "The dedication to Connie Rooke means only that she seemed to enjoy these poems more than I did and published some of them in *The Malahat Review*" ("Letter to the Editor," *NeWest Review*, 12, 2 [1986]: 1).

A partial explanation for her discomfort perhaps lies in the culturally inscribed notion that to be playful is to be frivolous, especially for women, who are not encouraged, as children or adults, to engage in a wide range of playful activities. As a child, the girl plays house and plays with dolls; as a teenager, she herself becomes the doll, a toy which she dresses up for others to play with. Child's play prepares for women's work of being wife and mother. In a culture where the value of work is measured only by production, women's work is historically coded only as reproduction, women's play as frivolous seduction. This may partially account for Webb's apparent discomfort with "Frivolities."

As well, there is the broader question, raised in the epigraph from Ghalib for the section, of the social value of poetry, of whether poetry is productive work or "idle amusement."

> *Now Ghalib, these verses are idle amusement.*
> *Clearly nothing is gained by such a performance.*

But Webb's title "Frivolities" is at once assertive and self-critical. The poems defy male/female and high/low culture codes about appropriate forms and behaviour with their emphasis on game-playing and the histrionics of "silk stockings," "entrapments," and "interstellar longings" (*WL*, 45), of falling in and out of hammocks (*WL*, 52). Memories about sexual and family relationships are collaged together in a carefree manner. A self-mocking, light-hearted tone diminishes the pain of memory. "Tonight, tonight, love, what shall we do tonight?" (*WL*, 46). Or: "The purple orchid he brought me / to wear at my reading // lies face-up in the blue-glazed bowl—/ a Ladyslipper with several eyes" (*WL*, 51). Speaking to Janice Williamson about the playfulness and eroticism of these poems, Webb comments:

> maybe my repressed eroticism is expressed through playfulness. . . . it was at a stage in my life where memories were returning. Perhaps it's a way of dealing with memories and just feeling that one can play with sexual material with a kind of wickedness. I was having fun writing these things which is a bit of a change. It was like a holiday, the holidays I never seem to be able to take in real life. (Williamson interview, 331)

The pleasures of this text range from the personal and private to the social and textual. They include, as well, the pleasure of resistance, subversion, and intervention.

Notes

1 For further discussion of Webb's use of the ghazal form, see Susan Glickman, "Proceeding before the Amorous Invisible: Phyllis Webb and the Ghazal," *Canadian Literature*, 115 (1987): 48-61, and Douglas Barbour, "Late Work at the Kitchen Table: Phyllis Webb's *Water and Light*," *West Coast Line* No. Six, 25, 3 (1991-92): 103-17.

2 For an illuminating discussion of the potentially liberating effects of using arbitrary formal structures, see Marjorie Perloff's chapter, "The Return of the Numerical Repressed." She cites Marcel Benabou, for instance, as follows: "constraint 'forces the system out of its routine functioning, thereby compelling it to reveal its hidden resources.'" And further that "'the paradox of writing under constraint [is] that it possesses a double virtue of liberation, which may one day permit us to supplant the very notion of inspiration'" (Perloff, *RA*, 140).

3 See Webb's discussion of the ghazal in "Ghazal-Maker," Rev. of *Sea Run: Notes on John Thompson's STILT JACK* by Peter Sanger, *Canadian Literature*, 112 (1987): 156-57.

4 See also John Hulcoop's article "Webb's 'Water and Light,'" where he suggests that Webb "can now extend her lines 'across the page' without resorting to oratorical yawp and without falling under the spell of a voice that imposes itself aggressively" (152).

5 I agree with Judith Butler's criticism of Kristeva: "Kristeva's description of the semiotic proceeds through a number of problematic steps. She assumes that drives have aims prior to their emergence into language, that language invariably represses or sublimates these drives, and that such drives are manifest only in those linguistic expressions which disobey, as it were, the univocal requirements of signification within the Symbolic domain" and further that "the semiotic . . . [the] domain of linguistic meaning distinct from the Symbolic . . . is the maternal body manifest in poetic speech" (*GT*, 81). However, I also find Kristeva's analysis helpful in pointing to the subversive potential of disruptive writing practices.

4

Shifting the Shifters—from "I/You" to "I/We"

One of the principal features of English poetic form that Webb questions and changes in her work is the traditional I/you grid of the lyric. Pronoun configurations define the speaker(s)' relationship(s) to other subjects and objects. Changing the pronoun structures can thus reconfigure power relations because pronouns establish the lines of connection and/or separation.[1] In poetry which, at least since the Romantics, has centred around the "I," the I/you configuration has been the primary relational grid in the poem. The writer who uses pronouns unselfconsciously will be automatically positioned within the sovereign "I"/receptive "you" structure of the lyric. Webb's challenges to that sovereign subject and subsequent investigations of various subjectivities can be partially understood by looking at how different pronoun configurations construct different relational grids in her poems.

First, let me outline the different configurations and their power dynamics.

(1) *I/you* usually constructs a relationship with "I" in a dominant position. "I" has control, has authority, occupies the centre. "You" is receptive, is the listener, the object of desire. This "I," however, is traditionally male. When a woman writer uses "I," she inhabits a space that has a long tradition of male dominance. She often feels uncomfortable, an impostor, a fake. Webb asks, in a poem titled "Performance," "Who is this *I* infesting my poems?" (*HF*, 67). The answers include: "*I* am the mask, the voice, the one who begins those lyrical poems, *I wandered lonely as a cloud*"; these answers suggest not only a performative "I" but also the ambivalent position of a female poetic "I."

If the lyric "I" is clearly female, the power dynamics shift. "I" often becomes submissive—the listener, the object of desire, and "you" becomes dominant, authoritarian, if not overbearing and abusive, as in

---

The notes to this chapter are on p. 87.

Margaret Atwood's opening poem in *Power Politics*: "you fit into me /
like a hook into an eye // a fish hook / an open eye" (1).

(2) *I/we*: As with I/you, this configuration also enacts various
power relations. It can become a homogenizing relationship that disem-
powers some members of the group by erasing difference, as in the royal
"we," where one person speaks for the group. This "we" assumes
homogeneity and *erases* difference, as, for example, in the joke about
the Lone Ranger and his Indian sidekick, Tonto: they are chased by
Indians until finally the Lone Ranger says to Tonto: "Well, Tonto, it
looks like we're surrounded," to which Tonto replies: "Whaddya mean
'we,' white-man." The Lone Ranger's "we" presumes a group identity
that erases Tonto's difference. However Tonto's "we" insists on his dif-
ference from the Lone Ranger.

I/we, as in the Lone Ranger's "we," is an appropriating structure
where the speaker presumes to speak for and about the experience of
others. This appropriative "we" has been challenged by writers of
colour and in feminist discourse by working-class women, by native
women, by women of colour, by lesbian women whose experiences
have at times been appropriated by the white, middle-class feminist's
assumption of shared identity. "Whaddya mean 'we,' white-woman."
I/we configurations thus raise the issue of identity politics.[2]

However, I/we may also configure a collaborative and hence
empowering group identity. Daphne Marlatt, in *Salvage* for instance,
establishes a lesbian identity by gradually shifting from a very solitary
lesbian "I" to a group-identified lesbian "we." The lesbian "I" writes
herself into language by constructing an "I/we" story. She works "to
combat this slipping away, of me, of you, the steps . . . what was it we
held in trust, tiny as a Venetian bead, fragile as words encrusted with
pearl, *mathetriai*, not-mother, hidden mentor, lost link?" (*Salvage*, 118,
ellipses in original). Marlatt's "I/we" configuration facilitates a move-
ment from an oppressed, silenced, unwritten "I" to an active,
empowered and "woman identified" subjectivity, to use Adrienne
Rich's term. This I/we is based on collaboration rather than domina-
tion. "I" aligns with others on a parallel track to produce a collective
"we"; it establishes an empowered collectivity.

(3) *We/they*: When "I" aligns with "we" to participate in a group
identity, several "we/they" stories are also generated. (a)"We/they" can
be a paranoid relationship, with the nameless, faceless "they" having
oppressive power. Or, (b) there can be an uneasy balance of power

between two binaries. Or, (c) the emphasis may be on an angry, accusatory relationship to a dominant group—the great grey "they." Or, (d) the emphasis can be on an affirmative, celebratory "we" position (as in women's writing the body, for instance) which displaces "their" story. Like the collaborative I/we configuration, this we/they story is empowering.

In Webb's poetry, the shifts from I/you to I/we and we/they structures enact, if not facilitate, a shift from a passive or submissive "I" to an increasingly active, pluralized, and group-identified subjectivity. That shift, in turn, empowers Webb and enables her to inhabit a social "we," but without erasing or appropriating difference within the group.

In Webb's early work, "we" rarely appears as pronoun and when it does, it is either the specific alignment of two lovers (*VT*, 35) or a very vague and general "we" who share existential despair ("Lament" and "Breaking," *VT*, 40, 46). There is little sense of group connections or alliances. More often, the I/you configuration predominates. I have already discussed the shifting and provisional nature of the speaker(s) in Webb's early work in the context of Webb's resistance to the sovereign "I" of the traditional lyric poem (see chapter 1). Here I want to look at the *relational* grid of the poems.

Prior to *Naked Poems*, the I/you configuration in Webb's work enacts a tentative and often passive "I" in dialogue or negotiation with a dominant "you." Whether as lover (*VT*, 44), or friend (*VT*, 54), or historical figures such as Picasso and Yeats (*VT*, 57-59), or as a vaguely threatening impersonal figure, "you" tends to occupy the dominant position. The *relational* network between I/you is one of negotiation or submission with the traditional roles of the lyric "I" and "you" reversed. In *Naked Poems*, however, the I/you configuration becomes more fluid and shifting as "I" and "you" explore and re-negotiate the power relations between two women in a lesbian relationship. However, in the last Suite of *Naked Poems*, the lover disappears altogether and the I/you negotiation is self-reflexive. *"What do you really want?"*, the speaker asks herself. She answers:

> want the apple on the bough in
> the hand in the mouth seed
> planted in the brain want
> to think "apple" (*VT*, 104)

Webb's lines suggest that eating the apple brings a welcome release *into* the world and an escape from the prison of paradise. The supposed Edenic paradise with Adam and Eve alone together is, in fact, an entrapment in an I/You enclosure.

Wilson's Bowl

Wanting to change the power relations, however, is only a starting point. The poems in *Wilson's Bowl* (1982) enact, among other things, Webb's continuing struggle to reconfigure the speaker's relationship to self and others, the struggle to escape the I/you enclosure of the lyric. In the first two sections, "I" is often unconnected, unattached to other pronouns. The only "we" is a loose association of misfits—the powerless and dispossessed of the opening poem:

> 'Loyal to the silence of our impasse . . .
> we look at each other . . . we do not go . . .
> in the faith that we are inconsolable . . .
> we are resting in this hell.' (*WB*, 14, Webb's ellipses)

Figures of an old lady, a young prince, the Flying Dutchman float around in a world of shadows, silence, and impasse. "I" is all but cut off from existence by the line break between "I / am"

> Insurrectionary wilderness of the I
> am, I will be, forcing the vision
> to something other, something out
> side the sleep of dreams riddled
> with remembrances. (*WB*, 15)

Here "I" attempts to escape the confines of memory and force a different future.

In the "Portraits" section (poems that speak to dominant male figures such as Socrates, Ezra Pound, Fyodor [Dostoevsky], and Rilke) "I" speaks indirectly or self-reflexively about these figures. Only Rilke and Fyodor are addressed directly as "you" and when Fyodor is addressed, "I" adopts the disguise of "a beetle in the cabbage soup they serve up for geniuses in the House of the Dead" (*WB*, 29). Pound, on the other hand, is presented in what Benveniste calls the impersonal historical narrative form, as "he" or "they," unconnected to "I." In the third section ("Crimes"), where Webb addresses general humanitarian issues of imprisonment, torture, and nuclear accidents, the pronoun "I" appears only once, as a parasitic figure drawing blood from the veins of heaven or hell (*WB*, 44), a metaphor that raises questions about the relationship of the poetic "I" to the world. Does the poet thrive (like a parasite) on the world's suffering? The "Letters to Margaret Atwood" (the prose poem that concludes the "Portraits"), however, are noticeably different. Written in the intimate I/you structure of the letter, they enact a collaborative, even conspiratorial relationship. Here "I" finds a comfortable connection to a female "you." She begins "Dear Peggy: What follows is a sort of hollow-eyed celebration. I couldn't make it to champagne, balloons and funny hats. You will understand why" (*WB*, 36).

The I/you configuration appears again in "A Questions of Questions," but with an elusive or oppressive "you," not the friendly, companionable "you" of the "Letters to Margaret Atwood." At first, Webb conducts a self-interrogation similar to the one at the end of *Naked Poems*, with a self-reflexive "you":

> and who are you in this
> school
> room
> torture chamber
>   whose are you?
>   and what of your
>   trials and errors?
> the judge
>   in his echo chamber
>   cannot know
>   and nor can you
>   you cannot answer (*WB*, 47)

Webb becomes her own interrogator, her own torturer, making the space inhabited by I/you an "echo chamber" of various selves. In the next poem, "I" speaks indirectly to a silent "it"—imaged as the ear in the shape of a question mark: "Does it know what I say? / Can it imagine my sentence?" In its refusal to speak, this silent ear eventually silences "I":

> I shut my mouth and open my eyes.
> Suddenly I do not love
> that ornament, that place.
> Turn your head.
> I want to see your face. (*WB*, 48)

In the next poem, "I" confronts a silent "you":

> The hello of your mouth is what I want
> the smile of your crooked pearlies.
> [. . .]
> Let's shutter ourselves in sleep.
> (Where did your mouth go?
> why didn't you say hello?) (*WB*, 49)

Further on in the sequence, "I" becomes silent in the face of torture and abuse: "I have nothing to say" is her response to "[E]xtracted toenails. /[. . .] Burns on the breasts. /[. . .] Electric shock. /[. . .] Beatings" (*WB*, 51). In the final poem of the sequence, "I" gives up her desire/demand for answers, recognizing that there is no "you" to provide answers. The I/you configuration is only an echo chamber of selves. Based on a desire for answers, it constructs a closed circle which is essentially narcissistic and/or solipsistic.

> The error lies in
> the state of desire
> in wanting the answers
> wanting the red-crested
> woodpecker to pose
> among red berries
> of the ash tree
> [. . .]
> and wanting the bird
> to be still and
> wanting it moving
> whiteflash of underwings
> dazzling all questions
> out of me, amazement
> and outbreathing
> become a form
> of my knowing, (*WB*, 52)

In this final section of "A Question of Questions," the pronoun/relational grid is between "I" and "it"; self and world. But they are placed on parallel tracks, rather than in the closed embrace of the I/you configuration: "I move and it moves / into a cedar tree" (*WB*, 52).

In my view the changes in pronoun configurations enact, if not construct, a change in epistemology, from the Cartesian "I," in which knowledge is produced by the autonomous self by means of control and domination of "you," to a participatory "I," in which knowledge is contingent and "I" participates in group identities and alignments. No longer signifying the unmarked (male) gender and unified individual self, "I" becomes a matrix of identities. Conceptually, release from oppression begins, as Webb explains in the Foreword to *Wilson's Bowl*, with recognizing the dominance of male power in her "educational and emotional formation"; syntactically, it begins with destablizing the dominant "I" and reconfiguring the pronoun networks in the poems. However, release and empowerment come slowly. In "Spots of Blood" (which follows "A Question of Questions"), at first "the blood pounds" and the "heart emerges" in anger and sympathy for the other women:

> The blood pounds at my temples.
> The women of the world parade before me
> in red slippers and red vests, back and
> forth, back and forth, fists clenched.
> My heart emerges from my breast for
> 14,000 rats and the citizens of Delft,
> for the women of the world in their menses. (*WB*, 54)

But at the end of the poem, "I" is Dracula's victim: "In the morning sun Count Dracula leans /against my throat with his own teeth" (*WB*, 55).

Dracula is just one of several (usually male) trickster figures who frequently appear in this book: a shape-shifting "you" that confuses, confounds, possesses, dispossesses. Whether Dracula, Raven, Vasarely, Alex, the Russian anarchist Prince Kropotkin, or the "Portrait" figures, they occupy the position of a powerful, dominating, overpowering "you." That figure becomes increasingly distanced, however, as the pronoun configurations shift. When the dominating "you" moves into a more distant, third person (as he, it or they), "I" finds some breathing space. "I" can feel connections, form alignments, join with others to become "we."

"Imperfect Sestina" (the poem that completes the middle section of *Wilson's Bowl*) enacts the struggle to change power relations through changes in alignments (*WB*, 72-73). Early in the poem, "we" are those who, Medusa-like, have "dreamt our demons into stone"; who have been empowered by desire; who have experienced illumination. This empowered "we" contrasts strikingly with the "we [who] are inconsolable" of the opening poem in the book. The rest of this poem is spoken by "I" who, empowered by group identity, speaks her anger, bitterness, suffering, confusion, and struggle:

> Can I really say I found even two cents at the crossing?
> There I was stabbed and pecked by spirit Raven.
> There in that marriage I turned into stone,
> and did not understand he carved me at his mirror. (*WB*, 73)

Unlike the detached, or passive, or silenced "I" of other poems, this "I" speaks loud and clear. Being part of "we" empowers her to speak, as a collaborative "I" empowered by group identity. The result, in this poem, is that "I" unmasks "you" as the trickster figure, or at least makes all the masks visible ("Now any mask can show me all those twins") and releases the "I" from the marriage (the I/you structure) that turned her to stone. In the last section, the twin selves come together (becoming "we") and turn away from the mirror ("you"). The new Eden "smells of cedar," suggesting an emergent physicality and sensuality not unlike the one called for at the end of *Naked Poems*. Raven (the trickster figure of Northwest Coast native mythology) is part of the scene too, but does not dominate. He retreats to a foetal position:

> Laughing and crying, twin meets at the crossing twin.
> They do not ask the mirror. Gold licks of illumination.
> Eden smells of cedar. Raven holds his wings and sucks his stone.
>   (*WB*, 73)

Water and Light

Because I have discussed *Water and Light* extensively earlier in this and the preceding chapter, I won't say much here about the pronoun configurations other than to point out that "I" appears frequently in this book, but mainly as a floating signifier, unattached to other pronouns. "You" rarely appears. As Sharon Thesen writes in her Introduction to *The Vision Tree: Selected Poems by Phyllis Webb*, "Even where the "I" is the subject, the "I" is in flux—not a point of reference but a moving line" (13). Detached from the I/you enclosure and its particular power relations, "I" enacts a subjectivity, including—and here is perhaps the most important change—a gendered subjectivity—instead of the unmarked (male) pronoun that causes so much difficulty for the woman writer. Especially in the "I Daniel" sequence, "I" speaks not from a position of mastery, nor as the dominant (or receptive) partner in an I/you configuration, but from positions formed and informed by linguistic, social, and historical contexts.

Hanging Fire

Hanging Fire is predominantly an I/we, we/they story, and the change in pronoun configurations has several effects on the relational grid within the poems. First of all, "I" does not depend on the binary I/you structure to exist. "I speak therefore I am," Webb writes in " 'Self City' " (*HF*, 24); the act of speaking creates the subject.[3] The speaking "I" has freedom to roam into various structures and relationships, to form alignments, to make connections, to adopt various guises and disguises, to perform different roles. The speaker(s) is/are witty, funny, angry, sad, ironic, sardonic, prosaic, poetic. There are prose poems, lyric poems, sound poems, shaped poems, playful dialogues, comic and serious impersonations. "I" often makes fun of her various poses and positions. In the midst of agonizing over the devastation caused by the eruption of Krakatoa, for instance, she wryly notes her voyeuristic position:

> God how I suffer to get this down as if I'd
> been there watching the lava hit and run after
> dogs and children and hens, cone island collapsing
> into the sea. Always this me. Tourist, back-packed,
> camera at ready, lens cap removed. (*HF*, 14)

In another, "I" inhabits a gamut of clichéd poetic roles:

> I've fallen over again
> into *despond*, occluded
> rage. I tear up another
> page of pilgrim's progress
> I lie on Donne's love's
> violet bank, say nothing
> all the day, nothing into
> the cliché-ridden night. (*HF*, 25)

Indeed, in *Hanging Fire*, "I" rather than "you" has become the shape-shifting, trickster figure, not only as the multivoiced "I" in the poems, but also in the cross-dressings performed by the writer in writing the poems. Webb's modus operandi in this book (as discussed in

chapter 1) is to start the poems with "'given' words phrases or sen-
tences that arrive unbidden in my head" (*HF*, 7): "I try to allow these
words that arrive unbidden to lead me into poems, and have been using
this sort of intense listening as a conscious process for about two years
now" ("MM," *LIHE*, 293). While these words are in some sense *sepa-
rate* from her (hence the quotation marks), she is the one who hears
them and writes them down. The "I" is both passive (listener) and ac-
tive (writer), as Webb observes in her essay "Message Machine." In the
essay, for instance, she is variously the voice of "Psychopomp . . . Mer-
cury in his guise as escort of the dead" (293) (which is the "given"
word at the start of the essay), the narrator of the essay, the victim figure
in the poem which she writes in the middle of the essay, and the critic
who analyzes the poem after it is written:

> Why are you so hard on yourself? a small voice asks, and the counter-
> tenor responds, look at that narrator of yours, and a first-person narra-
> tor too, like some rape victim being towed along on a journey she's
> only too willing to take.
> [. . .]
>   The voices are becoming confusing. Here's one that says, wait.
> Let's look at this whole thing more carefully. Is there a message here
> as in a dream, perhaps a reversal, disguise, an androgynous bi-play?
>   Well, OK, I say, an interpretation, I'm not against it. I am not
> 'me.' I'm really Psychopomp—cross-dressing would be a trendy way
> of describing this transformation now. ("MM," *LIHE*, 295)

The analytic voice also has several guises:

> The post-facto analytical intelligence sometimes performs with cool
> accomplished reserve, sometimes, like Glenn Gould, humming along
> with the music. There are other times when a gleeful and spiteful
> intentionality slashes a line across the page, knocks the cliché on the
> head, kicks the dogma under the table. ("MM," *LIHE*, 296)

"I" is indeed a trickster, shape-shifter figure who adopts various guises
and voices, who shifts according to which way the wind is blowing:

> Yes. No. Two words are better than one during the paradigm shift.
> Spit and hold your finger to the wind. Which way is blowing? Is
> blowing the lid off your head? Is prose. Poem? (*HF*, 53)

In a poem appropriately titled "Performance," "I" explores this
plurality of subject positions and relations. Although this poem appears
toward the end of the book, it was first published in 1984,[4] which
places it early on in the writing of *Hanging Fire*. The poem begins with

a question: "Who is this *I* infesting my poems?" In response, Webb cites a number of possibilities, from the "*I* hiding behind the trump type on the page of the book you are reading," to "a photograph of me on the cover of *Wilson's Bowl*," to the voice of the lyric poem—"*I* am the mask, the voice, the one who begins those lyrical poems, *I wandered lonely as a cloud*" (*HF*, 67), to the performative figure of the poet standing at the microphone. Who are these figures: "Is it I? *I* said, *I* say, *I* am saying—" (*HR*, 67). Further on, as she listens to various voices, the I of the poem self-destructs:

> *Listen*: Do you hear the *I* running away with the man in the green hat? Look again. *I* is off and diving into Fulford Harbour to run with the whales. *I* spout. *I* make whalesong. Passengers on the ferry swarm to starboard to see me disporting myself. *I/we* know they are out to get us. Yes, they are mad for education. They'll pen us up at Sealand and we'll die. We don't build big and we can't shoot. *I* commits suicide in the watery commune, the vocal pod. *We* swims on. (*HF*, 67)

Given Webb's early poem about suicidal impulses ("To Friends Who Have Also Considered Suicide" *VT*, 54), the suicide of "I" is especially interesting. Here the suicide becomes not a self-silencing act but a transformative one.[5] When the lyric "I" self-destructs, it ends the I/you enclosure that silences and/or disempowers the woman writer. When "*I* commits suicide" and "*We* swims on," there emerges a protean, polyvocal self(selves)—the "vocal pod" of the poem.

Two paragraphs later, another "we" enters the poem. This is the collaborative, group-identified "we" that I spoke of earlier in this chapter which, in this instance, also includes "you":

> I devise. You devise. We devise. To be together briefly with the page, the fallen timber. Or with me here standing before you wondering if the mike is on, if my mask is on, *persona*, wondering what to read next, or whether you'll turn the page. (*HF*, 68)

Though some of the familiar anxiety of the I/you structure lingers on, the emphasis on the performative and collaborative nature of reading/writing brings "I" and "you" together as "we."

Here, detaching "I" from the I/you configuration releases a plurality of speaking subjects and generates group connections. It also releases a sharper oppositional politics. When "I" joins with others to form a group "we," there is an implied, if not stated, we/they configuration. Indeed, many of the poems in *Hanging Fire* are angry and accu-

satory, including the poem where Webb hangs a curtain of fire on the
page, as a warning perhaps:

> hanging f   hanging f   hanging f   hanging f
>   ire   ire   ire   ire (*HF*, 39)

Human arrogance and genetic manipulations (*HF*, 13), experimenta-
tion with animals (*HF*, 28), commodity culture (*HF*, 69), "Delusional
systems" (*HF*, 36)—these are some of the targets (and sources) of that
anger. Although the pronoun "we" rarely appears in the book, "I"
speaks from a position of a group-identified subjectivity. Like the "I"
trapped in the Leaning Tower of Pisa in *Water and Light* together with
"you" and the "smelly tourists," the "I" becomes part of an intercon-
nected ecosystem: "we" feed in the same "biologic 'soup' "; swim in
the same river (22).

> Some of it makes sense, shape, meaning meandering river of biologic
> 'soup' on which fish, birds, insects feed that feed us. River on which
> we move undulant, forsaking all else for this infectious cruise.
> (" 'Seeking Shape, Seeking Meaning,' " *HF*, 22)

The I/you relationship is expanded into the social "we." In the pro-
cess, "you" as the opposing term in a binary opposition disappears. In a
poem dedicated to Salman Rushdie, who literally vanished from public
view, Webb writes of the disappearing "you":

> 'You are Nowhere'
>
> in the work. The work is kin.
> It's all in the family.
> [. . .]
> You are somewhere in the world
> of 'the fire next time'.
>
> I am trying to find you.
> You are nowhere. Somewhere (*HF*, 38)

While the poem obviously refers to Rushdie's going into hiding fol-
lowing the Ayatollah's call for his death, I think it also metaphorizes the
disappearing "you" in discourse. Just as the Ayatollah cannot find his
targeted opposition, the sovereign "I" loses "you" as the Other in the
socio-discursive field of the poem. Thus the pronoun structures in
Hanging Fire enact relational lines of connection, alignment, negotia-

tion. They also enact the fluid nature of those relations as "I devise. You devise. We Devise / To be together briefly with the page" (*HF*, 68).

Notes

1 I am indebted to Nicole Brossard's essay "Poetic Politics" for some of my ideas about pronoun structures, particularly her summary of the political implications of different pronoun combinations. Brossard writes:

"WE triggers emotions based on solidarity, memory, identification, complicity, proudness, or sadness.

THEY triggers emotions based on anger and revolt. Hatred also: THEY cuts the relation.

YOU (in the plural *vous*) triggers accusations, blame, reproach. It maintains the relation because it is a direct address. *You* calls for negotiation just as *they* calls for struggle.

We all have an I/We story and a We/They story. If you belong to a dominant group, *they* is either laughable, insignificant, or used as a scapegoat. If you belong to an oppressed group, *they* is targeted as enemy because they have proven to be a real threat or danger to your collectivity or your group" (80).

2 Marianna Torgovnick offers a very interesting anlysis of what she calls the "cultural we" in identity politics: "I do not object to the 'we' voice in and of itself. What I object to is the easy slide from 'I' to 'we' that takes place almost unconsciously for many users of the first-person plural or its equivalents—and is often the hidden essence of cultural criticism. This slide can make the 'we' function not as a device to link writer and reader, or as a particularized group voice, or even the voice of 'the culture,' but rather as a covert, and sometimes coercive, universal. I would like to slow down that slide to appreciate the full deceptiveness of the false cultural 'we,' and then examine its relationship to some current issues" (49).

3 See also Benveniste's argument that the subject exists only in language, as the "I" in discourse (Benveniste, 225).

4 "Performance" was first published in *Canadian Literature*, 100 (1984).

5 This idea comes from Janice Williamson's discussion of suicide as a transformative act. Williamson writes: "the language of suicide . . . shifts from incomprehension to transformation and acceptance" ("The Feminine Suicide Narratives of Phyllis Webb," *West Coast Line* Number Six, 25, 3 [1991-92]: 155-74).

5

Intertextual Dialogues:
Wilson's Bowl and *Hanging Fire*

The modernist notion of the text as self-sufficient objet d'art has been replaced, in much contemporary writing, by an emphasis on intertextuality. Both writer and reader are viewed as part of intertextual networks; texts are defined as relational and contingent; language processes are foregrounded rather than naturalized; and the word is seen as a constellation of meanings, produced by the *"intersection of textual surfaces"* (Kristeva, *KR*, 36) rather than as a stable meaning unit. John Frow explains: "The concept of intertextuality requires that we understand the concept of text not as a self-contained structure but as differential and historical. Texts are shaped not by an immanent time but by the play of divergent temporalities" (Frow, 45). Indeed, when Julia Kristeva developed the concept of intertextuality in her 1966 essay, "Word, Dialogue, and Novel," it was to emphasize intertextuality as a necessary precondition of all writing, following Bakhtin's notion of the " 'literary word' as a dialogue among several writings: that of the writer, the addressee . . . and the contemporary or earlier cultural context" (quoted in Kristeva, *KR*, 36). Kristevan intertextuality, however, refers more to a way of reading than to a compositional process: "every signifying practice is a field of transpositions of various signifying systems (an intertextuality)" (*KR*, 111) and that the writer and reader are thus always already within intertextual fields of meanings. It is simply a fact of writing, an a priori condition. But in Webb's work intertextuality becomes a compositional tool. She devises various ways of working with intertexts to deliberately transpose their signifying systems. Especially in her books of the past twenty-five years, the intertextuality seems quite proactive, part of her ongoing critique of history, tradition, and authority.

The list of more than a dozen intertexts that she provides in the "Notes to the Poems" at the end of *Wilson's Bowl*, for instance, suggests

---

The notes to this chapter are on p. 107-108.

a self-conscious intertextual dynamic in that book. That *Water and Light* is an intertextual intervention is signalled first by the subtitle *Ghazals and Anti Ghazals*, which points to the book's critique of the romantic tradition, and second by the epigraphs from *The Ghazals of Ghalib*, which form an intertextual Table of Contents for the book's five sections. Webb works with and against Ghalib's themes and forms to transpose the discourses of romance (as discussed in earlier chapters of this book). In *Hanging Fire*, the epigraph from Daphne Marlatt again emphasizes intertextual processes, including the erotic dimensions of intertextual relations[1]: "words call each other up, evoke each other, provoke each other, nudge each other into utterance . . . a form of thought that is not rational but erotic because it works by attraction" (Marlatt's ellipses). Also, Webb's opening explanation of her compositional method (of taking " 'given' words phrases or sentences" as titles and starting points for the poems) further signals a self-conscious use of intertextuality, while the numerous dedications, quotations, paraphrases, and at times deliberate misquotations throughout the book foreground the densely intertextual fabric of each poem.[2]

One also finds many intertextual compositional processes in Webb's poetry. Taking intertextuality in the Kristevan sense as the literal presence of one text in another, Webb uses the full palette of imitation, theft, translation, allusion, parody, paraphrase, pastiche, direct and indirect quotation, and naming. Taking intertextuality in a broader sense, as Michael Worton and Judith Still do (following Genette) in their Introduction to *Intertextuality: Theories and Practices*, to mean "everything, be it explicit or latent, that links one text to others" (22), Webb's range is even wider. Her work includes "paratextuality"— "relations between the body of a text and its titles, epigraphs, illustrations, notes, first drafts, etc."[3] As well, Webb's varied uses of the lyric, the haiku, the ghazal, the sestina, and other poetic forms engage what Genette calls "architextuality" by which he means relations between and within formal categories (cited in Worton and Still, 22-23). Webb's intertextual interventions operate along many lines of signification.

These interventions are made possible by the instability of the intertextual field. As Riffaterre explains, intertextuality "enables the text to represent, at one and the same time, convention and departures from it, tradition and novelty, sociolect and idiolect, the already said and its negation or transformation" (Riffaterre, 76). Or, as Worton and Still point out, "every quotation distorts and redefines the 'primary' utterance by relocating it within another linguistic and cultural context" (11). Any intertextual field is necessarily fluctuating and variable and thus can become a site for intervention. But the centrifugal effects of intertextuality vary considerably, depending on the writer's relation to history and tradition. For a writer who works primarily out of respect for tradition, or who challenges tradition from a position of authority and privilege (as, for example, in the case of male avant-garde writers), the intertextual networks contribute historical weight and authority to the new "linguistic and cultural context." Their effect is more integrative than disruptive. Even in the modernists' disjunctive, collaged intertextuality, the intertexts have an integrative function. In Ezra Pound's *Cantos*, for instance, his numerous citations from past "masters" anchor and validate his construction of an alternative tradition in twentieth-century culture. In Webb's poetry, however, while the weight of history and tradition is continuously undermined, the authority of "source" texts and "original" stories constantly questioned, hers is not a direct challenge to authority and stability, because she does not speak from a position of authority. Her intertextual interventions destabilize and reframe the past within continuing unstable intertextual fields of meaning.

Webb's poem "I Daniel" demonstrates this process. While based on the biblical book of Daniel, it is by no means a retelling of the "original" story. Webb skips the first part of Daniel's story altogether (the story of how Daniel's belief in God enables him to survive the lion's den and, with his companions Shadrach, Meshach, and Abednego, to survive Nebuchadnezzar's fiery furnace). Some details from the second section of the book of Daniel enter Webb's poem (where Daniel has a series of prophetic dreams, becomes Nebuchadnezzar's advisor, and eventually foretells several hundred years of history), but they are recontextualized within the contemporary debate about truth, vision, and the artist's relationship to society. Daniel's blind prophecy, explained in the Bible as God speaking through him, becomes, in Webb's poem, a metaphor for the contingent nature of truth and vision in the late twentieth century. The fragments from the Book of Daniel combine, in Webb's poem, into new meaning circuits.

Take the references to the "music" for instance: in the biblical story, the music signifies the worship of false Gods: it is Nebuchadnezzar's signal to his subjects to fall down and worship his golden idols.

then a herald cried aloud, To you it is commanded, O people, na-
tions, and languages, That at what time ye hear the sound of the cor-
net, flute, harp, sackbut, psaltery, dulcimer, and all kinds of music, ye
fall down and worship the golden image that Nebuchadnezzar the
king hath set up: And whoso falleth not down and worshippeth shall
the same hour be cast into the midst of a burning fiery furnace.
Therefore at that time, when all the people heard the sound of the
cornet, flute, sackbut, psaltery, dulcimer, and all kinds of music, all
the people, the nations, and the languages, fell down and worshipped
the golden image that Nebuchadnezzar the king had set up. (Daniel
3:4-6)

In Webb's poem, however, the music is generative. Indeed Webb has
commented that the impulse to begin the poem came from her discov-
ering the list of instruments; she was intrigued by the sound of the
words and started writing the poem.[4] Within the semiotic field of
Webb's poem, the music signifies a welcome artistic diversity: "I live
now and in time past// among all kinds of musick—sackbut, / cornet,
flute, psaltery, harp, and dulcimer" (*WL*, 35, *VT* 151).

The archaic spelling of "musick" does retain a trace of the "sick-
ness" of idolatry represented by the music in the Bible. But music in
Webb's poem signals creative listening and a wide-ranging sensitivity.
Where the local and particular are valued, as they are in the contempo-
rary world, the meaning of "music" changes. Hearing the instruments,
listening to the music—metaphors for a participatory position—
replace the muse or God as the basis of inspiration or vision. However,
the other meaning circuits are not totally erased. In the last poem of the
sequence, Daniel seeks transcendence (to "escape into the arms of
Gabriel") while the music plays on in a partial repeat of the list at the
beginning of the poem:

> It was only politics, wars and rumours,
> in the vision or dream:
>
> four beasts of terror with their
> numbers game. I play and trick my way
>
> Out of this scene into the arms of Gabriel
> who does not hear the tune performed
>
> on sackbut, psaltery, harp and dulcimer. (*WL*, 42, *VT*, 154)

The syntax here leaves Daniel's future position uncertain. Does he escape into the arms of Gabriel? Perhaps not. Does Daniel still hear the music? We don't know. Past, present, and future stories intermingle in an intertextual field, an intermingling that effectively dispels the notion of an original source or authority or story.

Other Daniel texts also enter the intertextual field of Webb's poem and bring with them other stories and visions about the artist in the twentieth century. The dedication of the poem to Timothy Findley recalls Findley's twentieth-century Daniel figure Hugh Selwyn Mauberley, the main character in Findley's novel *Famous Last Words*, who, while a prisoner in Fascist Italy, foretells a corrupt Europe (a story that he writes on the walls of his prison). Findley's Mauberley, in turn, resonates with Ezra Pound's ironic alter ego "Hugh Selwyn Mauberley," another visionary figure who claimed to see the truth and who was, like other Daniel figures, "out of key with his time" (Pound, 173). Yet another intertext is Pound's "The Pisan Cantos" in which Pound writes of his experience of isolation and suffering while imprisoned in Italy for anti-American radio broadcasts during World War II. A more recent intertext is E.L. Doctorow's 1971 novel *The Book of Daniel*. In Doctorow's novel, Daniel is the son of the Isaacsons (read Rosenbergs), political prisoners in the U.S. who were executed in the McCarthy era for allegedly being communists and committing treason. While they are Doctorow's "Beacon of Faith in a Time of Persecution" (22) and represent those who suffer from the ideological clashes that produce politically motivated executions, they are also, like the biblical Daniel, often confused and uncertain. Webb brings together these various Daniel stories into an aggregate intertextual structure of new and old meanings which redefine the artist/visionary in the twentieth century.

The distinctive feature of any aggregate structure is that it is built on linked particles and thus the combinatory processes remain visible. Similarly, in Webb's aggregate poetic structures, the reader can see Webb at work, making and changing meanings. A poem titled " 'Seeking Shape. Seeking Meaning,' " for instance, simultaneously enacts fragmenting and combinatory processes. Shape and meaning, she suggests in one section, come from particular linguistic and emotional "hooks":

> Cadence in scene, in the *seen*, seeking out pattern, finding where the
> eye catches, heart hooks, tangible order, a cadence. Tantrums of tears
> at such pure spirit, radiant things, on which the eyes close. (*HF*, 21)

At another point, she describes the effect of fragmentation as "to understand the parts, reify certain / curious particulars to our habit of framing." By fragmenting meaning into particles, we see how value systems are formed, how meanings are shaped or framed, how we are shaped by meanings:

> Some of it makes sense, shape, meaning meandering river of biologic 'soup' on which fish, birds, insects feed, that feed us. River on which we move undulant, forsaking all else for this infectious cruise" (*HF*, 22)

The volcanic eruption that begins the poem " 'Krakatoa' and 'Spiritual Storm' " also metaphorizes a necessary fragmentation of values and meanings, in this instance, as part of a major paradigm shift. The poem consists of many fragments of intertexts, again in an aggregate structure. They include lines from a newspaper report of the volcano erupting at Krakatoa, lines from the accounts of atomic bomb explosions (the "darkness at noon" at Hiroshima or the "desert bloom" of nuclear bomb testing), references to historical figures (Cassandra, Nostradamus), lines from a Wallace Stevens poem, and a dedication to Canadian writers Dorothy Livesay and bill bissett. At the start, the "heart hooks" and the "eye catches" on the geophysical, sexual, and ideological upheavals metaphorized as the volcanic eruption at Krakatoa:

> Hot magma
> indigo dawn
> wild yelps
> of pure physics
> crack open deep sea
> buttocks thrust up love lava
> world heart / broken /cardiac
> arrest.
> *Krakatoa. Krakatau.* (*HF*, 14)

Further on, she is "hooked" on the sound of the word "Spectacle" (of "marvellous sunsets for years") which calls up the homonym of spectacles as eyeglasses, which brings to mind Wallace Stevens' poem "Le monocle de mon / oncle." But Stevens' single-vision monocle is rejected, "sent flying into the eye / of the storm." The singular male sexuality in Stevens' poem, like the tunnel vision that insists on nuclear testing, is exploded in the recent "Spiritual Storm" of ecological, geophysical, nuclear, and sexual eruptions. Webb's responses are also fragmented: she feels compelled—"God I suffer to get this down"—but also detached—"Always this me. Tourist, back-packed, / camera at ready, lens cap removed" (*HF*, 14-16). Webb does not offer any new synthesis; the exploded particles remain in motion, as an aggregate of fragments. In linguistic terms, Webb's intertextual process is to work with the poem's semes (rather than its themes), the seme being " 'a minimal unit of signification,' comparable at the semantic level to what the phoneme is at the phonological level."[5] Semes combine to form sememes and to form polysemic structures. Focussing on semes allows Webb to fragment received cultural scripts and introduce alternative meanings.[6]

In gender terms, focussing on semes enables Webb to open the semiotic fields and create space for the female writing subject. It is a process that Rachel Blau DuPlessis aptly describes as changing the "taste" of words. Speaking of her desire to write a "poetry of shifters, a pronominal poetry, where discourses shift, times shift, tones shift, nothing is exclusive or uniform, the 'whole' is susceptible to stretchings and displacements," DuPlessis explains that she does so "[i]n part because of the gender contexts in which . . . words have lived, of which they taste" (144). Likewise, the "stretchings and displacements" in Webb's poems disturb those "gender contexts" and change the "taste" of the words. Her intertextual processes enact a "playful woman making a space to breathe," as she puts it, in explaining "the reasons I write" to an inquisitive editor:

> An editor asks me to put it all down: the reasons I write. And I thought "it" was a gift. Homo ludens at play among the killing fields of dry grasses. Playful woman making a space to breathe
> [. . .]
> What does he want? Contributions to knowledge? Civilisation and its discontents? Chaos among the order—or, oh yes, french doors opening onto a deck and a small pool where we can watch our weird reflections shimmering and insubstantial? The proper response to a poem is another poem. We burrow into the paper to court in secret the life of plants, the shifty moon's space-walks, the bliss, the roses, the glamorous national debt. Someone to talk to, for God's sake, some-thing to love that will never hit back. (" 'There *Are* the Poems,' " *HF*, 57)

Intersubjectivity: "someone to talk to, something to love"

As Webb implies in the above excerpt, her intertextual dialogues often question and challenge the power imbalances and the accompanying complex mix of "power and seduction" (*WB*, 49) in male-female social/textual relations. In the postwar period when Webb began writing, women were excluded from men's conversational circles, relegated to the "Ladies and Escorts" side of the bar. "[w]ho are you . . . whose are you?" she demands of a nameless, faceless "you" that seems a mixture of lover and oppressor; "Turn your head. / I want to see your face"; "Where did your mouth go? / why didn't you say hello?" ("A Question of Questions," *WB*, 47-49). Such questions assert her presence and demand that she be listened to by her literary and other fathers. They open spaces in the discursive field for the woman writer to speak, as she declares in a poem titled "Solitary Confinement":

> Let my tongue hang out
> to remember the thirst for life.
> Let my tongue hang out
> to deliver itself
> of the bitter curd.
> And spit
> give me water for spit.
> Then give me
> a face. ("Solitary Confinement," *WB*, 41)

Webb's intertextual dialogues are most often with father figures, but her demands for recognition ("give me / a face") cannot be fully explained as an Oedipal rebellion against the father. Hers is not a progressive development from dependence to independence that ends with the overthrow of the father.[7] Webb also continues to acknowledge, imitate, and listen to her literary forefathers and culture heroes. "Oh dear," she writes in an essay that notes the persistent presence of male mentors in her work, "why has old psyche thrown up yet another male figure, attractive, ambiguous, quick-silvery though he may be?" ("MM," *LIHE*, 293-94). At the end of the same essay, she ruefully notes:

> I've resisted writing this essay for months, possibly because my instinct to subvert the assigned exercise collided with my good-daughter mode. . . . After I decided I might as well give up on the attempt, and as the dead-line approached ever closer, I turned on the message machine: Hi, I'm Psychopomp, pomp, pomp, pomp— *et voilà* I

made it. My last two given phrases, by the way, were "Self City" and "Anaximander"—not again. ("MM," *LIHE*, 296)

Again and again, Webb both resists and is drawn to hegemonic, male figures and texts.

I find feminist psychologist Jessica Benjamin's concept of "inter-subjectivity[8]" is helpful in understanding this ongoing love/hate aspect of Webb's intertextual relationships, because in Benjamin's analysis, the power struggles are not resolved, self and other are not separated. Basing her analysis on pre-Oedipal relations, Benjamin posits "self and other as distinct but interrelated beings" engaged in a lifelong alternation between separation and identification (20). This model shifts attention to "the need for mutual recognition" within ongoing relationships rather than the need to break with the parental past (23). For Benjamin, the issue is "not how we become free of the other, but how we actively engage and make ourselves known in relationship to the other" (18); thus "assertion *and* recognition become the vital moves in the dialogue between self and other" (22). Whereas the Oedipal overthrow of literary forefathers is based on an assumption of male entitlement to positions of authority, Benjamin's model opens up the whole question of how power and authority are granted or assumed. Webb's mixture of resistance, critique, admiration and affection in her intertextual dialogues similarly foregrounds power relations and opens spaces for reconfiguring those relations. Benjamin's notion of ongoing processes of self-actualization and renegotiation within a continuum of subject-to-subject relations parallel Webb's combined defiant and commemorative intertextual relations.

In Webb's "Poems of Failure" and the "Portraits," her first sustained attempts at opening up textual/cultural spaces by means of intertextual dialogues,[9] I see this mixture of "assertion *and* recognition." In "Poems of Failure," Webb's intertext is the *Memoirs* of the Russian anarchist, Prince Kropotkin. Lines from the Kropotkin text resonate variously with Webb's experiences of shadows and prisons and impasses. But in contrast to the civic-minded, humanitarian Kropotkin ("The White Christ," *WB*, 21), Webb observes her own passivity, withdrawal, and inability to act. Shadows all but engulf her: "I grasp what I can. The rest / is a great shadow" (*WB*, 13, *VT*, 110). Yet Webb sees connections between her and Kropotkin's stories: Kropotkin's political anarchism offers a possible model for revolutionary poetic action by its anti-authoritarianism; Webb's poetic "anarchism" refuses

the authority of the lyric subject and the exclusionary position of the
Cartesian "I":

> Insurrectionary wilderness of the I
> am, I will be, forcing the vision
> to something other, something out
> side the sleep of dreams riddled
> with remembrances.
> k,k,k, the Prince in his dungeon
> exploring his way. *(WB, 15)*

Webb, like Kropotkin, is "imprisoned," in her case by the conceptual/
emotional impasse that she finds herself in: "What is locked in never-
theless pounds / at the gates" (WB, 17). Like Kropotkin, who was a
geographer, she too engages in mapping: she makes an intertextual
quilt, which serves as a poncho (perhaps for protection):

> I cut out diamonds from a pattern piece
> by piece. I sew two pieces, one purple
> one red, together, attach another making designs
> as I go. Mapping it into some kind of crazy
> poncho. I am absorbed in the fitting together
> of pieces. Troika the white cat watches.
> Red velvet on purple purple on red colours
> of the mystic and revolutionary. *The Politics*
> *of Experience, Love's Body, Psycho-*
> *pathology and Politics*, Trotsky's *Journal*, Pushkin,
> *The Possessed, Social Contract, Journey into Russia,*
> *Memoirs of a Revolutionist, The Romantic Exiles,*
> *Anarchism.* 'Eleanor Rigby.' *(WB, 18)*

However, at the end of the Kropotkin sequence, Webb still feels at an
impasse: in the final analysis, she is not like the revolutionary Kropot-
kin: "Not a case of identification. Easier to see myself / in the white cat
asleep on the bed. Exile" (WB, 21). In contrast to Kropotkin, her
" 'good masterpiece of work' / does not come" (WB, 21). By the end
of the book (when writing the Foreword), she comes to see that her
"failure" as not so much the result of personal shortcomings as of social
conditioning—specifically, the "domination of male power culture in
my educational and emotional formation."[10] She inevitably falls short in
any comparison with male figures since they already occupy a dominant
position.

"Portraits"

Webb's "Portraits" (written shortly after the Kropotkin sequence) of such venerable figures as Socrates, Dostoevsky, Ezra Pound, and Kropotkin, more directly challenge the authority of historical figures and texts and are thus more successful as intertextual interventions. Webb does this by focussing on the weaknesses and questioning the supposed strengths of these hegemonic figures. Indeed, these poems are more like anti-portraits because they deflate the heroic. The great Prince Kropotkin, for instance, is portrayed on his deathbed, his tongue silenced "('*la langue / paralysée et suis / incapable* . . .')" (*WB*, 28, Webb's ellipses). In her portrait of Dostoevsky, Webb at first imagines herself as "a beetle in the cabbage soup they serve up for geniuses / in the House of the Dead"—an unlikely position from which to take action. Indeed, she is "drowning fast." However, halfway through the poem she becomes more active, declaring "I'll leap into your foaming mouth and jump your tongue," and by the end she silences him: "Hold your tongue! You can't speak yet. You are mine, Dostoevsky" (*WB*, 29-30; *VT*, 118). In her portrait of Ezra Pound, Webb emphasizes his powerlessness—as a prisoner of war at Pisa and as a prisoner of "his fixed / obsession" (*WB*, 31; *VT*, 119). To the poet Rilke she says, "I speak your name I throw it away" (*WB*, 32; *VT*, 120); in "Vasarely" she declares, "I shift my gaze from the abode of adoration" (*WB*, 34; *VT*, 122), thus diminishing his power, although his paternalistic voice still speaks to her at the end of the poem: "*Pourquoi es-tu si triste, chérie?*" the voice asks, and then offers the (unwelcome) reassurance that the father figure will always be with her: "'*C'est toujours moi. / C'est moi. C'est Vasarely*'" (*WB*, 35; *VT*, 123). In Webb's "Father" portrait, the problem is masculine silence and aloofness rather than overprotective paternalism. Caught up in his Rosicrucian vision of a perfect world, he doesn't even see or hear her—"his eyes seeing beyond me / the Rosy Cross" (*WB*, 33; *VT*, 121). Webb's anti-portrait emphasizes his absence. In her anti-portrait of Socrates, while following the script of Socrates' life as told in Plato's *Phaedo*, Webb mocks Socrates' heroic rationalism, his supposed mastery and control as he prepares to drink the lethal hemlock: "Whoever died like that / with such good manners?" (*WB*, 26; *VT*, 116).

> What a dumb play
> for one who knew
> all the answers
> his questions

were answers.
'For is not philosophy
the study of death?' (*WB*, 27; *VT*, 117)

Webb's ironic questions initiate a reading backwards into the past against the grain of the hegemonic. She thus inserts a female subject into the male conversational circle in a subject-to-subject relation.

"Strange Attractors"

Another way of conceptualizing Webb's intertextual relations is via the notion of "strange attractors" that has been developed in recent chaos theory. In chaos systems, the movement of seemingly random particles into recognizable patterns is explained by the presence of "strange attractors"—defined as "any point in an orbit that seems to pull the system toward it" (Morris, 212). In the field of the poem, Roland Barthes named these "*siren* signifiers" (*RB on RB*, 145)—words that sing out, words that seduce, words that can't be resisted, like the song of the sirens that Odysseus encountered. However, while Barthes' term usefully emphasizes the erotic, seductive power of intertexts, it implies only a male experience, since the siren is traditionally female. I prefer the term "strange attractors," which implies the seductive, persistent, unpredictable nature of the attractors but without a gender tag.

In any case, in Webb's poetry, the "attractors" that push/pull the poems are usually father figures, trickster figures, or male muse figures—all of whom enact the contradictory qualities of strangeness and attraction. They include Kropotkin, Socrates, Rilke, Vasarely, Ghalib, Ghandi, Lenin, Wilson Duff, Wallace Stevens, William Carlos Williams, Ezra Pound, Anaximander, and Hermes, to name a few. Again and again, Webb responds to the push/pull of these figures with intertextual dialogues that are both commemorative and resisting, that combine assertion and recognition, to repeat Benjamin's terms. To take an example: Webb's poem " 'Thinking Cap' " is an intertextual dialogue with one of the major father figures of twentieth-century poetry—William Carlos Williams, a decidedly powerful figure in Webb's "intellectual and emotional formation." I quote the entire poem:

" 'Thinking Cap' "

The red hat
sails

through a rift
in my skull
out and over the
waiting audience
it's the colour
of red peppers
it's a flying
saucer
hovering there
spying and spritely
elvish in the coy
mood of not being
a red wheel
barrow
as mute though
as silent-speaking
this thing/spinning
over your head
preparing to land
fasten your seatbelt
lady and don't smoke
we're coming in
to Williamsland
to invade
the objects
to snatch the
after-image of
ol' Bill's plums—
you know—
the ones that
tasted so good
because they were
cold and beautiful
and couldn't

speak (*HF*, 64-65)

Here Webb both imitates (and thus honours) as well as rewrites two of
Williams' best-known poems, "The Red Wheelbarrow" and "This Is
Just to Say." The colour of Webb's thinking cap is the same as Williams'

wheelbarrow—which links Webb's poem to Williams—but her think-
ing cap is constantly on the move, signifying her intersubjective and
interventionist poetics. The cap "sails" out of her head toward the audi-
ence, then hovers "spinning" like a flying saucer, and veers off to invade
"Williamsland" where it disturbs the iconic objects, disturbs the
hegemonic position of Williams' imagist aesthetics, along with the ethic
of objectivity established by Williams, Ezra Pound, and other Modern-
ist writers. In contrast to Williams' red wheelbarrow which affirms the
truth status of the object, Webb's mobile "thinking cap" includes the
viewer's standpoint. In the above poem, for instance, Webb shows that
the values Williams assigns to objects (e.g., the plums) are connected to
his desire. Williams describes the plums, saying, "Forgive me they were
delicious / so sweet / and so cold" (354)—tasty objects, nothing more.
Webb's paraphrase of Williams, however, changes the descriptive terms
slightly, which shows how his desire feminizes the objects: "they tasted
so good / because they were / cold and beautiful / and couldn't speak."
Webb's paraphrase highlights the connection between plums and
women as objects of desire (signalled both by the fact that Williams
poem is written to his wife and by the association of plums with female
genitals) and thus reminds the reader of the long tradition of woman as
art object silenced by male desire. Webb expands the semiotic field to
include the "after image" of Williams' desire.

     Yet the Williams texts are also addressed affectionately. Webb imi-
tates the closing cadence of Williams' poem, for instance, even as she
protests his masculist bias,[11] although possibly I am now bringing my
own affection for Williams' poems—via the readerly axis of intertextu-
ality[12]—into the poem. Certainly, for me, meeting the plums and the
red wheelbarrow in Webb's poem is like meeting old friends. In any
case, the Webb / Williams interactions in the poem do not strike me as
the Oedipal battle where the rebellious young writer overthrows the
father. Instead, Webb creates an intersubjective relation that includes
both "recognition" and "assertion." Williams remains an "attractor"
even as Webb asserts her difference from him. The effect of this subject-
to-subject relation is to establish a textual, social space for female sub-
jectivity and agency within Williamsland.

     While the "strange attractors" in Webb's work are most often texts
by male writers, Webb does occasionally address women's texts. How-
ever, her dialogues with women's texts are more affectionate, more ad-
miring, less resistant, less violent. Also, the women are Webb's contem-
poraries, not figures from the past. Sisters rather than parents as role

models, whom she admires for their strengths: courage, expansiveness, and an ability to express anger, for instance. In "Gwendolyn MacEwen 1941-1987," Webb praises "[y]our last poems so big with cosmos & semen & gold" (*HF*, 61); in "Bronwen's Earrings," she admires Wallace's "touch of fantastic / as she moved her head / to follow the plot" (*HF*, 71). In the earlier "Letters to Margaret Atwood," she wonders if she can adopt Atwood's seditious stance: "After survival, what? the sedition in my own hand, will it be written down legibly, will I sign it and hand it over for someone else to fulfill" (*WB*, 38). In a reversal of the usual mentoring structure, Webb finds the example of young women poets especially helpful. In response to Smaro Kamboureli's question about her anger in *Hanging Fire*, for instance—"What made it possible for you to let this anger surface in this book?"—Webb explains, "I attribute it to the many feminist angry young women poets whom I've mentioned before. They gave me the sign, the sign that my time had come to be freer" (Kamboureli interview, 31).

In a recent poem, "Grapevine," a self-reflexive "she" is transformed by becoming intertwined with the grapevine of her own and other women's voices. The first intertextual reference in this poem is to an earlier poem of Webb's: the phrase "trying to write a poem" is from her 1966 *Naked Poems* (*SP*, 106). In quoting herself, Webb reiterates and recontextualizes her earlier statement that writing a poem can be a liberating action. Here the line becomes part of a "grape-vine" of women's talk, the gossip line that links various texts/voices. By climbing literal and figurative walls—like the literal and figurative grape-vine—she escapes emotional, textual, and social confines: her "tendrils in air" connect to the "grape eyeballs" on the grape vine, and connect her to Roberta Bondar in her spaceship in outer space:

> Climbing the wall / she is
> climbing the wall
>   "trying to write a poem"
>   (murmur of nutmeg)
>   tendrils in air
> grape eyeballs spy on Berlin
>   God's spyder
>   from her space window
>   Roberta Bondar
>   sees CANADA.
>   It is said. In her way.

            Along the vine.
    The word goes out
            Oka. Or August. Tendril.[13]

The tropes here are entanglement and entrapment, but also action and
agency. The result is a hybrid figure which includes both object and
subject. "The word goes out"; the grapevine of women's talk offers a
way to climb the walls, to escape confinement. Webb's collaborative
relationship with other women's texts provides pathways and trajec-
tories which can take her to outer space. The pun in "spyder" encapsu-
lates this hybrid space of combined object and subject positions: she is a
spy who looks on others, a spider that spins its webs (pun intended), but
God still "spied her"; she does not escape being looked at.

    Nor does Webb escape her "strange attraction" to male mentors.
In "The Making of a Japanese Print" (a sequence of poems that comes
at the end of *Hanging Fire*), Webb again works with a text by a male
writer. The intertext is *The Making of a Japanese Print* by the Japanese
intaglio artist Harunobu. The book is an explanation of his technical
processes in making a wood block print of a geisha figure named the
"Heron Maid." Webb describes Harunobu's processes of making the
woodblock while also "unmaking" the geisha figure and writing a con-
trary script for her. As with the William Carlos Williams' intertexts,
Webb both imitates and reconfigures the source text.

    Beginning with the womb-like "first circle," the first shape carved
into the wood, Webb follows the successive stages of imprinting the fig-
ure of the Heron Maid into the wood block. But while tracing these
technical processes, Webb simultaneously describes and critiques the
ideological inscription of the "feminine" on the woman's cultural
body: adding breasts, eyelashes, dark sandals, white chemise, father in
blue, flesh tint, and the artist's signature enacts both a physical and an
ideological process of inscribing the feminine. She suggests that Haru-
nobu's God-like position, his power to create a world, to give life to
inanimate objects enacts patriarchal technical / ideological mastery:

    What you see best
    is the ivory kimono
    coming towards you.
    It will stay in the same place
    always, Harunobu, brocading
    the threat of advance.

A mere press of your hands
and your death flies
into a silken shadow. (*HF*, 74-75)

Harunobu immobilizes the woman, brocades "the threat of advance," is
a "master" in all senses of the word.

In "*Imprint No. 3*," Webb shifts attention to her own responses to
the text, even confessing to some playful additions and fakery in her read-
ing of the figure, thus bringing herself into the meaning-making process:

A fake. There was no chair
no washy blue in the 'Heron Maid'.
I made it up for my own artistic
purposes. I was thinking of
Van Gogh, of myself sitting down
for the last time and getting
up again to make this confession. (*HF*, 76)

In the last poem of the sequence ("*Imprint No. 4*"), Webb, like
Harunobu, takes on the role of creating new life. But Webb reverses
Harunobu's process. The Heron Maid moves away from the wintry
"floating world" (the world of the geisha) where she is passive, cold,
silent. In Webb's final poem, the Heron Maid walks "off the path / into
summer." She becomes passionate (signified by the shift from winter to
summer), active, variable. Significantly, this new woman comes into
being by removing the traditional imprints of the feminine: "She un-
coils her hair / slips off her rings / imagines a different future" where

She'll have to change
habits and colors
wash off her fear.
Perhaps she'll look
for another job
cut her hair short
change her expression.
And, it's possible, die
some day in foreign arms
under the new dispensation. (*HF*, 77)

She changes her clothes, attitude, job, and perhaps even her sexuality:
the short hair suggests a masculinized figure, the "foreign arms" may be
racial or sexual.[14]

> A woman emerges at last
> on the finest paper, cursing
> his quest for the line
> and this damned delicate fan
> carved in her had
> to keep her forever cool
> factitious, apparently pleasing. (*HF*, 78)

But this emerging woman is still intertwined with Harunobu's "quest for the line"; she is not an ahistorical Botticellian Venus who emerges fully formed out of the sea foam. She is a hybrid figure formed by and within the historical constructions of the feminine. She may swear at Harunobu and the fan she is holding (symbol of her geisha role), but she is still holding the fan. Webb calls her "factitious"—a mixture of fact and fiction. The Heron Maid is part of the emerging woman even as the new (fictional) woman is redefining the geisha (fact). Webb's poem is similarly intertwined with Harunobu's text in a reciprocal, subject-to-subject relationship. Webb resists and follows his text in an ongoing intersubjective circularity within which she becomes a hybridized subject/object. As Smaro Kamboureli notes in an interview with Webb: "the woman in the print is almost frozen, a silent figure in someone else's creation, but in your poem . . . she comes alive, madly alive, because you give her a voice by giving her a poem." And Webb replies:

> I realize I am that woman. . . . She took a long time to emerge, that woman, cursing, because I have only really recently learned how to do that in my work. I've done it in my life, but I have not been able to get it into the work until recently. I think that's a big advance in *Hanging Fire*, that my anger really comes through, and I'm able to curse. (31)

But long before *Hanging Fire*, Webb began the intertextual interventions that would eventually enable her to speak her anger. Her intertextual dialogues, collaged voices, fragmented intertexts, recontextualized quotations, paraphrases with a difference, ironic juxtapositions, and so forth initiate an intersubjective (that is to say subject-to-subject) relation with hegemonic figures and texts. She opens the doors into the men's side of the bar, into the brandy and cigar domains, into the lyric enclosures of the self-sufficient male "I" and inserts a "playful woman making a space to breathe" (*HF*, 57). These various intertextual interventions enable the woman writer to dialogue with the past, to speak her anger, and, most importantly, to "imagine a different future."

Notes

1 See Michael Worton and Judith Still, eds., *Intertextuality: Theories and Practices* (Manchester: Manchester University Press, 1990), p. 2, for a useful discussion of the "erotic and violent aspect of . . . intertexual relations."

2 John Hulcoop provides a useful list of Webb's many intertexts in *Hanging Fire*: "A baker's dozen of Canadian poets . . . eighteen other poets—from Homer, Sophocles, and Shakespeare to Edith Sitwell, Odysseus Elytis, and Wallace Stevens. . . . Fourteen prose writers (from Cervantes and Bunyan to Kenneth Graham [*sic*] and Kundera), plus playwrights (Beckett, Max Frisch), philosophers (Anaximander, Descartes, Sartre), politicians (Ghandi, Lenin, Mao Tse Tung), psychologists (Freud, Jung), physicists, anthropologists, and literary critics all make appearances in sundry guises; so do composers as different as Verdi and Philip Glass, Stravinsky and Johann Strauss, Leoncavallo and Paul Horn; and visual artists Van Gogh, Matisse, Picasso, Douanier, Rousseau, and Harunobu" ("WBR," 234).

3 "Paratextuality" is Genette's term (*Palimpsestes*); the explanation is from Worton and Still, 22.

4 Comments at a public reading, Strathcona Park Lodge, 1986.

5 See the *Encyclopedia of Contemporary Literary Theory* for more discussion of sememes and semanalysis (621).

6 Riffaterre explains: "words correspond to sememes, and sememes contain, in a potential state of suspense, the semes that can, at any time, develop into a narrative. A sememe is an inchoate text" (74).

7 See John Hulcoop for a Freudian analysis of Webb's relation to her literary forefathers. He describes an Oedipal battle in which the neophyte writer becomes a "strong" poet by resisting and overthrowing her poetic mentors (*PW*).

8 It is important to distinguish between Jessica Benjamin and Julia Kristeva's uses of this term. For Kristeva, intersubjective means interpersonal: "The notion of *intertextuality* replaces that of intersubjectivity" ("Word . . . ," *KR*, 37). For Benjamin, intersubjective means social relations, which she differentiates from the "intrapsychic" (i.e., internal): "the crucial area we uncover with intrapsychic theory is the unconscious; the crucial element we explore with intersubjective theory is the representation of self and other as distinct but interrelated beings" (Jessica Benjamin, *The Bonds of Love: Psychoanalysis, Feminism, and the Problem of Domination* [New York: Pantheon, 1988], p. 20).

9 Webb's earlier work contains many direct and indirect references to other texts (Marvell, Yeats, Shakespeare, etc.), but the intertextual dialogues become more generative from *Wilson's Bowl* on.

10 See the Foreword to *Wilson's Bowl*, where Webb explains that the title
   "Poems of Failure" points to her failure to recognize the "dominance of
   male power culture in . . . [her] educational and emotional formation"
   until after she had finished the book.

11 Compare Webb's last four lines with the closing lines of Williams' poem:
   "Forgive me // they were delicious / so sweet / and so cold" (*Collected
   Earlier Poems*, p. 354).

12 See, for instance, "Missing You: Intertextuality, Transference and the Lan-
   guage of Love," by Sean Hand.

13 "Grapevine" has only been published as the broadside: " 'For Phyllis' A
   Tribute to Phyllis Webb, held at The Western Front in Vancouver, on Sat-
   urday, March 28, 1992" (Vancouver: Slug Press, 1992), 100 copies.

14 Brenda Carr comments: "Pushing the limits of this feminist fantasy, I
   wonder whether this eighteenth-century Japanese courtesan might find
   herself in the arms of a twentieth-century female poet from the West?"
   ("Genre Theory . . . ," p. 76).

6

Webb Criticism— A Re View[1]

The premise of this chapter is that aesthetic judgements are necessarily informed by social values. When the community of writers and readers is relatively homogenous, however, there is little awareness of or debate about those values. Good is good and bad is bad by common consent within a closed circle that in turn confers universality on its shared values by virtue of its homogeneity. In the postwar Canadian literary establishment of mostly white, middle-class, Euro-North-American, Christian males, for instance, "everyone" agreed that good poetry expresses an individualized, autonomous subjectivity; and that poetry has value because poets have greater access to truth than ordinary mortals by virtue of their acute sensibility. They are solitary, sensitive souls who live outside the economic mainstream (the starving artist, etc.), relatively uncontaminated by economic or social constraints. Indeed, it was generally agreed that the social function of the poet, as Matthew Arnold insisted in *Culture and Anarchy*, was to transcend the fractious everyday world of conflict and difference. In this paradigm, the particulars of gender, race, class, or history are viewed as largely irrelevant except as "background" information—perhaps helpful in defining the "special" (read limited) nature of female, or ethnic, or lower-class sensibilities—but never as factors in the critics' interpretation or judgement. Aesthetic judgements are based on sensibility and technique only. Such an ahistorical aesthetics effectively maintains the social order by erasing all but the "normal" subject from critical scrutiny.

Certainly, in the postwar Canadian literary establishment, the debates and disagreements centred around an aesthetics of form and technique.[2] Critical positions were neither historicized nor politicized until poststructuralist, Marxist, feminist, and postcolonial writer/theorists linked notions of "natural" and "universal" to historical moments and

---

The notes to this chapter are on p. 122-23.

cultural paradigms. Edward Said's now-famous call for *"interference"* at
the "Politics of Interpretation" session of the Modern Languages Asso-
ciation in 1981, for instance, proposed a politicized, interventionist
criticism that would examine the politics of representation and recover
histories "hitherto either misrepresented or rendered invisible" (30-31),
a process that includes "risking all the discomfort of a great unsettle-
ment in ways of seeing and doing" (32).

My purpose here is similar, but not so grand or far-reaching: I
examine how Webb's critics have unsettled some established "ways of
seeing and doing" literary criticism and have thus recuperated parts of
her work that were previously "either misrepresented or rendered invis-
ible" within a modernist/humanist critical context. Many critics of the
1950s, 1960s, and 1970s, I suggest, praised Webb in limited and limiting
ways, positioning her as an exemplary female version of the self-expres-
sive subject. I then note some feminist, interventionist readings in the
1970s and 1980s which diversify the Webb personae, although some-
times in equally essentialist terms. Finally, I consider several contempo-
rary instances of criticism that foregrounds its own processes and con-
texts even as it also takes process and context as the topic for discussion
in the poems. These latter methods, I suggest, construct a poly-
morphous, contextualized poetic self (selves) and thus provide a useful
range of entrances to Webb's texts, entrances which—in keeping with
the overall theme of this book—provide ways of seeing into the "dark"
that Webb makes available in her poems.

First, Principles

(1) *Objective*: b: Of, relating to or being an object, phenomenon, or
condition in the realm of sensible experience independent of individ-
ual thought and perceptible by all observers: having reality independ-
ent of mind (*Webster's New Collegiate Dictionary*, 9th edition).

In the modernist/humanist paradigm, the ideal literary critic—following
the Kantian aesthetics of detachment—was neutral, detached, im-
personal, unbiased. Don't use "I," declare the composition handbooks:
check your feelings at the door; no passions allowed here; no personal
pronouns either. Yes, of course, they say, you are expressing personal
opinion (after all you are an individual), but keep the personal out of
sight, out of mind, or you will lose credibility. Your task is to collect data
and interpret it for other readers, to maintain emotional distance in order
to find the universal meaning of the text. The poet, too, finds universal

meanings by objectifying the personal in concrete, objective, specific data, as in T.S. Eliot's objective correlative or Pound's notion of the self-sufficient image. Based on the ideology of scientific rationalism (of data-based truth), the method acquires ethical value because it leads to truth.[3]

(2) *Subjectivity*. One of the curious revolving doors of modernist/humanist aesthetics is that objectivity is the preferred method, yet *subjectivity* is the preferred content. Poems are valued as expressions of a unique, sensitive individual and the task of the critic is to both construct and interpret this artist/genius figure.

Sociologist Janet Wolff argues that reverence for the Cartesian subject as a unique, sentient being—of which the creative artist[4] is one of the highest forms—reflects not only the Enlightenment values of mind over matter but also the material conditions of the artist in Western culture since the nineteenth century. Wolff explains that the exalted position given to the artist in capitalist society relates directly to their marginal economic position: precisely because "the specific conditions of contemporary capitalist society are . . . hostile to artistic production" (10) she suggests, "the artist comes to be idealised as representative of non-forced and truly expressive activity" (18). But, she argues, this "concept of the artist/author as some kind of asocial being, blessed with genius, waiting for divine inspiration and exempt from all normal rules of social intercourse is . . . very much an ahistorical and limited one" (12). There is a "kernel of truth" in this definition in that industrial society "*has* marginalised artists. . . . But this does not mean that it is the essence of art to transcend life, and to surpass the real, the social, and even the personal" (12). The problem is that "one particular form of an historical figure is tranformed into a universal definition" (11).

Similarly, I would argue, in the postindustrial world of the late twentieth century, the numerous reconfigurations of the subject—as social, linguistic, historical, racialized—that have knocked the artist/genius off the Cartesian pedestal, relate to changes in material conditions of artistic production. At least since midcentury, government subsidies, university jobs, cultural industries, and a highly lucrative international art market have produced greater social and economic integration ("contamination" some would call it) of the artist. In my view, the shift in literary criticism to an ethics of the local with its accompanying attention to contextualized subjectivities is partially related to the above social changes.

Responses to Phyllis Webb's first five books—from *Trio* in 1954 to
Selected Poems in 1971—demonstrate the homogeneity of the postwar
Canadian literary establishment and its unselfconscious and unquestion-
ing application of Enlightenment values. Her work is valued insofar as it
reflects an "authentic" and "unique" subjectivity. She gets gold stars for
individuality, originality, sensitivity, and intensity (the signs of individ-
ual genius). As well, she is praised for specificity and concreteness:
which is to say for objectifying and universalizing the personal. Terms
such as "concrete," "objective," and "universal" inscribe value.

Desmond Pacey, for instance, in *Creative Writing in Canada: A
Short History of English-Canadian Literature*, praises Webb's skill in "find-
ing concrete images with which to express abstractions" (247). Here he
is repeating a judgement he formulated a few years previous in his
review of *Even Your Right Eye* (1956) where he praises Webb for "her
capacity to find the apt concrete symbol for idea or feeling" (113).
W.H. New, in an overview article on "Modern Canadian Writing,"
similarly praises her "tight control over imagery, her precision with lan-
guage, and her personal intensity" which "make her a fine lyric poet"
(126). Norah Story's description of Webb in the prestigious *Oxford
Companion to Canadian History and Literature* reflects the same general
view: Story applauds Webb's "striking use of imagery and . . . variety of
moods and forms to convey subtle and compressed insights into subjec-
tive experience" (825).

Others, however, while applying the same values, arrive at differ-
ent conclusions. They claim Webb's poetry is too subjective and per-
sonal, especially in her early work. John Corrington, for example, in a
review called "Nouveau Gnomic Poetry?" accuses Webb of "self-pitiful
observation" and of "counterfeit poems—following a poetic fad of
short, tight, Narcissistic form and content" (111-12). John Hulcoop
treats this accusation of self-pity extensively in his Introduction to the
1971 *Selected Poems*, where he argues that Webb gradually gains "con-
trol over those . . . impulses toward self-indulgence and self-pity" (24).
He traces an exemplary shift toward "impersonality" (34) and "self-
objectification" (37)—exemplary because she gains control of her
material and thus universalizes personal anguish. The poem "Lament"
is a watershed work, he argues, in which the voice becomes "more
carefully modulated, becomes less hysterical" (24). Hulcoop is careful to
locate Webb within Enlightenment values of control and detachment,
while also separating her from the negative excesses of female "hyste-
ria."

Likewise, Peter Stevens begins his review of *Selected Poems* with the somewhat damning title "Creative Bonds in the Limbo of Narcissism," but then goes on to applaud Webb's movement away from the self-obsession in her early poems (33). In a similar vein, Fred Cogswell complains about Webb's "solipsism" in a review of *The Sea Is Also a Garden* titled "Good but Not Great." But he praises *Naked Poems* two years later because Webb has become less subjective, relying instead on the "juxtaposition of concrete images" (69). Alan Pearson, however, complains that *Naked Poems* is too personal: Webb's "sensibility is so special" that "it almost completely evaded comprehension" (87). Pearson also, incidentally, offers an unusually straightforward assessment of the book's value in economic terms. He declares the book a waste of money because the reader gets only about 500 words for the price of $2.95 (87).

John Bentley Mays, in a 1973 article in *Open Letter*, questions not the monetary but the spiritual value of Webb's poetry. Although he purports to admire Webb's accurate representation of the late 1960s spiritual collapse ("contemporary civilized man's volitional and experiential destitution" [28]), the terms of praise are curiously negative: he supposedly admires her "exacerbated subjectivity" (15), the "polymorphous perversity of inner life" (24), the "melodramatic hollowness and overwrought stageyness" (15), or indeed her superficiality: it is the "kitsch, ultra, irresponsible, indiscreet aspects of her work—the small, tacky theatricality of so much of it—that compels us" (15). The above terms don't sound very laudatory to me. Likewise, he praises her anti-heroic stance, her lack of egotism, her refusal to provide answers and her willingness to present "decisive, unmitigated failure" (11-12), but again in terms that sound more damning that laudatory:

> we are left with her work as it is: not a monument to supreme effort, but a mirror of our own small motions and attempts to name, contain, transcend the history in which both we and she have found ourselves. . . . To go through the looking-glass of Phyllis Webb's writing is suddenly to find ourselves, not in a magical world of dream or realm of transcendent meaning, but in the same history we thought we had escaped, alone with the familiar problems of our world; *the same*. (12)

Toward the end of the essay, he speaks of the "interminable futility" (29) of such writing. Despite his claim to admire Webb's "failures," his descriptions imply the opposite. Certainly Webb herself,[5] as well as many readers took the essay to be a negative critique (Williamson, Mallinson, Hulcoop, Wachtel).[6]

As the above survey indicates, while there is some disagreement
about Webb's success in performing according to the rules, no one ques-
tions the rules themselves. Webb's sensitivity, her intellectual/emotional
intensity, her originality are always the evaluative criteria, along with the
related issues of control, precision, and objectivity. The critic's role
remains unquestioned: his/her role is to encapsulate the poet as objective,
sensitive (though controlled), detached, and contained.

With regard to Webb, such criticism essentialized her work in
gendered as well as modernist/humanist terms to produce a limited and
limiting view. The terms of praise often echo white, male, middle-class
definitions of the feminine: beautiful, emotional, melancholic, perhaps
even suicidal (but not too hysterical or excessive). Desmond Pacey's
review of *Even Your Right Eye* begins by equating Webb's personal and
poetic beauty: "*Monday's child is fair of face*—this is certainly Miss Phyllis
Webb, who in both person and poetry is very beautiful" (436). Such
characterizations were not limited to male reviewers. Journalist Gwen
Cash, in a lifestyle article on Webb in *B.C. Magazine* wrote "Phyllis
Webb . . . handles her wardrobe like her adjectives, with great discrimi-
nation" (17). While most criticism made no direct reference to gender,
the fact that the intellectual, the questioning, the affirming, the erotic
dimensions of Webb's poetry (i.e., the atypically female) were largely
ignored suggests an invisible gender construct at work. Take the pair of
poems "Breaking" and "Making," for instance. The concluding lines
of "Breaking" are often quoted to demonstrate Webb's characteristic
melancholia:

> What are we whole or beautiful or good for
> but to be absolutely broken? (*SP*, 55)

But the counterbalancing affirmations in the companion poem "Mak-
ing" are rarely mentioned:

> From the making made and, made, now making
> certain order—thus excellent despair
> is laid, and in the room the patches of the quilt
> seize light and throw it back upon the air.
> A grace is made, a loveliness is caught
> quilting a quiet blossom as a work.
> It does. (*SP*, 56)

The critic who is constructing a coherent (and female) subjectivity is
inclined to select only the melancholic statements. Or take *Naked*

Poems: they are often cited as evidence of Webb's exemplary sensitivity and delicate emotionalism (Davey, Hulcoop) without referring to their lesbian context[7] or their intellectuality. Brenda Carr and Susan Rudy Dorscht are the first to discuss them as lesbian love poems (*WCL* Number Six, 25, 3 [1992]).

Webb criticism of the 1960s and 1970s constructed a "Phyllis Webb" that had value insofar as she represented a female sensibility. The occasional nod to Webb's playfulness, or technical skill, or intellectual range and acuity could be contained within the gendered construct. The result was a curious kind of limitation. While Webb was highly regarded, the pedestal on which she was placed had a very narrow base.

Two interventionist reviews of the 1971 *Selected Poems*, however, do indeed raise questions about both gendered and other traditional values and mark the beginning of a revaluing of Webb's work. Julian Macfarlane who, in 1971, had just completed a master's degree in Chinese and Japanese poetics at the University of British Columbia, is able to see Buddhist and Confucian values in Webb's approach to processual and fluid subjectivity. In spoken Japanese, for instance, personal pronouns are rarely used; one does not focus on the self, in life or in a poem. Macfarlane finds a similar lack of an egotistical self in Webb's writing. Her poetry, he insists, is neither existential nor metaphysical: she focusses not on subjectivity, but on "the insufficiency of past tradition, of convention, of her history . . . as a source of poetic tools." She is obsessed not with personal issues, but with "the power and weakness of words" (1972, 55-56). He values her work for the dialogues with history, convention, and tradition.

Vancouver writer Hélène Rosenthal also offers an alternative reading of Webb's 1971 *Selected Poems*, in her case a reading that reflects Rosenthal's position as a woman writer/reader. Rosenthal equates the lyric self with male egotism and praises Webb's "complete lack of that egotistical pride we find over and over again in the works of celebrated male poets." While Webb "makes a place for herself in the pantheon of poets," she also "refuses the elevation." Webb's writing is communal and contextualized rather than individual and transcendent: she "speaks for us all, out of femininely felt responsibility for the quality of life" (1971, 7-8). In essentializing Webb as a "female" voice, Rosenthal's review operates in the same discursive field as other universalizing criticism and thus only changes the terms of praise, not the critical criteria or methodology. However, in arguing for "female" values, she at least raises the issue of gender bias in literary criticism as well as reversing some of the terms of praise.

Rosenthal's is the first of a number of feminist readings of Webb's work in the 1970s and 1980s which recuperate previously ignored or undervalued material and/or challenge the established critical methods. The second is Jean Mallinson's extensive analysis of "Ideology and Poetry: An Examination of Some Recent Trends in Canadian Criticism" (1978). While admitting that sexism is not the only cause of an "ideological bias,"[8] she notes that "culturally enforced expectations about attitudes appropriate to females" are part of the problem, especially in the case of John Bentley Mays' "venomous attack" on Webb in his 1973 article (93). Mallinson argues that Mays' critique of Webb has "probable roots in culturally determined expectations about the nourishing and comforting attitudes that it is thought appropriate for women to express" (94). When he writes: "If only she had given us one monumental poem, or had she loved or hated heroically" (quoted in Mallinson, 93-94), or further on when he laments the absence of the "earth mother" female (95), he is applying masculinist values. Mallinson argues that Mays' evaluative criteria reflect both male and female gender stereotypes (95).[9]

Janice Williamson's critique of Mays' position in a 1986 dissertation chapter on Webb (later revised and published in the Webb issue of *West Coast Line* in 1992) is even stronger. Williamson argues that in Mays' article, "cultural misogyny masquerades as aesthetic engagement": under the guise of a discussion of aesthetic value, Mays constructs Webb as " 'La Belle Dame Sans Merci' " who disempowers the (male) reader (*WCL*, 156). As an alternative to such a "limited and destructive reading" (*WCL*, 157), Williamson offers a rereading of Webb's "Suicide Narratives" as narratives of feminist "vitality":

> Rather than a representation in writing of woman's silencing, Webb's poems strategically push at the boundaries of language and form, voicing the contradictory internal division characteristic of the woman writer. Webb's "suicide poems" which bear the "crown of darkness" produce a complex and paradoxical reading of the vitality of writing woman. . . . (*WCL*, 171-72)

Alberta fiction writer Cecelia Frey, in a 1986 article, also traces an emerging feminist consciousness in Webb's work. In the early poetry, Frey finds a conflicted and divided self struggling against passivity and silence. The "pain, anguish and grief" that "comprise the informing mood of Webb's first three volumes" relate to "the female experience of reality" (41). Quoting Webb's line "[t]he self is a grave," Frey concludes that the "[t]he female in patriarchal society is buried alive" (41). Her reading of Webb's subsequent books traces Webb's gradual shift from passive to active female self, through *Naked Poems* where she withdraws "completely from male influence and control to the point where she cannot be located in the structures of western literary traditions" (44), to *Wilson's Bowl* which "is re-enactment and re-entry into voice" (46), and finally to the "fragmented, non-linear, non-logical, female" voice of *Water and Light* (48). In these ghazals—traditionally a male song to a female, sung in praise of love and wine—Webb reverses the gender roles and introduces the "female as writing subject intoxicated by the possibilities of poetry and language" in place of the "female as object" (37). Such feminist rereadings fracture the received judgements and recuperate a female history and experience, albeit one that is sometimes essentialized more than contextualized. Frey's narrative of the woman-as-victim being transformed into a liberated "fragmented, non-linear, non-logical" figure, for instance, depends on notions of female essence.

Webb criticism in the 1980s and into the 1990s has been quite wide-ranging—no doubt partially because of the diversity of Webb's books in this period: *Wilson's Bowl* (1980), *Selected Poems: The Vision Tree* (1981), *Talking* (1982), *Water and Light* (1984), and *Hanging Fire* (1990) are all very different books—and also because of a general shift toward an ethics of the local. Some critics continue to speak in the objective, neutral voice of the detached observer who judges according to unspoken and unquestioned values, whose role is to interpret the author's meaning, and who valorizes the individual creative genius. Peter Stevens talks of "essences" and "crystal clear poetry" in a review of *Wilson's Bowl* (*Windsor Star*, E7). Mark Abley's review praises the "mixture of anguish and serenity" that "distinguishes her finest work" (*Maclean's*, 52-53). W.J. Keith, also reviewing *Wilson's Bowl*, asks the familiar modernist question (echoing Yeats): "But what if the poem's acutely personal centre cannot hold?" (99). Indeed, Keith finds Webb sometimes "frighteningly subjective," but she succeeds in establishing "control" over "chaos" (100). John Hulcoop notes changes in "theme" and "voice" in Webb's later books—he finds a "liberation of self-as-woman from male socio-sexual, political, and poetic conventions" in the anti ghazals of *Water and Light* (Hulcoop, 157). But his

analysis remains formalist and his judgements continue to be based on
the modernist values of "mastery" (which provides control over chaos)
and originality (which produces a universal vision). Likewise, Bruce
Whiteman welcomes "A New Webb" in his review of *Wilson's Bowl*
and points to "a fullness and a variety that marks a real change of direc-
tion from her previous writing": Webb has entered a "new landscape
where the spirits do not throttle but rather talk." But his evaluative
terms have not changed. He praises her ability to create a "paradigm of
orderly chaos" (16). George Woodcock, writing in 1987 in *Northern
Spring: The Flowering of Canadian Literature*, perhaps best expresses this
critical position, arguing that "the clarity of her vision and the dedi-
cated impeccability of her craft" entitles her "to a first place not merely
among recent Canadian poets but in the whole poetic tradition of our
land" (265).

Increasingly, however, there is less valorizing of individual
"vision," less essentializing of the subject, less concern with "control"
of self and language and more talk about language processes and activi-
ties, more talk about contextualized meaning, more attention to fluid
subjectivity. Sharon Thesen, for instance, in her Introduction to *The
Vision Tree: Selected Poems by Phyllis Webb*, does not focus on Webb as
autonomous subject; first, she positions Webb's work and within the
historical definition of "West Coast writer":

> The designation "West Coast writer" often brings to mind, if not the
> radical shift in language and line away from the modernism of the
> Eastern Canadian writers of the 1950's and 60's and toward the pro-
> jective and redefined sublime of a new, post-modernist verse, at least
> an identifiable source and stance. (9)

She then offers a series of signposts in the form of single-word headings
and loosely connected paragraphs, signposts that mark diverse entry
points to Webb's texts: "Line" and "Ends" and "Desire" and "Compo-
sure" and "Shadow" and "Singularity" are some of her directional
signs. Thesen is not mediating or decoding the writing for us; she posi-
tions herself alongside the writing and invites us to join her in looking
at the poems. Although she says nothing about previous criticism of
Webb, Thesen's Introduction offers an unstated intervention by its
insistence on other terms.

Smaro Kamboureli's review of *Wilson's Bowl* challenges the
received interpretations directly: Webb's "writing act," she insists, "is
neither a narcissistic engagement with her book nor an oblique self-

defeat toward her critics" (87). Referring to the much-discussed "Poems of Failure," Kamboureli suggests that the poems enact a welcome failure, the failure of the ego. Welcome because the "failure" of the egotistical self facilitates "the surfacing of her poetic (infantile) self." The result, Kamboureli continues, is "the death of pure silence and the return of voice from the recesses of the throat to the page" (88).

Ann Mandel, reviewing *Wilson's Bowl*, along with Atwood's *True Stories* in *Fiddlehead* in 1982, also questions traditional values by arguing for "situated" and politicized meaning rather than "transcendent" truth. Drawing on Foucault's *Power/Knowledge*, she suggests that both Atwood and Webb are involved in "changing the means by which truth is produced" (65). In order to change power relations she suggests, they show that "[p]ower is not abstract any more than truth is; it is not a repressive negation of the body but an assertion of control on bodies, a notion central to Atwood's book and implicit in Webb's quarrels with visionaries and philosophers" (65-66). In a second review of *Wilson's Bowl*, Mandel also points to feminist issues in the poems, such as Webb's interrogations of male traditions. "Many of Webb's poems," she proposes, "are arguments with and rejections of male figures" as well as expressions of anger at their "refusal . . . to speak to her." Mandel also notes Webb's rejection of the male model of "egotistical competitiveness": "Webb has for the most part withdrawn from competition, leaving the white male gods of marble or flesh behind, retreating to mockery, to silence, and to the phenomenal world" ("Poetry of . . . ," 89). Mandel combines modernist and postmodernist critical values in valuing both Webb's individual "vision" and "truth," but arguing for a contextualized truth. Her conclusion, a quotation from Adrienne Rich, emphasizes a processual, variable truth within "these words, these whispers, conversations/ from which time after time the truth breaks moist and green" (91).

Others, such as Eleanor Wachtel, in a *Books in Canada* profile, emphasize not only contextualized truth, but also contextualized (and textualized) subjectivity. Wachtel calls for "a clear distinction between the poet and her work," arguing that "Webb's poetic persona is a construct, an artifact" (9). In a similar vein, Stephen Scobie objects to the reductiveness of Webb criticism that is based on a Webb persona derived at least partially from her personal life: "The greatest weakness of Webb criticism has been to present her as inward-turning and solipsistic, to the exclusion of that political world on which Jacobo

Timerman turns his astonished eye in 'Prison Report.' " "As recently as 1987," Scobie continues, "George Woodcock could still write that 'for Phyllis Webb, growing maturity as a poet has meant growing with-drawal—a narrowing of contacts with the world paralleling a narrowing of the circle of the creative self' " (63-64). Scobie himself emphasizes the fluidity of Webb's work which allows it be valued by both modern-ist and postmodernist critics (68).

A particularly amusing example of the hazards of conflating the writer and her work occurs in a review of *Water and Light* by the late Michael Estok. Recognizing the seductive and erotic quality of many of the poems in *Water and Light* (also their similarity in form and tone to *Naked Poems*), Estok assumes they were written to a lover. The dedica-tion of one section of the book to Connie Rooke leads him to con-clude that these are lesbian love poems (Estok, 12)—to which Webb felt compelled to respond: "Frankly," she writes,

> I am mystified as to how Professor Estok came to the conclusion that these poems are about a love affair which "turns sour." They are not about a love affair, sweet or sour and, I hope by this letter to prevent further misreading of this section. . . . The poems were not written as a sequence, there is no intended plot-line, and the dedication to Con-nie Rooke means only that she seemed to enjoy these poems more than I did and published some of them in *The Malahat Review*. (*NeWest Review*, 12, 2 [1986]: 1)

On the subject of conflating the writer and her work, Stephen Scobie usefully argues not so much for separating the two as for recog-nizing the performative role of the personal in contemporary culture. Noting the current obsessive attention to "personality," he suggests the critic should recognize that the "writer's public image . . . *is* a text and must be read as such" (61). In defining personality as textual and "staged," Scobie locates the self in social and linguistic contexts, con-texts that foreground but at the same time decentre subjectivity: "post-modernism foregrounds the presence of the writer . . . but scatters any sense of unity in that self by making it part of the textual play" (65).

In the *Festschrift for Phyllis Webb*, published in 1992 as an issue of *West Coast Line*, I (as editor) likewise proposed to "foreground the pres-ence of the writer," but not as a unified construct nor a reductive ver-sion of the personal.[10] The Webb letters, manuscripts, poems, inter-views, and photographs—together with the tributes and critical essays—constitute a textual field that includes but is not defined by the personal. Also, I suggest, Sonja Skarstedt's painting, reproduced on the cover of the issue presents a performative Phyllis Webb complete with wry smile and opaque eyes partially concealed behind dark glasses and multicoloured robes. Unlike the static beauty of the figure in Joe Plaskett's portrait done more than thirty years previous, with its troubled alter ego hovering in the background,[11] Skarsted's figure radiates vibrancy and energy. Her portrait argues with Plaskett's by repeating the portrait structure but changing many details, to suggest a self-conscious, performative subjectivity rather than the passive receptivity of Plaskett's figure. The photographs throughout the issue further expand the visual field to include many Phyllis Webbs: as a demure young woman at Kingston in 1955; in casual conversation with her mother in 1958; smiling at her cat circa 1980; and more recently, in conversation with Smaro Kamboureli or sitting in a reflective pose with a bookcase behind her. The visuals foreground the performance of person(s), the person as text.[12]

Also, the subtitle, *You Devise. We Devise*, taken from Webb's poem "Performance" (which is reprinted in the issue as the first item), proposes a self-conscious critical process. Many of the essays, tributes, and interviews are indeed done with an awareness of the reader's role in constructing meanings or subjectivities. They emphasize the contexts of their various "devisings." Douglas Barbour examines Webb's *Water and Light* within the ghazal tradition; Brenda Carr connects Webb's lyric practice to feminist issues; Susan Knutson contextualizes "Phyllis Webb's Semantic Geometry" in relation to traditional rhetorical tropes; Janice Williamson considers "Webb's Suicide Narratives" in the context of feminist sociologists' analyses of women's suicides. If the criticism is personalized, it is via the reader not the writer: Susan Rudy Dorscht begins her article in the first person with the "compelling questions" of "[h]ow the discourses of compulsory heterosexuality typically dress and address me and whether I can undress and be naked" (54); Stephen Scobie's discussion of Webb's poem "Breaking" takes the form of a series of personal diary entries; Aritha van Herk responds to the "textual seduction" (184) that she finds in *Naked Poems* with a playful/ serious, poetic/prose investigation of meanings in the poem. The critic is self-conscious, often performative; she becomes a coproducer of the text's meaning and complicit in any judgement of its value.

Indeed the validity of the truth-claims depends on the extent to which they are contextualized. Having recognized that claims to universality or neutrality too often disguise an ethnocentricity that appro-

priates, devalues, and/or erases difference, these and many other con-
temporary critics focus as much on the processes of producing meaning
as on the results of their critical analysis. And the measure of "good"
criticism is in the correctness and completeness of those processes.

Also, Canadian criticism in general has shifted in the last decade to
address social and political contexts of poetry, the critic's role as copro-
ducer of meaning, the politics of representation in a multiracial society
still dominated by white males, the politics of canonization, and the
relationship between methodology and ideology.[13] In Webb criticism,
as in the discourse around subjectivities that have been previously "ren-
dered invisible" or viewed reductively as representations of an exotic
other (Said, above), the effect has been a welcome shift in focus from
essentialized and individual to polyvocal and social subjectivities. The
effect of such criticism has in my view been a welcome expansion in
the viewing frames so that more aspects of Webb's work can be seen
and valued.

Notes

1 This chapter is based on a paper which I gave at "Interventing the Text" at
the University of Calgary in May, 1991. A shortened and revised version
also appeared as my preface to "You Devise. We Devise: A Festschrift for
Phyllis Webb," *West Coast Line* Number Six, 25, 3 (1991-92): 14-17.

2 See Dudek and Gnarowski's *The Making of Modern Poetry in Canada* for
details of some of these debates.

3 Typically, the ideology is both expressed and concealed within the defini-
tion: i.e., the notion that objectivity by definition excludes moral issues
prevents any discussion or even awareness of its ethical status. Similarly,
with regard to poetry, as Antony Easthope explains: "What makes poetry
poetry is what makes poetry ideological" (*PD*, 22).

4 I use the term artist as a generic term that includes writers.

5 Note also Webb's reference to her "critical wounds" in the Foreword to
Wilson's Bowl.

6 Frank Davey, however, argues that everyone misread the Mays' essay,
mainly by missing the irony in it (see "The Struggle for Phyllis Webb," in
CLP). In my view, the negative descriptions of Webb's work override the
supposed ironic frame of the essay and his obsessive reiteration of her fail-
ures bespeaks a barely veiled misogyny.

7 While some critics may, as Frank Davey suggests, have refrained from men-
tioning the lesbian content because of "the polite conventions that gov-
erned literary criticism at that time, rather than reading practices" or
because of a "concern that attention to the lesbian aspects of the poem
could have unfortunate social or employment repercussions for Webb"

("The Struggle for Phyllis Webb," in *CLP*, note 5, 243), my own experience with students reading these poems suggests a reading bias as well. Most students assume they are heterosexual love poems and simply ignore or read over details such as "your blouse" that gender the lover.

8 Mallinson defines "ideological criticism" as "a criticism which not only interprets but also ignores, rejects, and misreads poems and judges poets on philosophical or quasi-philosophical grounds" (93).

9 Frank Davey argues that Mallinson quotes Mays out of context, which diffuses the irony of the essay ("The Struggle for Phyllis Webb" in *CLP*, 210-14). However, I find Mallinson's analysis helpful in showing Mays' unstated gendered values.

10 These intentions may not necessarily be clear to all readers. See Frank Davey's critique of my preface to the issue. He argues that I claim "Phyllis Webb" under the banner of a feminist project: "a relatively inclusive post-modernism yields to a certain kind of feminist need to invent a Webb rescued from men by women" ("The Struggle for Phyllis Webb," in *CLP*, 240).

11 See chapter 7 for a description of Plaskett's painting.

12 Frank Davey takes a different view of the effect of inclusion of personal photographs. He finds both my preface and the photographs reductive: "Butling follows Wachtel and Williamson in giving special emphasis to the need for criticism to acknowledge a 'separation between the writer and her work,' arguing that criticism will otherwise 'be reductive' and lose any sense that the selves presented in literature 'are constructed of and in language.' This is a particularly ironic claim for an editor to make after having assembled a collection that collages critical essays with personal letters, interviews, the reminiscences of friends, tributes, and photographs of Webb with her mother, her books, her cat, and on the Salt Spring Island beach gazing at the petroglyph 'Wilson's Bowl' " (*CLP*, 232).

13 See, for instance, *Canadian Canons: Essays in Literary Value*, edited by Robert Lecker (Toronto: University of Toronto Press, 1991); Frank Davey, *Canadian Literary Power* (Edmonton: NeWest, 1994); or *Colour. An Issue*, *West Coast Line* Numbers 13/14 (Spring-Fall 1994), or any number of issues of *Fireweed* magazine.

Phyllis Webb,
painting by Joe Plaskett

7

The Bio as Text

I have chosen to leave biography until the end of the book in order to position biography as context rather than cause. That is to say, I do not want to locate the writer's life as the primary ground that explains or illuminates the poetry, nor to suggest that the poetry is a direct expression of the life. Nor do I wish to contribute to the mystique of personality, the *People*-magazine approach to biography, where personal details are exaggerated, glamorized, or mystified in the interests of cultivating star status. On the other hand, I am not suggesting that the poetry be viewed, as the modernists and New Critics would have it, as a sanitized objet d'art existing quite separately from time, place, and messy (or tidy) personal lives. Instead, I focus on the social, economic, political, and geographic contexts within which the writing was produced, to suggest that poems and writers are part of social realities while also emphasizing that a biography is itself a text, constructed from other texts—in this instance constructed by myself from letters, essays, prefaces, interviews, and articles by Webb, and from articles by journalists and literary critics. I have included numerous quotations to emphasize the textual sources of the biography and to suggest its status as a parallel text or intertext rather than as primary ground.

Geography and History—Victoria/Vancouver: 1927-50

Born in Victoria on April 8, 1927, the youngest child and only girl in a family of three, Webb lived on the Pacific Coast of Canada for the first twenty-two years of her life. Her parents, Mary Patton and Alfred Wilkes Webb, settled in Victoria, British Columbia, in the 1920s. Her mother was born in Nova Scotia, but grew up on Vancouver Island, in Willington, B.C. She later moved to Victoria where she met and married Webb's father, who had come to Canada from England after World War I. He had been a cavalry officer in the war. When Webb was in the second grade, the family moved to Vancouver (her father, who worked for the Bank of Canada, was transferred there); but after her parents divorced in the mid-1930s, Mary Webb, with the three children, moved back to Victoria. Her father, in the meantime, moved to Ottawa, returning to Vancouver some fifteen years later when he retired in 1945.

In Victoria, Webb attended Monterey Elementary School (grades one and two) and later, St. Margaret's Girl's School (grades seven to twelve). St. Margaret's, a private school in Victoria, is known both for its quality education and its rigorous training in social decorum. As Webb explained to Leila Sujir, there she was taught to be the exemplary female: to keep quiet about her thoughts and feelings ("there are all those things you must not say"), to be gracious and decorous ("to be a very nice person . . . well-behaved and all that" [35]). Only later did she become aware of "what silences have been imposed. . . . the unnatural silences that Tillie Olson speaks of in the book, *Silences*" (35). However, even as a child, Webb resisted the prescribed "nice girl" role. She describes herself as being like her birth sign, Aries: "Fiery, difficult . . . Aries like to be in the spotlight. We're a bit bossy. Supposed to be creative and sensitive" (Wachtel, 8). Indeed Webb's school years were troubled ones. Often she "felt inadequate, stupid, inferior. There was always some subject that baffled me, like science." But she excelled in history and English, winning the history prize when she graduated. Webb summarizes: "I had a terrifying teacher who hated me in math, because I couldn't do it, and loved me in English. I went to doctors with psychosomatic ulcer symptoms—I had emotional blocks. . . . I don't think I would have made it at a regular school" (Wachtel, 8). Webb graduated from St. Margaret's school in 1945. She then enrolled at the University of British Columbia in September of that year, along with the many war veterans who went to university after the war, a fact that produced an atmosphere of serious debate about political, economic, and social issues and contributed to a wide-ranging undergraduate education for Webb.

Political Activities: 1945-49

While still in high school, Webb developed an interest in politics that would later lead to her to join the CCF[1] party: a high school social-studies teacher at St. Margaret's took the class to visit the British Columbia legislature while it was in session. Webb describes the event to Janice Williamson:

Harold Winch, the Leader of the Opposition, was presenting his reply to the budget speech. . . . This had quite a dramatic impact on me because he was a very dramatic speaker and person. . . . I was so impressed with Harold Winch's presentation that I became involved with the CCF at that time. I began to learn about socialism. (Williamson interview, 323)

Webb is alluding here to the fact that for many years her interests were largely determined by the men in her life: she joined the CCF party partially because of her attraction to Harold Winch as, later on, she pursued a career in writing partially because of F.R. Scott's support and encouragement. The horrors of World War II also helped form her political consciousness; she describes the war as "one of *the* formative experiences of my youth," partially because "my oldest brother, Walter, was in the war—he joined up at seventeen, and was overseas." But more generally "the horror and insanity of war, and of politics, turned me to socialism in my seventeenth year" (letter to John Hulcoop, cited in Hulcoop, 5).

The CCF party position on minority rights also appealed to Webb, again for both personal and ethical reasons. She explains: "In 1945, the CCF had been demanding, among other things, votes for Asiatics and native Indians. That plank in the party platform was for me a springboard, and I jumped in" (*NBBS*, 107), partially because she felt "an identity with minority issues—the Japanese and the Indians had no vote"—and an identity with the underprivileged and rejected—"I think I felt like a minority myself . . . being poor and having no daddy" (Butling interview). When she went to the University of British Columbia in 1945, she became involved in an organization called The Parliamentary Forum, where students would meet, make speeches, and debate issues. She also helped form the student CCF party at UBC and joined the CCF constituency association in Victoria in 1947. As well, she took introductory courses in government and economics at UBC and an upper-level course in the history of economic thought. This latter course was, in Webb's view, as interesting for its omissions as its inclusions: the professor refused to include the ideas of Karl Marx in the course syllabus.

Literary Contexts: 1945-50

Webb started writing poetry in high school, some of which was published in the school magazine.[2] Her subjects, she explains, were typically adolescent "I guess the unconscious subject matter was junior erotica" (Wachtel, 9). Then, at the University of British Columbia, she became part of an off-campus writing group led by poet Earle Birney. The group included novelist Robert Harlow and writer/editors William and Alice McConnell of Klanak Press, among others. But not until Webb left university did she take herself seriously as a writer.

> I wrote in high school,[3] and all the way through university, I guess. I didn't take myself very seriously, until I met Frank Scott, and he thought I was a poet, from what he saw. And then other people began to pay attention to me, so I began to pay attention. (Scobie interview, 2)

Through the writing group at UBC and through her first-year introduction to literature course with Professor John H. Creighton, Webb discovered other Canadian writers, even other Canadian women writers, which provided her with invaluable role models. Creighton's course, Webb explains, included work by "Dorothy Livesay and Earle Birney and E.J. Pratt and F.R. Scott and [A.J.M.] Smith. But the one who entranced me the most and made me feel I wanted to be a poet was P.K. Page" (Sujir interview, 31). Webb continues:

> I think it was very lucky that I happened to take this particular course at U.B.C. . . . because it seemed very important to me that those models were there and that being a poet was a possible life for a Canadian. And I hadn't really thought of it until that time. Though I had, of course, written. (Sujir interview, 32)

Inspired by Professor Creighton's dynamic teaching in the first-year course, Webb went on to take his upper-level modern literature course, where she was introduced to such modernist luminaries as Virginia Woolf, James Joyce, and Somerset Maugham. Webb's talk on Virginia Woolf, which she gave to the UBC Letters Club, shows her developing interest in modernist aesthetics.[4] Members of the Letters Club at that time included the writers Robert Harlow, Hilda Thomas, Mario Prizack, and Helen [Gowans] Pereira.

Other highlights of her academic life included a course in aesthetics, an introductory psychology course where Freud was covered intensively, and literature courses such as G.G. Sedgewick's on Shakespeare and professor/poet Roy Daniells' popular Milton and the Metaphysical Poets. As John Hulcoop notes in his biographical sketch of Webb, many of the writers that she studied at UBC—Shakespeare, Donne, and the metaphysical poets—became important influences in her later writing

(14-16). Also worth mentioning is Vancouver musician and art con-
noisseur Harry Adaskin's music appreciation course, a course much
loved by a whole generation of UBC students, myself included. Harry
and Frances Adaskin not only gave professional performances of classical
sonatas in class (Harry on the violin, Frances on the piano), they also
regularly invited the students to their home for more music and discus-
sion. In the Adaskin home, Webb first saw paintings by the Group of
Seven as well as by contemporary Vancouver artists. She had already, of
course, heard of Emily Carr while growing up in Victoria:

> My brother [Gerry] was painting, when I was in my teens, and Emily
> Carr was one of the people he worshipped and he did quite a lot of
> paintings that were very influenced by Carr. I used to hear all those
> stories about her too. . . . When I went to UBC I used to visit the
> gallery [Vancouver Art Gallery]—quite often on Saturdays—just to
> go and sit in the gallery surrounded by Emily Carrs. She was a big
> emotional influence. . . . She really spoke to me. (Butling interview,
> 1986)

Reading contemporary Canadian and British writers, discovering liter-
ary role models, seeing contemporary Canadian visual art, participating
in political and literary organizations, being introduced to the ideas of
Freud and Marx, arguing the merits of various economic systems—
these were the main ingredients of Webb's undergraduate years. How-
ever, notwithstanding the UBC yearbook's prediction that "she would
be the first female prime minister of Canada and that . . . she'd put
chintz curtains in the House of Commons" (Wachtel, 8), she had little
sense of purpose or direction. In the midst of the postwar rush to re-
establish domestic order, and the accompanying growth of the middle-
class family, there were few career paths for women. As I noted earlier,
Webb tended to let herself be influenced and directed by others, espe-
cially the men in her life:

> When I was younger my intellectual concerns seemed to have some-
> thing to do with the man that I was involved with and even my pro-
> fessors at UBC had a big influence on me. I was very susceptible to
> male influence, and I think that was because I lost my father at such
> an early age through divorce. (Butling interview, 1986)

CCF Candidacy

Harold Winch was still a major influence in her life when she graduated
from UBC with a bachelor's degree in English and philosophy (on Fri-
day the 13th, 1949). At his suggestion, Webb entered the British Co-
lumbia provincial election campaign as a CCF candidate in Victoria,
along with two other women candidates: "It was a three-seat constitu-
ency. The CCF put up three women candidates of varying ages, one
really quite old, one for the middle, and one very young. That was
quite innovative at the time" (Williamson interview, 323-24). The
party platform in 1949 was also quite innovative. Although the issue of
the vote for minority groups was settled before the election (Chinese,
Japanese, and native Indians were granted the right to vote in 1948), the
party platform addressed social and economic problems of the under-
privileged and the working class. They promised improved health care;
an air ambulance system for remote areas; tax reform; "a square deal for
the farmer" (which meant flood control and marketing boards); im-
provements for workers such as two-weeks holiday with pay and
"union security on the job"; and various improvements in forestry,
mining, and fishing industries (*CCF News*, April 27, 1949).[5] Webb her-
self was billed as a recent university graduate who, as the "youngest
women ever [twenty-two years old] to run for the CCF," would repre-
sent the youth of 1949. A party press release describes her as follows:
"Recently she [Webb] spoke on Town Meeting of the Air on the topic
'Is youth going Socialist?' answering an emphatic 'yes.'"[6]

Webb, of course, did not win the seat in the election (June 15,
1949) and turned instead to a typical career path for women. She took a
secretarial training course in Victoria, got a job with the public works
department in Vancouver, and moved to a West End apartment in Van-
couver. However, later in 1949, she met F.R. Scott while attending the
CCF National Convention. (Scott, a founding member of the CCF par-
ty, was attending the convention in his capacity as national chairman.)
Ironically, it was Harold Winch who introduced Webb to Scott, who
then replaced Winch as Webb's close friend and mentor for most of the
next decade. Webb repeatedly emphasizes her debt to Scott whenever she
talks about her formative years as a writer. As she says to Eleanor Wachtel,
"Frank Scott influenced my life enormously. He was a socialist when I
was, he had a broad knowledge—a Renaissance[7] man they used to call
him" (Wachtel, 11). Scott advised her to pursue a career in writing and
for that purpose to move to Montreal, which she did in 1950.

1950–60: Montreal, London, Paris

I have chosen to treat the 1950s as a unit in Webb's life because of the tidy geographic markers: the decade is marked by her move from Vancouver to Montreal in 1950 and her return to Vancouver from Paris, via Montreal and Toronto, in 1960. During this decade (from age twenty-three to thirty-three), Webb lived an exceptionally patchwork life. She lived in Montreal, Toronto, Victoria, London, and Paris. She had no regular job and often lived on very little money, supporting herself by freelance work and occasional jobs as a secretary in a half-dozen different places and by writing reviews, talks, drama scripts, and feature presentations for CBC radio. She attended McGill University in Montreal to do a qualifying year for graduate work. Webb also read widely on her own during this period, becoming variously involved in such different topics as the French theatre, Gide's "philosophy of risk," Buddhism, the poetry of Marianne Moore, Rilke, and the new British poetry. She argued poetics constantly with Louis Dudek, Frank Scott, Earle Birney, and others. She published "Falling Glass" in *Trio* (1954), *Even Your Right Eye* (1956), and completed most of *The Sea Is Also a Garden* (1962). She also suffered from depression and ill health, partially brought on by her complicated relationship with Frank Scott.[8]

The patchwork nature of her life comes partially from personal imperatives, from a desire to be independent, to resist the 1950s emphasis on the middle-class family and domesticity and to be a writer; it also came partially from the lack of career options for women combined with the "unnatural silences" that are imposed on women (Sujir interview, 35) and partially, I would argue, from the modernist notion of the artist as one who lives on the edges of the economic mainstream. In any case, the 1950s was both a very productive and a very troubling decade for Webb. The following is a detailed account of her activities. Again I do not want to imply a direct cause/effect relationship between the life and the work, but rather to locate the poems within social, economic, and historical contexts.

Mentors and Modernism

When Webb arrived in Montreal, Frank Scott introduced her to the group of writers who met occasionally at the home of Irving and Betty Layton, or at John Sutherland's apartment, to read and discuss poetry. The group,[9] which included Louis Dudek, Irving and Betty Layton, Gael Turnbull, Eli Mandel, Miriam Waddington, and, later on, Leonard

Cohen and Al Purdy (Williamson interview, 321) was vital to Webb's developing self-confidence as a writer: "I had a great deal of encouragement and acceptance into this very interesting literary circle,' she explains to Stephen Scobie (interview, 2); it was a "multi-generational group" that brought neophyte writers such as herself into the community of more established writers such as Sutherland, Dudek, and Scott who had the power to legitimize young writers by providing group acceptance, theoretical respectability, and access to publishing.[10] Partially as a result of the contacts Webb made through this group, Webb's poems began to appear regularly in the various little magazines of the time, including *Northern Review, CIV/n, Contemporary Verse, Combustion, PM Magazine, Forge*, and *Fiddlehead*. In 1954, Raymond Souster at Contact Press published her first collection—titled "Falling Glass"—in *Trio*, a book that included the "trio" of Gael Turnbull, Eli Mandel, and Phyllis Webb.

As well as boosting Webb's confidence, opening up publishing avenues, and providing a community—"my connections were a mixed poetic, sexual, and communal thing" (Williamson interview, 322)—the group provided Webb with a much-needed education in poetics. F.R. Scott continued to read and critique her writing, to provide support and encouragement, and to recommend poets to read. He introduced her to the work of Marianne Moore, for instance, who became an important influence for Webb in the 1950s. Moore was one of the few women poets of whom Scott and Dudek approved, Webb explains to Janice Williamson, because "she was a highly intellectual poet" (321-22). Webb has commented that even in as recent a book as *Water and Light*[11] (a book which she dedicated to Scott) Scott's influence is still evident in "the classical influence, that clean line, and the social" (Butling interview, 1986).

Webb also credits Louis Dudek with teaching her a great deal about poetics:[12]

> I was very naive about poetry at that stage, and I really do thank Louis [Dudek] for educating me in poetics. He had a much broader theoretical stance; he had a much larger view of poetry than anyone else I knew. He was also a propagandist for a Poundian or Williamsesque approach to poetry. (Scobie interview, 1)

Fortunately for the literary historian, some of Dudek's advice to Webb was in written form—in letters to Webb in 1951-52 (when Webb worked as a secretary to the principal at Macdonald College outside

Montreal and Dudek was at Columbia University in New York City) and again when she lived in London and Paris. In a ten-page critique of several of Webb's early poems, Dudek alternately scolds, admonishes, praises, lectures. His comments show both his commitment to a modernist (and masculinist) aesthetic and his paternalistic, mentoring relationship to Webb. He describes Webb's poem "Earth etc" (presumably "Earth Descending") as "entirely too subjective." He objects to another poem because "one reads some private lives into it—not the business of poetry. Must be intimate-universal." "When you write about poetry—or yourself" he continues, "it must be raised to a universal." He also stresses organic form ("make rhythm always speak your thought, never such a pattern as this") and plain language ("I'd say one ought to try to make one's meaning as plain as possible; obscurity, if any, can only result from the difficulty of an idea itself, and from the people's inability to follow the poetic way of communication"). He ends the letter with the following rather harsh summation:

> Most of the poems really miss the best aim of poetry. Some are already fine. Surprising, since the technique is very uniform, does not show a drive to experiment, to discover the necessary form for the available complexity of personality, life, imagination. . . . and does not show any immersion in successive fields of influences.

As a corrective, he recommends

> an intense reading of one or two poets at a time in order to absorb their quality. e.g. Yeats would give a richer atmosphere; these poems are too dry in language & in the emotive state they choose to evoke; or William Carlos Williams, to give them more luminous imagery, more physical and zestful movement—out into the world. Not read them to imitate. But to expand one's own range of knowledge of *what the poetic experience can be*. (Dudek to Webb, October 23 [1951 or 1952], Dudek papers, NL)

While admitting at the end of the letter that possibly hers is "a kind of poetry that I have no faculty to criticize, being different from it," his lecturing tone throughout admits no such equivocation. His tone is stern, confident, but at the same time friendly, in keeping with his mentoring role. Webb's letters in turn indicate a combination of compliance and defiance, a mixture of affection, resistance, awe, and admiration. One letter begins "dear damned and damning Louis"; in another, affection and fear are combined in a quick shift of phrase: "The poem—though I don't like all that title—moved me very much.

It is a really fine piece of work. O, but I fear for you. I think I mean I
fear you" (Webb to Dudek, nd., Dudek papers, NL). In retrospect, she
describes herself as "not always a willing student, certainly not a com-
placent one. My history of friendship with Louis has been argumenta-
tion, against his dogmatism and didacticism" (Scobie interview, 1).

Webb seems to have taken Dudek's advice to read Yeats and Wil-
liams, the most obvious indications being her "Poems from Dublin,"
(written circa 1956) and her use of William Carlos Williams' line for
the title of her 1962 collection *The Sea Is Also a Garden*. However, she
criticizes as well as admires Yeats, noting his stultifying effect, for in-
stance:

> Old Yeats, your cold, bitter
> lyrical, marble lines
> drive me into innocence, the better
> rage—the rest I can divine
>
> with my "divining heart." I feel
> in the cold wash of the rain
> your cool and consonantal seal
> upon the honeyed hive of brain—(*VT*, 59)

Likening Yeats to a cold shower that stops the action of the brain hardly
suggests unqualified admiration. Yet she was obviously still drawn to
Yeats—she describes her trip to Ireland in 1956 as a "literary pilgrim-
age to do homage to Yeats and Joyce" (typescript, "Dublin Delight,"
NL) and the "Poems of Dublin" end with an image of ducks swimming
in a pond, an image that simultaneously does homage to Yeats (recalling
poems such as Yeats' "The Wild Swans at Coole") while offering an al-
ternative movement away from Yeats' "cold, bitter, marble lines" to-
ward the "immediate, sensate":

> at the pond's edge,
> their heads turned back
> into immediate, sensate, sinking necks
> of purple and green fluffed and rebellious plumage. (*VT*, 59)

More recently, in " 'Thinking Cap' " (*Hanging Fire*, 1990), Webb criti-
cizes a similar coldness in the poems of William Carlos Williams. In the
latter poem, however, Webb's critique is much more active and inter-
ventionist: the poet invades "Williamsland" and reactivates the objects:

we're coming in
to Williamsland
to invade
the objects
to snatch the
after-image of
ol' Bill's plums—
you know
the ones that
tasted so good
because they were
cold and beautiful
and couldn't

speak (" 'Thinking Cap,' " *HF*, 65)

Here Webb overrides the imposed silences of a masculinist aesthetic and reenergizes those "cold and beautiful" and silent objects in Williamsland.

In recent years, Webb has reflected on the role of male mentors in the formation of her poetics, as Susan Glickman reports:

> speaking at the League of Canadian Poets panel discussion of "The Female Voice in Canadian Poetry" (Regina, 1984) she wondered whether her early acceptance by the predominantly male literary establishment had in some way inhibited her development as a poet, encouraging too great a reliance on masculine approval and the literary techniques which seemed to ensure it. (54)

In the 1950s, however, that "early acceptance by the predominantly male literary establishment" provided much needed literary education and external validation of herself as a writer.

"The Poet and the Publisher"

Equally important to Webb's education in poetics and to her relative early success as a writer was a research project on the state of publishing in Canada. Webb began the project in 1951 by sending out a questionnaire to sixteen writers, a group that included three women (Anne Marriott, P.K. Page, and Dorothy Livesay) and thirteen men. Ten of the sixteen replied. She then sent a summary of the responses to various publishers and academics such as Lorne Pierce (Ryerson Press), John Gray (McClelland and Stewart), and Robert Weaver at CBC. Initially conceived as a possible masters thesis, the first formal presentation of her findings was in the form of a seminar paper which she gave in Arthur Phelps' Canadian literature class at McGill in 1953 (Webb to Gray, July 27, 1953, quoted in Knight, 45). She subsequently wrote three papers titled "The Poet and the Publisher." The first one, published in *Queen's Quarterly* (61 [Winter 1954-55]) was a summary of the results of her survey on the state of publishing in Canada; the second one was a "brief account of a similar survey that she had recently completed in England" (Whalley, xi) which she delivered at the Canadian Writers' Conference on "The Poet, His Media, and the Public" at Queen's University in July 1955. The conference, organized by F.R. Scott and others and funded by a grant from the Rockefeller Foundation, brought together for the first time writers, editors, publishers, librarians, and booksellers from across the country.[13] According to George Whalley, editor of the conference proceedings, Webb's *Queen's Quarterly* paper "was widely discussed" at the conference, "providing a nucleus of factual evidence in an area where conjecture, partiality, and resentment are more usually encountered" (xi). Following the conference, Webb wrote the third and final version. As Whalley explains, "[s]o interesting and provocative were these [Webb's] two reports that the Committee invited Miss Webb to prepare a combined report on the publishing of poetry in Canada and England" (xi) to be included in the publication of the conference proceedings in 1956. This version was also broadcast on CBC radio in November 1955.

Through her work on the project, Webb met and/or corresponded with the major Canadian publishers and writers of the 1950s, a fact that may have helped get her poetry published and certainly contributed to a lively social and intellectual life. The significance of Webb's project to Canadian cultural history is also considerable: as Lorna Knight explains, the project "served as a focus for concern and a catalyst for solutions" for many writers and publishers in the 1950s (43).[14] Many of the suggestions that Webb presented in her paper (suggestions that came from the questionnaire and from her correspondence with publishers) were debated at the 1955 Conference and incorporated into the conference resolutions (such as inexpensive editions of Canadian books, subsidies for publishers and writers, more Canadian literature in school and university curricula, increased "purchases of new Canadian writing for distribution" overseas, and a cash award to accompany the Governor General's Award [Whalley, 8-9]). Many of the conference resolutions were, in turn, acted upon by the Canada Council when it was formed in 1957.

For Webb, the project also marked the beginning of her career as a cultural/literary journalist. Throughout the 1950s, 1960s, and into the 1970s, Webb supported herself through a combination of freelance journalism and secretarial work. Her radio work began in 1953, when Robert Weaver invited her to submit some of her poems for broadcast on *CBC Wednesday Night*. Three poems were broadcast on October 30, 1954, for which she received $34.50.[15] Such a fee, though no doubt an elixir for the ego, would barely pay the rent, even in 1954. From 1950-54, Webb also worked as a secretary to the principal at Macdonald College of McGill University (at Saint Anne de Bellevue), and as secretary to the chairman of the Biochemistry Department at McGill in Montreal.

Webb's radio work and occasional magazine articles not only provided money to live on; they also provided intellectual food for her poetry in the sense that freelance work gave her some freedom in choice of topics. Presumably she would have some choice of books to review, for instance, for such programs as *Critically Speaking*. Her feature broadcasts on Rilke, Dylan Thomas, the New English poets (in 1957), François Sagan, Van Gogh, and others on such programs as *CBC Wednesday Night* certainly reflect her interests. She also took part in panel debates on current topics on both CBC radio (*Now I Ask You*) and CBC television (*Fighting Words*).

In the fall of 1953, Webb enrolled at McGill University in Montreal as a qualifying student for the graduate program. Her courses included a Canadian literature survey (one of the first in a Canadian university) with Professor Phelps, using the A.J.M. Smith anthology, *The Book of Canadian Poetry*. In another of those serendipitous historical accidents, some of the lectures in the course were given by Constance Beresford-Howe who was a teaching assistant for the course. Not only were her lectures excellent, according to Webb, but here again (as with P.K. Page and Virginia Woolf in the 1940s) Webb found a female writer/role model. Webb also took a Chaucer course with the well-known Chaucer scholar, Professor Joyce Hemlow. Thus, notwithstanding the preponderance of male mentors in Webb's life in the 1950s, she found a few women role models as well, a fact which may have bolstered the incipient feminism of poems such as "Poet" and "Earth Descending" (*Trio, SP*).

England—1954-55

In the spring of 1954, Webb decided not to enter graduate school at McGill and, instead, to travel for awhile. She left for England (the day after *Trio* was published) to travel in England and Ireland. Webb left Montreal partially to go on the "literary pilgrimage" that I described above and partially to get away from her continuing complicated relationship with Scott. However, she was joined by Scott for a brief holiday in Paris in the summer of 1954 where they had "four . . . days of pure miracle" (Webb to Dudek, September 5, 1954, Dudek papers, NL) and he then came back to London with her. In "A Walk by the Seine," Webb writes:

> But you and I slowing
> our words to a muted tone
> (for beauty silences the horse-drawn
> carriages of wisdom), meshing
> light and leaves in that imperial notion
> of stasis and dream, move and stand,
> like love and death, at the river's edge (*EYRE*, 24)

Shortly after, they again decided to go their separate ways, as Webb explained to Dudek in a letter two weeks later: "Frank has finally faced the dilemma of our situation, and has given his answer as No" (Webb to Dudek, September 22, 1954, Dudek papers, NL).[16] Webb stayed on in London and eventually worked for awhile as secretary to the head of the Psychology Department at the London School of Economics.

While in England, Webb became interested in the philosophy and the "moral stance" of André Gide:

> I was very attracted to French writers when I was living in England. . . . I was fascinated with Gide: I think it is more a way of thinking, and a moral stance, and a kind of insistence that he had on the narrow path, the narrow road; and the whole philosophy of change that he had, that you must not *stay* anywhere. I think it's a statement about the mind more than about actual journeying. That became part of *my* philosophy, of risk, that I must not stay in one place. (Scobie interview, 2)

Webb's poems of this period often take intellectual and emotional risks: "I'm doing some rather different writing over here," she writes in a letter to Dudek in 1955, and "I quite like it." She then enclosed "Double Entendre" in the letter, adding that it was dedicated "to the memory of André Gide" (Webb to Dudek, January 23, 1955, Dudek papers, NL). The poem enacts a mental/emotional journey through a series of double entendres and other kinds of doubles, including a doubling of the self in "real" and imaginary mirrors:

> the portrait of the artist
> > holding a mirror,
> or Gide
> > in his *Journals*
> > > writing of Stendhal's) (*VT*, 42)

"Two Versions," "Poems of Dublin,"[17] and other poems in *Even Your Right Eye* (1956) similarly enact an intellectual and emotional restlessness. In "Sunday Morning Walk," the speaker observes that "my Sunday morning walk . . . takes me to several answers / and no conclusions"; she acquires "a collection of unknowns" (*SP*, 48). Indeed the dialectic structure of much of Webb's early poetry (discussed in detail in chapter 1) can also be related to Gide's philosophy of risk in the sense that the perpetual oscillations enact a desire not to "stay in one place" in the poem, in the mind, in the world.

Montreal—1955-57

Webb returned to Montreal in 1955 in time to attend the Canadian Writers' Conference at Queen's University in July and give her paper "The Poet and the Publisher." In 1956, she published her first full book, *Even Your Right Eye*, with McClelland and Stewart. Late in 1956, she moved to Victoria to stay with her mother "indefinitely" as she says in a letter to the CBC dated January 4, 1957, because of health problems (typescript, Webb papers, NL). However, early in May of 1957, she was back in Montreal (Webb to Salverson, Webb papers, NL) and stayed until the fall when she left for Paris. While in Montreal, Webb resumed her freelance secretarial work—"It paid well and left time between jobs for writing" (Cash, 17)—and also worked for a few months as a full-time secretary in the Biochemistry Department at McGill. It was in that job that Webb first became aware of animals being used in research experiments, a practice that she has angrily denounced on several occasions, most notably in the opening poem of *Hanging Fire*, " 'A Model of the Universe' ":

> Or shady dealings in the lab.
> A hand-made mouse with cancer

for generations, patented,
marketed, sold, as transgenetic
engineering steers us to the
unity of all things. (*HF*, 13)

Paris—1957-58

In September of 1957, Webb received a Canadian Government Over-
seas Award and spent the next year and a half in Paris where she lived
the typical expatriate artist's bohemian life, living first in cheap hotels
and then subletting a one-room studio on rue de Seine that "belonged
to an Israeli artist who spent six months of the year in Paris and six
months in Spain" (typescript, "The Garret," Webb papers, NL).
Webb's descriptions of her life in Paris in a series of articles that she
wrote for the *Victoria Times* in 1959[18] and in an interview with journal-
ist Cultus Coulee (published in *The Gulf Island Driftwood* in 1971) em-
phasize the bohemian flavour of her Paris life. Her garret was a "walk-
up" on the seventh floor in an old (seventeenth-century) building; she
had an excellent view from her balcony of "the fine steeple of St. Ger-
main des Prés Church, the top of the Eiffel Tower, . . . a wonderful
complex of rooftops, and garret windows with flowering plants and liv-
ing cats," but the room itself was less enchanting. There was no running
water in the room, cold water available down the hall, and a "Turkish"
toilet (typescript, "The Garret," Webb papers, NL). When her lease
was up at the garret, Webb chose to move to a less bohemian but more
practical studio at the Cité Universitaire, a residential complex for inter-
national students and artists:

> I must admit that my reasons for going to live at the Cité weren't
> exactly inspired. I was running low on money and a room there
> would cost about $22 a month. I wanted to be warm in winter, and I
> also wanted good conditions for work. (Typescript, "The Cité Uni-
> versitaire," Webb papers, NL)

As for her writing projects: in her interim report to the Awards Com-
mittee of the Royal Society of Canada, dated Paris, July 14, 1958,
Webb summarizes:

> My main occupation during these past months has been the prepara-
> tion of a new manuscript of poems. The work has been slow, retarded
> as it was by continuing ill-health which will force me to stay in France
> for an unspecified period of time. However, the coming year will in a
> sense be useful for completing my book, for assimilating my various

and divided interests and focusing them, and for continuing my study of the French contemporary theatre and its authors, which has been the most stimulating intellectual experience France has offered. (Carbon copy, Webb papers, NL)

Webb's study of the French Theatre of the Absurd included plays such as Pirandello's *Henry IV* and writers such as Arthur Adamov, Artaud, Ionesco, de Nerval, Sartre, and others (Hulcoop, 15). Webb did not find much of interest in French poetry. Nor was "there . . . anything very exciting happening in England at that time" (Butling interview), but she made contact with Danny Abse in England who had published Webb's "Sacrament of Spring" in his magazine *Poetry and Poverty* in 1954.

Living in Paris during the political crises that preceded General de Gaulle's takeover in 1957 provided an important "education in politics. . . . I was never able to forget that a brutal colonial war was in progress" (typescript, "Paris," Webb papers, NL). On one occasion, when she and two other Canadians—the painter Joe Plaskett and the poet Daryl Hine—"decided to hear General de Gaulle explain his new constitution at the Place de la République," they had to run for their lives when the police fired shots and tear gas into a crowd of protesters (typescript, "Riot," Webb papers, NL).

Webb wrote few poems while in Paris. On the basis of publication dates and internal evidence, I presume her Paris poems include "To a Policeman Guarding the National Assembly" (*Delta* No. 6 [January 1959]; *SIAG*, 32); possibly "Propositions" (*Threshold*, 3, 1 [Spring, 1959]; *VT*, 42); and "In a Garden of the Pitti Palace" (*Tamarack Review*, 22 [Winter 1962]; *SP*, 73). Poems published in 1959 in the *McGill Chapbook*, 190 ("Galaxy," "Images in Crystal" [*EYRE*, 10-11], and "Ishmael" [uncollected]) were written in Montreal before she went to Paris.[19] In Paris, as she explains in the interim report cited above, her writing was "retarded by continuing ill-health"—both physical and mental. Much of her time and energy was spent in therapy with psychologist Lucy Jones (to whom *The Sea Is Also a Garden* is dedicated, together with Webb's mother, Mary Webb).

The portrait of Webb done by a close friend in Paris—New Westminster painter Joe Plaskett—provides a visual representation of Webb's troubled psychological state during this period (see page 124). It shows a divided self—the female split subject that feminist theorists often speak of—with the public figure of woman-as-*object* of the gaze at the centre of the painting and the repressed *subject* who speaks to and through the public mask looking on from the sidelines. The public self faces the viewer with striking composure and elegance, anticipating and accepting an admiring viewer. The private self looks quizzically at the public figure from the edge of the painting. The space between is filled with tensions. The public figure bespeaks a composed silence while the private self is reflective and questioning. The two figures are united, however, by the similarities in their hands. The long, bony, skeletal hands in both are strikingly languid, even lifeless. But they also express/possess potential power and agency, if only by association with bird claws and witches gnarled hands. Double-coded, they represent the subject/object tensions in the female split subject. Plaskett's portrait is, of course, an artist's construction, not a direct representation of the person Phyllis Webb. But it does offer one artist's view—also a close friend—of Webb's troubled mental/emotional state, a state that Webb also describes in a letter to Louis Dudek written from Paris. Webb writes of a paralyzing silence and passivity:

> You said . . . "Even a dying man can bless the living, not because he believes in life for himself, but because he believes in life for others." But I didn't believe in life for others, or in anything else, and all your good advice in the letter seemed to miss my most awful point: that nothing either within or without made sense, and further, I had no energy to make the senselessness a 'passionate subject.'" (Typescript, Webb to Dudek, August 17, 1958, Dudek papers, NL)

But Webb's Paris life was not all depression and illness. In a radio talk written on "a pleasant wave of nostalgia" after returning to Canada, she speaks of the delightful ambiance of her favourite Paris café, The Old Navy:

> It was my café because the prices were moderate, it wasn't too big, and I liked the clientele—a mixture of writers, actors, dramatists, students and no-gooders. Here I met one of the leading avant-garde playwrights [Arthur Adamov]. . . . Around him one could usually find a group of young people, most of them actors, some of them critics and playwrights too. They would talk at length with great animation about plays, politics and heaven knows what—but one felt that tremendous intellectual energy was applied to whatever subject was under discussion. I was awed by these displays of passionate intellection. (Typescript, "A Talk for Radio," Webb papers, NL).

There she enjoyed that favourite Paris pastime—people watching:

> I'd study the faces and notice the way different languages influenced the contours of the face, especially the shape of the mouth and the curve of the cheek line. . . . I'd watch the way people met in cafés and formed groups. (Typescript, "Cafés," Webb papers, NL)

Life in Paris also nurtured Webb's long-time interest in existentialist philosophy, an interest that began with her study of philosophy at UBC, although Webb also describes herself in a letter to John Hulcoop as an "intuitive existentialist" (Introduction, *SP*, 30).[20] Kierkegaard, Heidegger, and Nietzsche are frequent intertexts in Webb's writing. Several poems in *The Sea Is Also a Garden* (1962), such as "Breaking," "Making," "A Tall Tale," "Sitting," or "To Friends Who Have Considered Suicide," address the existentialist debate about Being and Nothingness (see chapter 1), although not without some characteristically Webbian ironic or comic twists and turns.

Vancouver (1960–63): Literary and Social Contexts

In the spring of 1959, Webb returned to Canada, first to Montreal and then to Toronto where she did freelance work for McClelland and Stewart as a copy editor and for CBC as a script reader. In 1960, she moved to Vancouver and got a job teaching first-year English at the University of British Columbia. She was hired by poet and professor Roy Daniells, then head of the English Department, as a full-time teaching assistant on the understanding that she would later start graduate work. However, it became a standing joke between them that this was a pretence: every year she would write him a formal note asking him to waive the study requirement so that he could renew her contract (Butling interview). Webb held sessional appointments at UBC for three years, earning a salary of about $400 to $600 a month for an eight-month period, depending on how many courses she taught (the sessional salary was $1,600 per course). A UBC year-end financial statement on March 31, 1963 lists her total salary as $3,221 (UBC archives).

At UBC, Webb became part of a literary/social group of gay and lesbian writers who taught there, including Jane Rule, Helen Sonthoff, and John Hulcoop. Webb's circle of friends and acquaintances also included some other lively members of the UBC English Department, such as Warren and Ellen Tallman, George Woodcock, and Earle Birney, as well as a group of visual artists who taught at the Vancouver School of Art: Roy Kiyooka, Jack Shadbolt, Toni Onley, and Takao

Tanabe (who published *Naked Poems*). This latter group reflects a continuing presence of visual art and artists throughout Webb's life.

Webb also met the avant-garde American writers who visited Vancouver in the early 1960s: first Robert Duncan who gave a series of lectures on Ezra Pound, and William Carlos Williams and H.D. at the home of Warren and Ellen Tallman in 1961;[21] then Robert Creeley when he taught English and creative writing at UBC for a year in 1962-63; then Charles Olson, Allen Ginsberg, Denise Levertov, and others when they were hired as guest instructors to teach a poetry seminar in the summer of 1963 at UBC. Webb prepared a radio program titled "Five Poets," based on interviews she conducted with Olson, Creeley, Ginsberg, Duncan, and Levertov while the poetry seminar was in progress. The program included readings and comments by the writers, woven together by Webb's commentary in which she outlines the events in the 1950s that brought these writers together. Webb also provides summaries and explanations on the key points in Olson's "Projective Verse" essay, comments that are surprisingly insightful given the difficulties posed both by Olson's unconventional style and innovative concepts. Webb's explanations show that she had an unusually clear grasp of Projective Verse concepts as early as 1963. "Composition by field," she explains, means that "the poem is begun without formal preconceptions." And further, "[w]hether or not Olson had in mind a wild field or a magnetic field or a psychological field . . . composition by field allows the poet to work in the open and in the unknown in the manner of an explorer. . . . the ecology of the field alone delimits the subject" (typescript, "Five Poets," Webb papers, NL). Her explanation of two other key points in Olson's "Projective Verse" essay—"FORM IS NEVER MORE THAN AN EXTENSION OF CONTENT" and "ONE PERCEPTION MUST IMMEDIATELY AND DIRECTLY LEAD TO A FURTHER PERCEPTION" (Olson, 148-49) are also surprisingly insightful: "Clearly, the poet cannot rest on his oars. Constantly aware of every element in his poem—the syllable, the line, the image, the sound, the sense—he has to listen attentively to his own intelligence; and his own breath" (typescript, "Five Poets," NL).

Webb's program was never aired, however, because Robert Weaver, the Special Program Officer for CBC radio, cancelled it: "I swung my whip and cancelled 'Five Poets'" he writes in a letter to Webb dated January 27, 1964. He continues:

In case you haven't heard, I think that in fairness to the Vancouver
people I should tell you that it was all my doing. . . . while I thought
that you did your best to make understandable much of the *fatuous
nonsense* that the poets were talking, I still thought it turned out to be
little more than fatuous nonsense and almost impossible to listen to. In
fact they were almost all incoherent. (Weaver to Webb, Webb papers,
NL; emphasis added)

Webb replies that "I don't see what you mean by fatuous nonsense"
and then goes on to defend both the quality and the relevance of the
program: "I personally thought there was fascinating material in some
of the interviews, and I really feel a simple kind of regret when I think
that no one was able to hear Olson, for instance, read 'The Distances.' "
Finally, she notes her personal interest: "I cared about the program, and
it took two months of pretty steady work" (carbon copy, Webb to
Weaver, February 3, 1964; Webb papers, NL).

Weaver's rejection of the program typifies a negative attitude that
was to persist for many years, especially in central Canada, toward both
the new American poetics and the upstart Vancouver writers who were
likewise arguing for open forms and a particularized stance in writing.
Certainly, some editors welcomed the new writing: Raymond Souster
published *New Wave Canada* in 1965 with the claim that "within the
covers of this anthology is the most exciting, germinative poetry writ-
ten by young Canadians in the last hundred years of this country's liter-
ary history." George Bowering, Frank Davey, and Lionel Kearns were
included in the Ryerson Press *Poetry 64* anthology; they were also pub-
lished by Louis Dudek in *Delta* magazine. Webb herself also showed her
support for this new writing through radio reviews and interviews and a
series of television interviews done in 1967 that included bp Nichol
and bill bissett.[22] But many writers, editors, and critics in the Canadian
literary establishment rejected the new poetics. Earle Birney, for in-
stance, in a letter to Webb in 1964, is very critical of Duncan, Olson,
and Creeley. He seems resentful of their influence on the young Van-
couver writers and dismisses them as "pretentious," "unskilled," and
"ignorant" teachers who were primarily interested in generating
uncritical followers. However, writers such as Daphne Marlatt, Bob
Hogg, Gladys Hindmarch, and Fred Wah—who studied with Creeley
at UBC as well as Creeley's contemporaries (such as Webb) or other
young writers such as George Bowering and Frank Davey who took the
summer poetry course at UBC in 1963 with Olson, Duncan, Creeley,
and others—tell a different story. They often praise these writers, not

only for introducing them to the new American poetics, but also for encouraging individual development rather than direct imitation. For myself, Robert Duncan's wide-ranging intelligence—which I first encountered in his rambling, disjunctive lectures in Vancouver in 1961— so excited and fascinated me that I decided to forego a planned year in France and go to graduate school instead. Likewise I found Olson and Creeley to be extraordinarily exciting teachers, both at the 1963 summer poetry workshop and in courses that I took from them at the University of New Mexico (Creeley) and the State University of New York at Buffalo (Olson). In my view they were also excellent readers of their poetry; like Webb, I regret that the Canadian radio audience was denied the chance to hear them read their work.[23] To my mind, Birney's and others' objections to the supposed incoherence is a red herring, diverting attention from the real issue of who or what would dominate the Canadian literary world. The obvious excitement on the part of many young writers about Black Mountain poetics threatened to destabilize the Canadian literary establishment, which is to say the issue was more ideological than formal. The literary establishment resisted the concepts by attacking the forms in which the ideas were expressed.

Webb's relation to the literary wars of the 1960s is, however, peripheral. Her writing was not seen as part of the new poetics by the literary establishment. Webb was not associated with the *Tish* writers, who began publishing their "Poetry Newsletter" in Vancouver in 1961, although she was very supportive of their work.[24] The first section of *Naked Poems* was published in one of the most prestigious little magazines of the time, *The Tamarack Review*, edited by Robert Weaver— ironically, at the same time that Robert Weaver cancelled Webb's "Five Poets" radio program (fall 1963).

But Webb's interview program with Olson, Duncan, Creeley, Levertov, and Ginsberg, together with her comments on form and line in "Polishing Up the View" (*Talking*), an article based on a 1963 interview of Webb by Dorothy Livesay, indicate the extent and the seriousness of her research into the new poetics. The literary establishment may not have associated her with the new American poetics, but she herself was closely involved.[25]

Webb had not written much in the early 1960s, except to put together *The Sea Is Also a Garden* for publication in 1962. But in the spring of 1963, in an application for a Canada Council travel grant of $2,000, she outlined two projects: "The first, probably to be titled NAKED POEMS, will be a small volume of small poems. In inspiration

they will perhaps derive from Sappho, Creeley, and, most importantly
from Chinese and Japanese forms"; the second "SCORPION AND BULL
will be a book of big poems," with both cosmic and comic dimensions:
the poems would include "social satire" in the form of "a critique of
language" together with "serious poetry of somewhat cosmic propor-
tions." To accomplish the above, she proposed first to attend the sum-
mer poetry seminar at UBC because she could learn "new verse tech-
niques" from "some of the leading experimental poets" who will be
there; second to travel briefly to Toronto and Montreal "mainly to
re-establish contact with Canadian poets and to get my bearings on the
problem"; third to go to New York "to absorb something of the Zeit-
geist necessary to accurate satire"; and finally, to spend some time in
San Francisco because "some of the poets who most interest me live
there, and I would expect to find such a milieu nourishing" (typescript,
Webb papers, NL). Webb got the grant and proceeded as planned, trav-
elling to Montreal and New York and then staying in San Francisco for
the winter of 1964-65 until she accepted a job with CBC in Toronto in
the spring of 1965.

The first half of the project was completed within two years: Webb
had already completed Suite I of *Naked Poems* in the spring of 1963; she
continued to work on them in San Francisco in the winter of 1964, and
finished them later that year in Toronto. They were published by Van-
couver artist Takao Tanabe at his Periwinkle Press in 1965.

Naked Poems marks a major shift in Webb's work both formally
and thematically (as discussed in chapter 1), a shift which one might ex-
pect would enable her to move easily into the larger forms that she had
proposed for the second project. But the "book of big poems"—which
expanded to include a series of poems on the Russian anarchist Prince
Kropotkin—had a slower gestation and went through many changes.
Not until the early 1970s (1970-73) did she publish "Poems of Failure"
(which incorporate the earlier Kropotkin project), most of the "Por-
traits," five sections of "A Question of Questions" and some of the
"Crimes" poems."[26] With these poems, Webb completed some aspects
of the proposed "book of big poems": she uses longer lines and larger
forms; she offers a "social critique" in her questioning of excessive
rationality, of rigid political, personal, and social structures, of culture
heroes, and of war crimes. The poems also often include the projected
mixture of comic and cosmic. The writer as a beetle in Dostoevsky's
cabbage soup who threatens to jump into his mouth to "improve" her-
self is one such example (*WB*, 29-30), or the trickster figure ("my

deceiving angel's / in-shadow'') in "A Question of Questions," who
counsels patience and trust and then "flies off / with my head" (*WB*,
52; *SP*, 128-29).

Toronto and the CBC (1964-69)

In 1964, Webb took a job as Program Organizer at CBC in Toronto
where she developed the radio program *Ideas* (with William A. Young
and Janet Somerville), an FM-radio program, with selected portions
carried on AM. The program developed out of CBC's *University of the
Air* (which Webb had been hired to run) and *The Learning Stage*, run by
Young. The two programs were brought together as the *Ideas* series. In
1967, Webb became executive producer, a position which she held for
two years (except for a six-months leave of absence in 1967). Webb also
prepared educational television programs for CBC, including a centen-
nial project on "Modern Canadian Poets," consisting of interviews
with twenty-six poets over a period of thirteen weeks. The poets
ranged from the well-established, such as A.J.M. Smith and F.R. Scott,
to experimental young writers such as bp Nichol and bill bissett. Webb
"wrote, organized and hosted them all" (Coulee).

The *Ideas* series which Webb produced consisted of in-depth in-
terviews and/or feature broadcasts on many of the major artists and
intellectuals of the 1960s. Figures such as Austin Clarke, R.D. Laing,
Norman O. Brown, Northrop Frye, Marshall McLuhan, Paul Good-
man, Daniel Berrigan, Martin Luther King, Isaac Asimov, Leslie Fied-
ler, and Glenn Gould were featured on the program. The job was de-
manding and exhausting and thus in some ways prevented Webb from
writing—John Hulcoop cites "nervous exhaustion" brought on by the
excessive demands as the job as one reason for Webb's inability to write
during this period (Hulcoop, Introduction, *SP*, 7). Also she suffered
from physical and mental health problems related to an undiagnosed
thyroid deficiency and to hypoglycemia (Wachtel, 9) which com-
pounded the difficulties.[27] But I think Webb's work for the *Ideas* series
also contributed to the eventual success of her poetry project. The
people she met and the research she did in connection with her job
informed her own project of developing a social critique. Her work
there helped to politicize and radicalize her thinking. R.D. Laing's
analysis of the family as a functional (or dysfunctional) social unit, for
instance, relates to Webb's investigation of family relations and the role
of father figures in her poetry—in "Father," in the "Portraits," and in

other poems written during the early 1970s (*WB*, 25-35). Indeed, Webb cites R.D. Laing's *The Self and Others* in the list of source texts at the back of *Wilson's Bowl* (87).[28] She also cites Laing's *The Politics of Experience* as an important intertext for the "Kropotkin Poems" in her Canada Council application in 1968 for a grant to work on those poems: "I will be concerned essentially wit[h] this *Politics of Experience*. . . . it has been another fervent desire of mine for some time to move from what has been called a 'solipsist' position to a more open one" (typescript of application, Webb papers, NL). Or, Norman O. Brown's philosophy of *Love's Body* as an all-encompassing social and spiritual construct resonates with Webb's discussion of "the 'body politic' and 'love's body' as interchangeable polymorphous analogues in an ideal world" in the Foreword to *Wilson's Bowl*.

However, not until Webb also developed a feminist analysis of her dependent relation to male authority figures (including many of the figures featured in the *Ideas* programs) and of the sometimes debilitating effects of such a dependency was she able to enter into the transformative dialogues with male authority that started her writing again.[29] Webb describes this moment of recognition to Leila Sujir:

> when I was trying to write the Kropotkin poems. . . . I read . . . Adrienne Rich's book *Of Woman Born: Motherhood as Experience and Institution* [1976]. It was, for me, a structural revelation of the society, which I at the time compared to the Marxian analysis . . . where you just suddenly see the whole structure. I brought myself up as a Marxian and a Freudian. And at this stage in my life, a genuine shift began to take place where I could no longer accept these analyses. (Sujir interview, 34)

Similarly, in response to Janice Williamson's question "when did the issue of gender in writing become more present in your thinking?" Webb explains:

> not until the early seventies. That's a very long time for me to start thinking about where some of my problems in writing were coming from, like the silences and the difficulty in carrying off a programmed poem or book. Finally, I had this overbearing sense that there had been too many fathers, literary or otherwise. I know by 1969 it was conscious, and I wrote a little piece in which I dispatched the fathers to the river Lethe, and I saw them sail away. (Williamson interview, 322)

Webb also speaks of women's fear of success as part of the problem:

Success is very threatening to me, and to a lot of women. When it
hits, you're really scared that (a) I didn't deserve it, and (b) now they'll
get me. . . . When I was made executive producer of CBC's *Ideas* in
the '60s and got a $1,000 raise, I went into a severe depression. Then I
read an article in *Time* that said this was quite a normal reaction.
Pathetic, isn't it, that women aren't taught how to handle success.
(Quoted in Wachtel, 8)

Vancouver and Salt Spring Island

Late in 1967, with six months' leave of absence from her CBC job,
Webb moved for the first time to Salt Spring Island, to recover from the
physical and mental-health problems referred to above. During that
time, she also took a three-week trip to the Soviet Union (prompted by
her interest in the Russian anarchist prince Kropotkin). In 1970, when
she was forty-three years old, she returned again to Salt Spring Island
and bought a house. She has lived on Salt Spring for most of the time
since then, at several different locations on the island. The geography of
this Pacific Coast island appealed to Webb, both because the West Coast
is her "psychic homeland" and because of her empathy for islands:

I grew up on an island—Vancouver Island. I was born in Victoria and
grew up there and my one ambition when I was a teenager was to get
off that island. . . . And then halfway through my life my ambition was
to get back onto an island, preferably a Gulf Island, and everything
just kept turning up Salt Spring. . . . it's very important to me in some
deep way, I think, to be on an island. . . . Sometimes I think it may be
as basic as my mother was here, or that this is where I grew up, but I
think it is the sea. It is my original landscape, and I think that really
profoundly pulled me. . . . And it's so quiet here and peaceful, in a
purely physical sense. I feel safe on this island. I feel protected from
other people. (Munton interview, 82-83)

In conversation with Stephen Scobie, she adds that she feels "very com-
fortable with those familiar images, the sea, the green" which may
indeed have "tantalising psychological ramifications" (interview, 2), but
at the very least provides a physical and psychic home.

The cover photograph on *Wilson's Bowl*—of Webb standing near
the shore at the edge of the photograph looking toward the sea—offers
one image of that geographic and psychic home. The sea, the rocky
coastline, and the petroglyph bowl filled with seawater can be read as
both physical and psychological spaces. The visual rhyme between the
small circle of seawater in the bowl and the wider expanse of the sea

enacts the connection between the individual psyche and the oceanic unconscious in Jungian philosophy, while the off-centre figure of the writer (hidden in the fold of the cover) enacts her de-centred position in the poem. Webb quotes Roland Barthes in her Foreword to *Wilson's Bowl* to explain this relationship between the writer and the poem: " 'I am both too big and too weak for writing. I am alongside it, for writing is always dense, violent, indifferent to the infantile ego which solicits it.' " Webb's poem "The Bowl" also explores the multiple connections of the bowl/poem/psyche/sea. Webb's bowl/poem offers, not the welcoming hospitality of "a loving cup," but a meditative space in language where the landscape and the psyche intermingle:

> This is not a bowl you drink from
> not a loving cup.
> This is meditation's place
> cold rapture's.
> Moon floats here
> belly, mouth, open-one-eye
> any orifice
> comes to nothing
> dark as any mask
> or light, more light / is
> holy *cirque*.
> Serene, it says silence
> in small fish
> cups a sun
> holds its shape
> upon the sea
> howls, 'Spirit entered
> black as any raven.'
> Smiles—
> and cracks your smile.
> Is clean. (*WB*, 64; *VT*, 132)

Intermingling of physical and psychic space becomes integral to Webb's work from *Wilson's Bowl* on. As here, Webb's bowl/poem intermingles water, light, darkness, masks, silence, reflections, smiles, depths, trickster figures, sun and moon, reader and writer.

Similarly, the poems in *Water and Light* (1984) are imbued with multiple resonances between landscape, mindscape, and wordscape. As Doug Beardsley writes on the back cover, "[t]he poet's immediate land-

scape is evoked, her neighbours, particular circumstances, private refer-
ences," together with "the personal associative leaps of her singing
mind." Particulars of the Pacific Coast landscape are again intertwined
with the movements of mind and language in *Hanging Fire* (1990). Sun-
light, moonlight, marshlight (the deceptive light known as *ignis fatuus*),
and "delusional systems" converge in a poem called " '*Ignis Fatuus*.' "
The following are the opening and closing lines of the poem:

> Sunlight sprays through rain; wind tumbles surf,
> globe of a morning moon glows down-here, where
> we need all the light we can get.
>
> [. . .]
>
> *Ignis fatuus*, foolish fire, jack-o'-lantern, will-
> o'-the-wisp. Marsh light from decomposing matter.
> Delusional systems. Us. (*HF*, 36)

Politics and Economics: 1970s

In 1968, Webb returned to her CBC job, but resigned a year later when
she was awarded a Canada Council Senior Arts grant. She also left her
CBC job, she explains to John Hulcoop, partially because she did not
want to align herself with the establishment. In Webb's view, "if I had
stayed [at the CBC] I would have become reasonably powerful and
fairly well off for a single person, and I felt that my sympathies were on
the side of the powerless." If she "became too affiliated with power it-
self and money," she would be going against her basic sympathies (Hul-
coop interview, 6). After quitting her job, Webb lived in Vancouver for
a while, then moved to Salt Spring Island in 1970, then back to Van-
couver for a year in 1972. In Vancouver, she again supported herself by
freelance journalism, producing some of the best work of her journalist
career. She wrote "Phyllis Webb's Canada" for *Maclean's* (October
1971; *T* and *NBBS*); she did radio reviews for John Merrit's programs
Critics at Large and *Critics on Air*; she read her poems on Robert
Weaver's *Anthology*; and wrote four in-depth feature radio programs:
"Waterlily and Multifoliate Rose: Cyclic Notions in Proust" (*Ideas*,
1971; *Talking*), "The Question as an Instrument of Torture" (*Ideas*,
1971; *Talking*), "Fate and the Unconscious" (*Ideas*, 1972; *Talking*), and
the award-winning "Rejoice in the Lamb: The Offering of Christo-
pher Smart (*CBC Tuesday Night*, 1972).[30] She also worked as executive

secretary for the Burnaby Arts Council for six months in 1972. Webb continued to work as a freelance broadcaster until 1975 when she took a job as bookstore manager for Volume II Bookstore on Salt Spring Island for a year.[31]

In 1978, Webb turned to teaching creative writing which, except for a writer-in-residence appointment at the University of Alberta in Edmonton and the occasional award or grant, was her principle means of support until she retired in 1990. She taught English and creative writing courses at the University of British Columbia and the University of Victoria in the 1970s. In 1978-79, she was a visiting assistant professor at the University of Victoria; from 1982-85 and again in 1986-87, she was a part-time sessional lecturer. In 1990, she was appointed an adjunct professor. She also taught summer courses at The Banff Centre in 1981, 1983, 1984, and 1985.

To her surprise, teaching not only provided a means of support but proved to be a stimulus to her writing, as she explains to Stephen Scobie in a 1983 interview:

> When I first started teaching Creative Writing, it had a quite exhilarating effect. That was when I really started writing again, when I was teaching at UVic, four years ago. For some reason, it seemed to stimulate me to write—much to my surprise, because I thought it wasn't supposed to do that. I thought teaching killed all your creative energies. But because I was *thinking* about writing so much, I was simply moved to write. (5)

On at least one occasion, teaching also provided an opportunity to investigate new theories and ideas. Among Webb's papers at the National Library is an outline for an eight-week course called "Mind and Market-Place: Consuming Concepts." Webb offered the course through the Centre for Continuing Education at UBC in the fall of 1971. The purpose of the course, according to Webb's proposal, was to examine the "built-in obsolescence" of ideas, the relation between mind and market place, what produces the "mental junk heap" that parallels the junk heaps of material goods in a consumer society:

> A characteristic of our books, machines, our grown-up toys is built-in obsolescence. The junk heap is a heraldic symbol of North American consumer society. . . . This workshop will attempt to understand fads, styles and fashions in ideas. What is obsolescence and what are its uses: what can we learn from some mechanical and scientific models? . . . The rise and fall of culture heroes; the fate of "movements," and the absorption of dissent. . . . how do we accommodate the mental junk

heap and the disenchantment of the broken-back paper-backs of last year's dream? (Webb papers, NL)

"The aim of the workshop," she continues, "is to become obsolete in eight weeks and understand why." This workshop reflects Webb's own propensity for subversive activity. While the tone here is playful, as is often the case in Webb's work, she is raising important ethical issues. Her course notes include a subheading "[t]he ethic for change" and the following list:

> the prizing of the process of discovery itself
> the prizing of the here and now and with it the imperative
>   Start from where you are!
> the priority of experiment
> the projective use of the past. (Webb papers, NL)

The above list challenges the ideology of progress (damaging to both the environment and to the mind) that produces junk heaps of consumer goods as well as the notion of outdated ideas. Remaindered books or remaindered ideas—both are by-products of an ideology of progress.

As the above course outline indicates, Webb's political activism resurfaced in the 1970s, this time with the newly formed feminist consciousness described earlier in this chapter, together with a renewed concern for human rights and environmental issues. In 1970, she launched a formal protest against CBC Vancouver with the B.C. Civil Liberties Association for sexist hiring policies. They had refused to consider her for summer relief announcing because of a policy of not hiring women announcers. In a letter to Robert McGall, Regional Director of the CBC, she protests against "the idea that the authority of the news must be endowed with a male voice" (Webb to McGall, June 29, 1970; Webb papers, NL). Her letter to John Stanton, president of the B.C. Civil Liberties Association cites biased and irrational hiring policies as the basis for her complaint:

> I have never before bothered to apply for a staff job in Vancouver because of the well known prejudice against women. With the arrival of Mr. Robinson's letter, I feel the time has come to place a particular instance of bias before the Civil Liberties Association. . . . If Mr. Robinson's refusal on the basis of "no women announcers" and the mysterious announce functions they are incapable of performing is typical of the thinking—or more accurately the feeling—among those in a position to hire at CBC Vancouver, then the situation is indeed serious. (Webb to Stanton, June 16, 1970)

As a result of Webb's protest, the B.C. Civil Liberties Association launched an investigation that led to the CBC Vancouver office changing its policy.

Webb also challenged the male bias in Canada Council awards when she was a member of the Canada-Scotland Writers-in-Residence Exchange jury. In a letter dated January 25, 1982 to the Arts Advisory Panel for the Canada Council, which she sent via "Katherine Benzekri, Writing and Publication Section of the C.C., asking her to pass it along to the panel," she calls for an affirmative action policy. The reception to this proposal was disappointingly cool, as she later explains to Sharon Nelson: "Kathy Benzekri herself did not take my suggestion of affirmative action in that committee meeting seriously: a competition is a competition and one should choose the best. C'est tout" (Webb to Nelson, April 11, 1982, Webb papers, NL).[32]

Beginning in the early 1970s, Webb also became interested in the Greenpeace protests against nuclear testing. In 1971, she applied to join the crew of "an 80-foot halibut packer named the Phyllis Cormack, renamed Greenpeace, [which] sailed off with a motley crew for the Alaskan island of Amchitka to protest an American five-megaton underground nuclear explosion" ("Protest," 38). Though she was not selected to be a crew member, she followed the Greenpeace I and II voyages to Alaska and Greenpeace III "from New Zealand [to] the site of French nuclear test . . . near the South Pacific atoll of Mururoa" (38) with great interest. In an article on Ben Metcalfe, journalist and "propaganda minister for Greenpeace protest mission" (38), she describes her response to the first Greenpeace mission to protest nuclear testing in the South Pacific:

> I became a spectator, convinced the whole thing was an all-male conspiracy. I sat back and waited for the blast. It came. I felt it in my spine. The house didn't even twitch, but the earth shuddered. I was glad those too small ships of fools, male chauvinist or not, had done what they could do, which wasn't much, but it was symbolic and beautiful and it was courageous. ("Protest," 38)

The images and the discourse generated by the Greenpeace movement—of mushroom clouds and various environmental disasters—form another intertextual field for Webb's writing, particularly in *Hanging Fire*, where the poet's anger over these issues finds voice(s).[33] At the time, in "Lines for Gwen [MacEwen], Lines for Ben [Metcalfe]," the

"I" seems temporarily silenced on the subject. The poem concludes
with a silent and solitary "I":

> Gwendolyn was writing in the dream
> *I am in the heat of childbirth*
>
> she at her standing-desk self-possessed
>   1,3,5,7
> she wrote again and split
>
>   as I woke
> without a word. (*WB*, 80)

Webb's political activism continued into the 1980s and included
working for Amnesty International, for both political and literary rea-
sons, as she explains to Stephen Scobie:

> I became involved with Amnesty International when I went to the
> Writer and Human Rights Congress in Toronto in 1981. . . . I think
> the reason I became so involved with it was that, unconsciously, I was
> still working on that prison image, which is so dominant in my poe-
> try, and perhaps I saw a way out of my own prison through working
> for those who are in prison. This is a meaning I have laid on after the
> fact. I came back from that Congress with a lot of energy for activities
> beyond the very narrow circle of my regime—with a new release of
> energy, which allowed me to organize a group on Salt Spring. It's the
> kind of energy I used to have when I was younger, and belonged to
> the CCF, and ran for the CCF: it was the kind of political energy I
> haven't had for a long time. (Scobie interview, 6)

Webb's political activism of the 1970s and 1980s—whether as teacher,
or Amnesty International worker, or Greenpeace sympathizer—connects
with her critique of oppressive power structures in many of the poems in
Wilson's Bowl. In the poems, her subversive activity takes the form of ques-
tioning cultural authority figures—Pound, Dostoevsky, Kropotkin,
Socrates, and others—or setting up intertextual fields that foreground,
loosen, and/or dislocate power relations (see chapter 4).

Northwest Coast Native Art and Myths

While living on Salt Spring Island, Webb became interested in native
rock carvings (petroglyphs) and paintings (pictographs), particularly
when she came across the petroglyph bowl near Fulford Harbour, later

named "Wilson's Bowl" by Lilo Berliner (*NBBS*, 113). That interest brought Webb into contact with Beth and Ray Hill, authors of *Indian Petroglyphs of the Pacific Northwest* (1974) and Lilo Berliner, a reference librarian at the University of Victoria who had been studying petroglyphs and pictographs for many years. Webb explains: "It was because of my own new discovery of petroglyphs in 1970 that I was introduced first to Lilo Berliner and then to Beth Hill, who was working on her book" and further that these contacts led to a "strange network of connections [which] was to affect all our lives in ways we could not foresee" (*NBBS*, 111).

Webb became personally involved in this "strange network of connections" when Berliner left her letters from UBC anthropologist Wilson Duff on Webb's doorstep just before she walked into the sea to commit suicide (in 1977). Webb was left with the puzzle of twin suicides (Duff committed suicide six months before Berliner, in August of 1976) and the puzzle of a relationship based entirely on letters (they never met in person). In Webb's essay, "A Correspondence"—written in 1977 for inclusion in a memorial collection on Duff (*The World Is as Sharp as a Knife*) but not, in fact, published until 1982 (in *Talking*), Webb "fulfill[s] what I felt must be Lilo's intention," to have the correspondence published (*NBBS*, 129). Webb's essay includes excerpts from the Duff/Berliner letters, excerpts from Duff's essay "Nothing Comes Only in Pieces," and Webb's commentary on the various puzzles that the correspondence explores. She describes the Berliner-Duff relationship as a "fascinating . . . dialogue between two persons who never met and yet could share ideas, intuitions, feelings, secrets and jokes" (*NBBS*, 112) and the Duff essay as "a ground theme and reference point in these letters" (*NBBS*, 114). She explores the theme of Duff and Berliner as "twins," a theme that begins with Duff addressing a letter to "Lilo, my 'twin'" in January 1975 (*NBBS*, 126) and later that year exclaiming in another letter:

> I have the feeling that I am almost ready to state Duff's Law. It will be an equation, with "I am You. That is You" on the one hand, and "The World is As Sharp As A Knife" on the other. The world is a single twin, caught in the reciprocal act. (Cited in Webb, "A Correspondence," *NBBS*, 129)

Duff describes a similar complementarity in the famous twin stone masks that were the centrepiece of the exhibition of Indian sculpture curated by Duff in 1975 (*images stone b.c.: Thirty Centuries of Northwest*

Coast Indian Sculpture). The twin stone masks are identical except for the eyes—one has open eyes, the other closed.[34] Duff describes the masks in his catalogue essay as representing two complementary sides of human nature in a reciprocal relationship: "the one, 'eyes open', the other, 'eyes closed.' . . . They are twin stone faces, recognizing each other in each other" (26). Webb concludes her essay by commenting on a similar complementarity between Duff and Berliner, noting that "[a]lthough twins, they were not identical . . . [Lilo] was a Jungian and oriental. Wilson was a Freudian and western" (*NBBS*, 129).

These various texts (the letters, Duff's essays, Webb's essay) form an intertextual field for many of the poems in *Wilson's Bowl*. Also, as Webb explains to Leila Sujir, the "Wilson's Bowl" poem

> was a way of dealing with death, writing that poem, or two deaths, and . . . with my own suicidal impulses which the death cured me of. I was right up against the facts of that particular suicide, having to deal with police and things. . . . it was an exorcism. (Sujir interview, 36)

It is important to note, however, that Webb's treatment of the Duff/Berliner material is quite different in the poems than in her essay. The essay is descriptive and analytical; the poems are transformative and critical. The "twin" motif, for instance, informs Webb's poem "Imperfect Sestina." However the twin in this poem is no soulmate; it is an oppressive (male) alter ego that all but consumes its other half to serve its own egocentric needs:

> There I was stabbed and pecked by spirit Raven.
> There in that marriage I turned into stone,
> and did not understand he carved me at his mirror. (*WB*, 73)

Here, she enacts a woman's negative experience of so-called reciprocal relationships. She sees not a complementary relationship, but an oppressive structure; not the perfect fit imaged by the male carver of the two masks, but a power imbalance in the sense that there is neither the perfect fit of the sestina rhyme pattern (hence "Imperfect Sestina") nor the "perfect" balance of male/female in a reciprocal relationship. The "I" of the poem angrily protests the oppressive structure and focusses on the cracks in the structure, the moments of "illumination"—the word "illumination" literally breaks the sestina pattern. Webb explains:

> The imperfections in "Imperfect Sestina" which begin to occur in
> the fourth stanza with the word "illumination" came about through
> speed of writing and the workings of the unconscious. I have learned
> to pay attention to so-called mistakes, and this one told me that "illu-
> mination" wanted to take over the poem. I therefore reinforced the
> mistake by repeating the word insistently, disrupting the compulsive
> sestina form with another compulsion which shed more light. ("Up
> the Ladder: Notes on the Creative Process," *NBBS*, 34)

That "compulsion" is to question, to break through the rigidity of tra-
dition, in both verse forms and thought patterns. Similarly, in "Twin
Masks," Webb points to a masculinist bias, asking "if a woman could
have made them / the two stone masks"; and she "feel[s] the weight of
the rock reject me" (*WB*, 70).

   Webb's references to Haida art and myths might now be ques-
tioned as appropriative, but at the time she was viewed as someone
whose interest in aboriginal cultures helped to generate both an interest
in and a respect for those cultures. Also, it should be noted that the
Haida legends enter her work via her involvement with the Lilo Ber-
liner/Wilson Duff correspondence, not as exotic "material" brought
directly into a poem without any awareness of how such uses perpetuate
an exploitive relationship between white and native cultures. Webb's
use of Haida art and myth thus differs substantially from that of writers
such as Susan Musgrave (in her sea-witch poems) or bill bissett (in some
of his chant poems). I would argue that Webb does not try to be
"native" nor to represent a native perspective; she translates rather than
appropriates, and her translations involve respect for and knowledge of
the material as well as an awareness that there can be no direct transfer
in either direction.

Publications, Recognitions, Awards: 1980s and 1990s

Since the publication of Webb's *Selected Poems* in 1971, Webb has
received considerable public acclaim and recognition. She was awarded
the B.C. Library Association Prize in 1972 for "the writer who has
made the greatest contribution to the poetry of B.C. in the past five
years" (Hulcoop, *PW*, 8). She was also offered an honorary degree
(which she declined) from Simon Fraser University in 1975 "in recog-
nition for outstanding contribution to Canadian Literature" (Hulcoop,
PW, 8). She also declined an honorary degree from the University of
Victoria. While the 1970s was also a period of "critical wounds," as
Webb puts it in the Foreword to *Wilson's Bowl*,[35] with the publication

of *Wilson's Bowl* in 1980, Webb's reputation as an outstanding poet was firmly established. Cecelia Frey lists twenty reviews of *Wilson's Bowl* in her Webb Bibliography (compared to thirteen for the 1971 *Selected Poems* and seven for *Selected Poems: The Vision Tree* in 1982). Critics as various as Douglas Barbour, Bruce Whiteman, Lola Tostevin, W.J. Keith, Smaro Kamboureli, Ann Mandel, and Stephen Scobie all speak highly of the book. Douglas Barbour, for instance, describes her as "one of the finest poets now writing in English" ("Canadian Poetry Chronicle," 1982, 44); Lola Tostevin finds "some of the finest poetry" that she has read "in a long time" (15); W.J. Keith describes the book as both "impressive and exalting" (102); and Bruce Whiteman declares it "in almost every respect a fine book" (16).

Also in 1980, Webb was honoured with a private award. The award came from a group of writers who felt she should have won the Governor General's award for *Wilson's Bowl*. The award, organized by bp Nichol and Michael Ondaatje, with help from Margaret Atwood and P.K. Page, consisted of a gift of $2,300 and the following statement about Webb's work:

> . . . your poetry has meant a great deal to us . . . [and] continues to move us and surprise us with its heart and craft. We want to emphasize that this gesture is a response to your whole body of work as well as to your presence as a touchstone of true, good writing in Canada, which we all know is beyond awards and prizes. (Quoted in Wachtel, 8)

Throughout the 1980s and into the 1990s, Webb has continued to receive considerable public recognition and praise, although *Water and Light*, *Talking*, and *Hanging Fire* were not as widely reviewed as *Wilson's Bowl*. In 1980-81, she was invited to be writer-in-residence at the University of Alberta; in 1982, *The Vision Tree: Selected Poems by Phyllis Webb* won the Governor General's award for poetry. Also in 1982, she was awarded a Senior Arts grant from the Canada Council. Webb has read at many national and international festivals, including Toronto's International Festival of Authors at Harbourfront, the Adelaide Festival in Australia, the New Zealand International Festival of the Arts, the Lahti International Writers Reunion in Finland, and the New Literatures in English Association Conference in Essen, Germany. The 1980s was also a productive decade for Webb, with six books published in eleven years: *Wilson's Bowl* in 1980; *The Vision Tree: Selected Poems by Phyllis Webb*, *Talking*, and *Sunday Water: Thirteen Anti Ghazals* in 1982; *Water and Light* in 1984; and *Hanging Fire* in 1990. In 1992—the year of her sixty-fifth birthday—she was made an officer of the Order of Canada, she was nominated for the Canada/Australia Literary Prize (a nomination which she declined because she felt writers of colour should be among the nominees), and she was honoured by a group of literary friends with a day-long "Tribute to Phyllis Webb" and birthday party at the Western Front in Vancouver. The latter event was held in conjunction with the publication of *"You Devise. We Devise" A Festschrift for Phyllis Webb* (*West Coast Line* Number 6).

———

Obviously a biography of a living writer has no conclusion. Webb continues to live on Salt Spring Island. She declines invitations to give public readings but occasionally gives talks, such as a lecture on "Poetry and Psychobiography" at the Vancouver Institute in 1993, or a paper at the conference in honour of Robin Blaser's life and work in Vancouver in 1995 ("The Crannies of Matter: Texture in Robin Blaser's Later 'Image Nations'"). She contributed a short prose reminiscence—"Tibetan Desire"—to an anthology celebrating Leonard Cohen's sixtieth birthday (1994). These and other prose pieces have been recently collected in *Nothing But Brush Strokes* (1995).

In the summer of 1993, she surprised herself by unexpectedly taking up watercolour painting and she has since been absorbed in learning how to use watercolour paints as well as experimenting with collages of cut-up photographs. A selection of this visual work was published in *NBBS* as "The Mind's Eye: A Photo-Collage Essay" (74-82). Webb explains that this

> shift in consciousness to the visual occurred after I'd decided not to do any more overseas travel as a writer or anything of a public nature. Almost a Buddhistic withdrawal of identity, a test, and a risky move for someone with an unstable ego. I did experience moments of initiatory psychic jeopardy before the painting and collaging began.
>
> When they began, *circles*—moons, suns, gongs, bicycle wheels—emerged as a dominant theme, especially in the collages. I started with a series called "Tibetan Desire" (a phrase from Leonard Cohen's *Beautiful Losers*) which featured a brass gong. The petroglyph bowl referred to in the title of my book, *Wilson's Bowl*, glowed, moon-bathed, through another sequence. Just recently I completed "The Greg Curnoe Cycle," all bicycle wheels and parts. Jung's spiri-

tual mandala of maturity; Vaughan's "great ring of pure and endless
light"; the Wheel of Fortune, life's cycle. (*NBBS*, 86)

The stunning series of images that constitute what Webb calls a "A
Photo-Collage Essay" (*NBBS*, 74-82) indicate Webb's restless, inquir-
ing intelligence intensively at work in this new medium.

Finally, as a way of ending without concluding this chapter (and
book), I will quote a poem that Webb read on the steps of the B.C. leg-
islature on Thanksgiving Day, 1993—a poem that in a sense brings this
biography full circle in that Webb's political awakening occurred in the
B.C. legislature some fifty years previous, in 1943.

Webb wrote the poem to protest the B.C. government's decision
to allow logging to continue in Clayoquot Sound on Vancouver Island.
However the poem not only scolds the loggers and protestors alike to
leave the trees alone; it also serves as a reminder to the reader and/or
biographer to stand back a little, to not hold the poet too closely, to
leave the poet, like the trees, to "grow old in peace":

THE TREE SPEAKS

Get off my back,
I've had it up to here
with the humans,
let me grow old in peace,
fall over and die gracefully;
though I sometimes think
a quick cut of the chainsaw
is better than death by fire,
always a possibility.
Suffering. We know about
suffering. Growth is suffering.
But you know that.
And don't give me your stupid
human hugs. Listen to me now,
talking out of character like
a member of the human race,
look what you've brought me to,
so low that I'm only a foolish
projection of some old woman poet.

I have to listen to the ants,
beetles, lichen, chipmunks, mosses,
moulds using my bark—and don't strip
it off me for your baskets, either.
Do you hear the raven up there
in my top-most boughs, tricking
and treating? I like that. I like
the feel of all that.

No, I don't want your hugs, I'm
sorry, or the chainsaw gangs,
or tongues of flame. Don't want
this poisoned voice. That old
woman poet can have it back.
For obvious reasons,
I've got to save my breath.

Let me winter back into pure
tree-life, species specific,
blowin' in the wind,
uttering only rarely a bleak,
humanoid word
of thanks, of praise.

                 –October 7, 1993
           (author's typescript, printed here with her permission)

Notes

1 CCF stands for the Cooperative Commonwealth Federation, the Canadian socialist party, formed in the 1930s in Saskatchewan on a platform of social and economic reform. It later became the New Democratic Party. It was the official opposition party in B.C. in the 1940s.

2 A typescript of a poem titled "Ego" in the Webb papers at the National Library has a note at the bottom of the page stating "published school magazine 1944."

3 Quotations from this interview are taken from Stephen Scobie's typescript, which he has kindly provided me with. The published version is considerably shorter.

4 A copy of this paper is in the UBC archives.

5 See Ken McCarter, "Party 'Platforms' and 'Manifestos' in B.C. Provincial Elections, 1903-1975," unpublished research project at the University of B.C. 1976, UBC Special Collections.

6 Angus MacInnes Memorial Collection, Box S1, folder 8, UBC Special Collections.

7 See Sandra Djwa's biography for details of Scott's career as a writer, law professor at McGill, political activist, and civil libertarian (*The Politics of the Imagination: A Life of F.R. Scott* [Vancouver: Douglas & McIntyre, 1987]).

8 Scott had become Webb's lover as well as mentor, while also continuing his family life with his wife and son.

9 The composition of the group varied depending on who was getting along with whom, who was in town, and so forth. In some "Notes by *PW*," that Webb kindly sent me on this chapter, she remembers that "John Sutherland did not come to Irving's. He was Betty Layton's brother and there was some kind of feud on between Irving and John. We also met at the Sutherlands' but I doubt if Irving came."

10 Paradoxically, members of the group represented both centre and margin in the literary world. Dudek, for instance, as an editor (*CIVn, Delta*), reviewer, and university professor was part of the establishment with the power to legitimize and validate the young writer. On the other hand, as an advocate of socialist politics and the open-form poetics of Ezra Pound and William Carlos Williams, he represented the avant-garde poetics of the 1950s. Similarly, F.R. Scott was seen as both a radical (because of his socialist politics and legal fights for minority rights in Quebec) and a mainstream figure (as an editor, professor, and literary critic). See Webb's comments re: the canonizing power of this group in the Skarstedt interview (*Zymergy*, p. 48-49).

11 In this same interview, she continues, "I look at the Ghazals and although they're very different from his work, there is a connection—he liked to write in those forms" (Butling interview).

12 Webb also credits Dudek and Layton with introducing a "Marxist branch of Canadian literature, or neo Marxist": "One of the things I've been noticing in the development of Canadian poetry since the early 50s is that Layton and Dudek . . . were representative of or trying to write a kind of social critique" (interview with Eli Mandel for *CBC Anthology*, thirtieth anniversary celebration, 1976; Webb papers, NL).

13 See Sandra Djwa's biography of F.R. Scott for a detailed account of the conference (*The Politics of the Imagination*, p. 275-85).

14 For a more detailed discussion of the project, see Lorna Knight " 'With all best wishes, high hopes and thanks': Phyllis Webb, Canadian Poetry, and Publishing in the Early 1950s," *WCL*, Number 6 (1992): 43-53.

15 The poems, as listed on the CBC contract, were "Curtains," "Cats in Snow," and "The Colour of the Light" (Webb papers, NL).

16 In fact, their liaison did not finally end until 1958, after Scott again visited her in Paris.

17 An early version of this poem was published in *The Canadian Forum* in August 1956. The revised version appears in *SIAG* (1962).

18 Typescripts of these articles have the following titles: "Cafés," "Paris," "The Cité Universitaire," "Riot," "Fencing," and "The Garrett." The typescripts are undated, but all but one have a Toronto address on them and in one she refers to "having lived for a year recently" in Paris, indicating that they were written in Toronto in 1959 (Webb papers, NL). They were published in the *Victoria Daily Times*, August 3-7 and 10, 1959.

19 Letter to Pauline Butling, May 13, 1992.

20 See John Hulcoop's Introduction to the 1971 *Selected Poems* for a detailed discussion of Webb's existentialism (p. 27-31).

21 Duncan's three talks were audiotaped by Fred Wah. Copies of the tapes are in the Special Collections at Simon Fraser University.

22 Videotapes of these interviews are in the National Library.

23 Audiotape recordings of the readings and lectures given at the Poetry Seminar at UBC in 1963 are available in the Special Collections at Simon Fraser University.

24 For instance, Webb was one of the judges for the MacMillan Poetry prize at UBC which was awarded to Fred Wah in 1963.

25 See also Webb's comments on what she learned from these writers, cited in chapter 1, as a further indication of the extent of her involvement.

26 The specific titles are "Poems of Failure: Preface to the Kropotkin Poems"; "From the Kropotkin Poems: Ezra Pound"; "From the Kropotkin Poems: Kropotkin"; "A Question of Questions 1-5"; "For Fyodor"; "I Can Call Nothing Love"; "Antisong"; "From the Kropotkin Poems: Solitary Confinement"; "From the Kropotkin Poems: Treblinka Gas Chamber"; "Letters to Margaret Atwood." For publication dates and places, see Cecelia Frey's Annotated Bibliography in *The Annotated Bibliography of Canada's Major Authors*, vol. 6, p. 401.

27 For further discussion of Webb's silence during this period, see John Hulcoop's analysis of political/aesthetic issues (*Phyllis Webb and Her Works*, p. 43-48); Eleanor Wachtel's comments on the debilitating effect of Webb's CBC work on her writing (12); Janice Williamson's feminist analysis of suicide and silence in "The Suicide Narratives of Phyllis Webb"; Cecelia Frey's discussion of Webb's developing feminist consciousness in "The Left Hand of Phyllis Webb"; and my discussion of the power issues in "Paradox and Play in the Poetry of Phyllis Webb."

28 Laing, in turn, thanks "Phyllis Webb and Jeff Anderson . . . for making everything as easy as possible for me at all times" in preparing his 1968 Massey lectures, later published as *The Politics of the Family* by the CBC in 1968.

29 The portrait poems on Ezra Pound and Kropotkin were published in 1970 and "A Question of Questions" was published in 1971, corroborating Webb's comment that by 1969 she had initiated a transformative process.
30 Webb, together with the program producer Robert Chesterman, won an Ohio Radio Award for the program on Christopher Smart.
31 This information is taken from a resumé of Webb's included in the Webb papers at the National Library.
32 See Sharon Nelson's article "Bemused, Branded, and Belittled: Women and Writing in Canada" for an analysis of the gender bias in literary awards and grants (*Fireweed*, 16 [1982]: 65-97).
33 John Hulcoop describes *Hanging Fire* as "Webb's Book of Revelation, a volume full of revolutionary violence" ("Webb's Book of Revelation," p. 242).
34 See *images stone b.c.: Thirty Centuries of Northwest Coast Indian Sculpture*, an exhibition originating at the Art Gallery of Greater Victoria (Saanichton, B.C.: Hancock House, 1975).
35 For further discussion of Webb's "critical wounds," see Hulcoop, *Phyllis Webb*, p. 22-23; Williamson "The Feminine Suicide Narratives of Phyllis Webb"; Jean Mallinson "Ideology and Poetry: An Examination of Some Recent Trends in Canadian Criticism"; and chapter 6 in this book.

Chronology of Phyllis Webb

1927   Born in Victoria, B.C., April 8.

1945   Graduated from high school (St. Margaret's Girl's School), Victoria, B.C.

1945   Became a member of the provincial CCF party.

1945-49   Studied at the University of British Columbia, majoring in English and philosophy; graduated with a Bachelor of Arts degree (spring 1949).

1949   CCF candidate in the provincial election, Victoria, B.C.

1949   Attended the CCF National Convention in Vancouver where she met F.R. Scott.

1950   Moved to Montreal and became part of the literary group of Louis Dudek, Frank Scott, Irving and Betty Layton, Eli Mandel, Miriam Waddington, and others.

1950-57   Worked as a freelance secretary and began doing radio journalism.

1951   First publication of her poems in *The Cataraqui Review, Northern Review,* and *Contemporary Verse.*

1953-54   Enrolled as a qualifying student for the graduate program at McGill University.

1954   Publication of *Trio* (with Eli Mandel and Gael Turnbull) by Raymond Souster (Toronto: Contact Press).

1954-55   Lived in London; travelled to Ireland and France.

1955-57   Moved back to Montreal.

1955   Presented a paper on "The Poet and the Publisher" at the Canadian Writers' Conference at Queen's University: (a continuation of "The Poet and Publisher" published in *Queen's Quarterly* [Winter 1954-55]).

1956   Publication of *Even Your Right Eye* by McClelland and Stewart.

1957-59   Received a Canadian Government Overseas Award which enabled her to live in Paris for a year and a half.

1959   Worked in Montreal and Toronto for McClelland and Stewart as a freelance copy editor and for CBC radio as a script reader.

1960-63 Moved to Vancouver and worked as a teaching assistant in English at UBC.

1962   Publication of *The Sea Is Also a Garden* by Ryerson Press.

1963   Attended the UBC summer poetry seminar with Charles Olson, Robert Duncan, Robert Creeley, Denise Levertov, Margaret Avison, and Allen Ginsberg; interviewed Olson, Duncan, Creeley, and Ginsberg for CBC radio (never broadcast).

1963-64 Received a Canada Council Junior Arts grant to travel to New York and San Francisco.

1964-67 Moved to Toronto to work for CBC as a Program Organizer in the Public Affairs Department.

1965   Publication of *Naked Poems* (Vancouver, B.C.: Periwinkle Press).

1965-69 Started (with William A. Young) the CBC radio program *Ideas*; worked as program organizer (1965-67), and executive producer (1967-69).

1967   Travelled to the Soviet Union and lived on Salt Spring Island, B.C., while on six months' leave from the CBC.

1967   Hosted a series of programs for CBC television on Canadian writers (including Scott, Livesay, Atwood, bissett, and Nichol).

1969   Received a Canada Council Senior Arts grant, quit her CBC radio job, and returned to B.C.

1969-70 Lived in Whitecliff, outside Vancouver.

1970-89 Lived mostly on Salt Spring Island.

1971   Publication of *Selected Poems* by Talonbooks.

1972   Awarded the B.C. Library Association Prize for *Selected Poems* (for "the writer who had made the greatest contribution to the poetry of B.C. in the past five years").

1972   Won an Ohio Radio Award (together with the producer Robert Chesterman) for the CBC feature broadcast "Rejoice in the Lamb: The Offering of Christopher Smart."

1970-76 Supported herself with freelance radio work and temporary jobs.

1976   Read Adrienne Rich's *Of Woman Born*.

1976-77   Taught at the University of British Columbia.

1978-79; 1982-85; 1986-87; 1990
          Taught creative writing at the University of Victoria.

1980-81   Writer-in-residence appointment at the University of Alberta in Edmonton.

1980   Publication of *Wilson's Bowl* by Coach House Press.

1982   Publication of *The Vision Tree: Selected Poems* by Talonbooks; awarded the Governor General's Award for poetry; publication of *Sunday Water: Thirteen Anti Ghazals*, Island Writing Series (Lantzville, B.C.); publication of *Talking* by Quadrant Editions, Montreal; awarded a Canada Council Senior Arts grant.

1984   Publication of *Water and Light* by Coach House Press.

1989   Moved to Victoria; attended the Lahti International Writers Reunion in Finland.

1989-93   Appointed adjunct professor at the University of Victoria (no teaching except for fall 1990).

1990   Publication of *Hanging Fire* by Coach House Press; moved back to Salt Spring Island.

1991   Attended the Association for the Study of the New Literatures in English Association Conference in Essen, Germany.

1992   Attended the Adelaide Festival in Australia and the New Zealand International Festival of the Arts.

1992   Appointed an officer of the Order of Canada.

1992   Honoured at a Tribute to Phyllis Webb—held at The Western Front, Vancouver, B.C.

1992   Publication of " 'You Devise. We Devise.' A Festschrift for Phyllis Webb," *West Coast Line* Number Six, 25, 3.

1993   Nominated for Canada-Australia Literary Prize (declined).

1995   Publication of *Nothing But Brush Strokes: Selected Prose* by NeWest Press, Edmonton.

Works Cited

Books by Phyllis Webb

Webb, Phyllis. *Even Your Right Eye*. Toronto: McClelland and Stewart, 1956.

_____ . *The Sea Is Also a Garden*. Toronto: Ryerson, 1962.

_____ . *Naked Poems*. Vancouver: Takao Tanabe/Periwinkle Press, 1965.

_____ . *Selected Poems 1954-1965*. Edited and introduced by John F. Hulcoop. Vancouver: Talonbooks, 1971.

_____ . *Selected Poems 1954-1965*. Edited by John F. Hulcoop. Vancouver: Talonbooks, 1972.

_____ . *Wilson's Bowl*. Toronto: Coach House Press, 1980.

_____ . *Sunday Water: Thirteen Anti Ghazals*. Lantzville, B.C.: Island Writing Series, 1982.

_____ . *Talking*. Montreal: Quadrant Editions, 1982.

_____ . *The Vision Tree: Selected Poems by Phyllis Webb*. Edited and introduced by Sharon Thesen. Vancouver: Talonbooks, 1982.

_____ . *Water and Light: Ghazals and Anti Ghazals*. Toronto: Coach House Press, 1984.

_____ . *Hanging Fire*. Toronto: Coach House Press, 1990.

_____ . *Nothing But Brush Strokes: Selected Prose*. The Writer as Critic Series, V. General editor, Smaro Kamboureli. Edmonton: NeWest Press, 1995

Webb, Phyllis, Gael Turnbull, and Eli Mandel. *Trio*. Toronto: Contact Press, 1954.

Articles and Uncollected Poems by Phyllis Webb in Books and Periodicals

Webb, Phyllis. "The Poet and the Publisher." *Queen's Quarterly*, 61 (Winter 1954-55): 498-512. Rpt. (revised) in *Writing in Canada: Proceedings of the Canadian Writers' Conference, Queen's University, 28-31 July, 1955*. Edited by George Whalley with an introduction by F.R. Scott. Toronto: Macmillan, 1956, p. 78-89.

_____ . "Protest in Paradise." *Maclean's*, June 1973, p. 38-39, 73-77.

_____ . "Talking the Line: Phyllis Webb in Conversation with Douglas Barbour and Stephen Scobie." *Writing*, 4 (Winter 1981-82): 22-25.

_____ . "Following." *Canadian Literature*, 100 (Spring 1984): 351-53.

_____ . Letter to the Editor. *NeWest Review*, 12, 2 (October 1986).

————. "Ghazal-Maker," Review of *Sea Run: Notes on John Thompson's STILT JACK* by Peter Sanger. *Canadian Literature*, 112 (Spring 1987): 156-57.

————. "Message Machine." In *Language in Her Eye: Views on Writing and Gender by Canadian Women Writing in English*. Edited by Libby Scheier, Sarah Sheard, and Eleanor Wachtel. Toronto: Coach House, 1990, p. 293-96. Reprinted in *Nothing But Brush Strokes: Selected Prose*, The Writer as Critic Series, V. General editor, Smaro Kamboureli. Edmonton: NeWest Press, 1995, p. 136-42.

————. "Three Radio Talks." *West Coast Line* Number Six, 25, 3 (Winter 1991-92): 95-102.

————. Letters to Daphne Marlatt: October 15, 1982; December 30, 1982; January 24, 1982 [*sic*] [1983]. "Phyllis Webb and Daphne Marlatt: A Selected Correspondence." *West Coast Line* Number Six, 25, 3 (Winter 1991-92): 89-94.

————. "Grapevine" [Broadside]. Vancouver: Slug Press, March 28, 1992.

————. "A Bow to the Numinous." Review of *The Holy Forest* by Robin Blaser. *Books in Canada*, April 1994, p. 27-28.

Interviews with Phyllis Webb

Butling, Pauline. Interview with Phyllis Webb. Strathcona Park Lodge, 1986. Unpublished.

Hulcoop, John. "P.W. Interviewed by John Hulcoop." September 1980, Vancouver, B.C. [Broadcast on CBC Radio *Anthology*, April 25, 1981]. Typescript in Webb papers, National Library.

Kamboureli, Smaro. "Seeking Shape, Seeking Meaning: An Interview with Phyllis Webb." *West Coast Line* Number Six, 25, 3 (Winter 1991-92): 21-41.

Munton, Ann. "Excerpt from an Interview." *West Coast Line* Number Six, 25, 3 (Winter 1991-92): 81-85.

Scobie, Stephen. Typescript of interview, 1983. "Canada's Finest Poet." *Victoria's Magazine (Monday)* April 1983: 17-18.

Skarstedt, Sonja A. "Hanging Fire. An Interview with Phyllis Webb." *Zymergy*, 9, 5, 1 (Spring 1991): 35-49.

Sujir, Leila. "Addressing a Presence: An Interview with Phyllis Webb." *Prairie Fire*, 9, 1 (Spring 1988): 30-43.

Williamson, Janice. "Read the Poems, Read the Poems. All Right?" Interview with Phyllis Webb. In *Sounding Differences: Conversations with Seventeen Canadian Women Writers*. Toronto: University of Toronto Press: 1993, p. 321-39.

General Reference

Abley, Mark. Review of *Wilson's Bowl*. *Maclean's*, March 30, 1981, p. 52-53.

Ahmad, Aijaz. Introduction to *The Ghazals of Ghalib: Versions from the Urdu by Aijaz Ahmad, W.S. Merwin, Adrienne Rich, William Stafford, David Ray, Thomas Fitzsimmons, Mark Strand, and William Hunt*. Edited by Aijaz Ahmad. New York: Columbia University Press, 1971.

Arnold, Matthew. *Culture and Anarchy, 1867*. Cambridge: Cambridge University Press, 1960.

Atwood, Margaret. *Power Politics*. Toronto: House of Anansi Press, 1971.

Bakhtin, M.M. *The Dialogic Imagination*. Edited by Michael Holquist, translated by Caryl Emerson and Michael Holquist. University of Texas Press Slavic Series 1. Austin: University of Texas, 1981.

_____. *Problems of Dostoevsky's Poetics*. Edited and translated by Caryl Emerson. Theory and History of Literature, 8. Minneapolis: University of Minnesota Press, 1984.

Barbour, Douglas. Review of *Selected Poems 1954-1965, Quarry*, 21 (Winter 1972): 61-63.

_____. "Major Poet, Major Work." *The Edmonton Journal*, January 24, 1981, p. C4.

_____. Review of *Wilson's Bowl*. *The Toronto Star*, March 21, 1981, p. F2.

_____. "Canadian Poetry Chronicle XI," Part 2 (Review of *The Book of Fall* by Ken Norris, *Artemis Hates Romance* by Sharon Thesen, and *Wilson's Bowl* by Phyllis Webb). *West Coast Review*, 17, 2 (1982): 37, 44-45.

_____. "Lyric/Anti-Lyric: Some Notes about a Concept." *West Coast Review*, October 17, 1982, p. 44-63.

_____. "Foremothers: Phyllis Webb." *Contemporary Verse*, 12, 2 (1989): 44-46

_____. "Late Work at the Kitchen Table: Phyllis Webb's *Water and Light*." *West Coast Line* Number Six, 25, 3 (Winter 1991-92): 103-17.

Barthes, Roland, *The Pleasure of the Text*. Translated by Richard Miller. New York: Hill and Wang, 1975.

_____. "The Death of the Author." *Image—Music—Text*. Translated by Stephen Heath. London: Fontana, 1977.

_____. *Roland Barthes by Roland Barthes*. Trans. Richard Howard. New York: Hill and Wang, 1977.

Belsey, Catherine. *Critical Practice*. New Accents Series. London: Methuen, 1980.

Benjamin, Jessica. *The Bonds of Love: Psychoanalysis, Feminism, and the Problem of Domination*. New York: Pantheon, 1988.

Benveniste, Emile. *Problems in General Linguistics*. Miami: University of Miami Press, 1971.

Bhabha, Homi K. "Signs Taken for Wonders: Questions of Ambivalence and Authority under a Tree outside Delhi, May, 1817." In *"Race," Writing, and Difference*. Edited by Henri Louis Gates, Jr. Chicago: University of Chicago Press, 1986, p. 163-84.

Bloom, Harold. *A Map of Misreading*. New York: Oxford University Press, 1975.

Brossard, Nicole. *The Aerial Letter*. Toronto: The Women's Press, 1988.

_____. "Poetic Politics." In *The Politics of Poetic Form: Poetry and Public Policy*. Edited by Charles Bernstein. New York: Roof Books, 1990, p. 73-86.

Brown, Norman O. *Love's Body*. New York: Random House, 1966.

Bryson, Norman. "The Gaze in the Expanded Field." In *Vision and Visuality*. Edited by Hal Foster. Dia Art Foundation: Discussions in Contemporary Culture Number 2. Seattle: Bay Press, 1988, p. 87-113.

Butler, Judith. *Gender Trouble: Feminism and the Subversion of Identity*. Thinking Gender Series. New York and London: Routledge, 1990.

Butling, Pauline. "Paradox and Play in the Poetry of Phyllis Webb." In *A Mazing Space: Writing Canadian Women Writing*. Edited by Shirley Neuman and Smaro Kamboureli. Edmonton: Longspoon/NeWest, 1986, p. 191-204.

_____. "Phyllis Webb as a Post-Duncan Poet." *Sagetrieb*, 7, 1 (1988): 57-78.

_____. "I Devise. You Devise. We Devise." Preface to *West Coast Line* Number Six, 25, 3 (Winter 1991-92): "You Devise. We Devise: A Festschrift for Phyllis Webb." A special issue guest edited by Pauline Butling.

Carr, Brenda. "Genre Theory and the Impasse of Lyric? Reframing the Questions in Phyllis Webb's Lyric Sequences." *West Coast Line* Number Six, 25, 3 (Winter 1991-92): 67-79.

Cash, Gwen. "Portrait of a Poet: Victoria's Phyllis Webb." *B.C. Magazine*, April 6, 1957, p. 17.

Clifford, James. *The Predicament of Culture: Twentieth-Century Ethnography, Literature, and Art*. Cambridge: Harvard University Press, 1988.

Chiba, Reiko. *The Making of a Japanese Print*. Rutland, VT and Tokyo, Japan: Charles E. Tuttle, 1959; 8th printing 1978.

Cogswell, Fred. "Good But Not Great," Review of *Poems*, by Alan Dugan, *The Plink Savoir*, by Robin Mathews; *Image of Life*, by Charles Shaw; and *The Sea Is Also a Garden*, by Phyllis Webb. *The Fiddlehead*, 55 (Winter 1963): 68.

_____. Review of *Naked Poems*. *The Fiddlehead*, 68 (Spring 1966): 69-70.

Corrington, John. "Nouveau Gnomic Poetry?" Review of *Naked Poems*, *Northwest Review*, 7 (Spring 1966): 111-12.

Coulee, Cultus. "Phyllis Webb . . . Salt Spring Poet." *Gulf Island Driftwood*, May 13, 1971, p. 9.

Davey, Frank. "Phyllis Webb." In *From There to Here: A Guide to English Canadian Literature since 1960*. Erin, ON: Porcépic, 1974, p. 261-65.

————. "The Struggle for Phyllis Webb." *Canadian Literary Power*. The Writer as Critic Series, IV. General editor, Smaro Kamboureli. Edmonton: NeWest Press, 1994, p. 197-244.

Doctorow, E.L. *The Book of Daniel*. New York: Bantam, 1971.

Dorscht, Susan Rudy. "Poems Dressed in a Dress and Naked: Sweet Lines from Phyllis." *West Coast Line* Number Six, 25, 3 (Winter 1991-92): 54-63.

Djwa, Sandra. *The Politics of the Imagination: A Life of F.R. Scott*. Vancouver: Douglas and McIntyre, 1987.

Drucker, Johanna. "Women / Writing / Theory: what is at stake?" *Raddle Moon*, 11, 6 (1992): 17-19.

Dudek, Louis. "Always Phenomenal/Epiphenomenal," Review of *Wilson's Bowl*. *The Canadian Forum*, August 1981: 29-30.

————, and Michael Gnarowski, eds. *The Making of Modern Poetry in Canada: Essential Articles on Contemporary Canadian Poetry in English*. Toronto: Ryerson Press, 1967.

Duff, Wilson. "IMAGES: A Way of Seeing and a Way of Thinking, Introduction to *images stone b.c.*" *Thirty Centuries of Northwest Coast Indian Sculpture*. An exhibition originating at the Art Gallery of Greater Victoria. Saanichton, B.C.: Hancock House, 1975, p. 12-22.

————. "Nothing Comes Only in Pieces." In *The World is as Sharp as a Knife: An Anthology in Honour of Wilson Duff*. Edited by Donald N. Abbott. Victoria: British Columbia Provincial Museum, 1981, p. 315-24.

Duncan, Robert. *The Opening of the Field*. New York: Grove Press, 1960.

————. "Ideas of the Meaning of Form." In *The Poetics of the New American Poetry*. Edited by Donald Allen and Warren Tallman. New York: Grove, 1973, p. 195-211.

DuPlessis, Rachel Blau. *The Pink Guitar: Writing as Feminist Practice*. New York and London: Routledge, 1990.

Easthope, Antony. *Poetry as Discourse*. New York and London: Methuen, 1983.

————. *Literary into Cultural Studies*. London and New York: Routledge, 1991.

Encyclopedia of Contemporary Literary Theory: Approaches, Scholars, Terms. General editor and compiler, Irena R. Makaryk. Toronto: University of Toronto Press, 1993.

Estok, Michael. "Regeneration and Enlightenment." *NeWest Review*, 11, 9 (May 1986): 12.

Findley, Timothy. *Famous Last Words*. Toronto: Penguin, 1982.

————. *Not Wanted on the Voyage*. Toronto: Penguin, 1984.

Frey, Cecelia. "Phyllis Webb, An Annotated Bibliography." In *The Annotated Bibliography of Canada's Major Authors*. Edited by Robert Lecker and Jack David. Vol. 6. Toronto: ECW Press, 1985, p. 389-448.

————. "The Left Hand of Webb." *Prairie Fire: A Celebration of Writing by Canadian Women*, 7 (Autumn 1986): 37-48.

Frow, John. "Intertextuality and Ontology." In *Intertextuality: Theories and Practices*. Edited by Michael Worton and Judith Still. Manchester: Manchester University Press, 1990, p. 45-55.

Glickman, Susan. "Proceeding before the Amorous Invisible: Phyllis Webb and the Ghazal." *Canadian Literature,* 115 (Winter 1987): 48-61.

Goodman, Paul. *The Empire City*. New York: Bobbs-Merrill, 1959.

Hand, Seán. "Missing You: Intertextuality, Transference and the Language of Love." In *Intertextuality: Theories and Practices*. Edited by Michael Worton and Judith Still. Manchester: Manchester University Press, 1990, p. 79-91.

Hulcoop, John. Introduction to *Selected Poems 1954-1965 by Phllis Webb*. Vancouver: Talonbooks, 1971, p. 9-41.

————. " 'Bird Song in the Apparatus': Webb's New Selected Poems." Review of *The Vision Tree: Selected Poems*. *Essays on Canadian Writing*, 30 (Winter 1984-85): 359-70.

————. "Phyllis Webb." In *Dictionary of Literary Biography 53: Canadian Writers Since 1960, First Series*. Edited by W.H. New. Detroit: Gale, 1986, p. 372-79.

————. "Webb's 'Water and Light.' " *Canadian Literature*, 109 (Summer 1986): 151-59.

————. *Phyllis Webb and Her Works*. Toronto: ECW [1991].

————. "Webb's Book of Revelation: Lifting the Lid Off Krakatoa and Spiritual Storm?" In *Inside the Poem: Essays and Poems in Honour of Donald M. Stephens*. Edited by W.H. New. Toronto: Oxford University Press, 1992, p. 230-45.

Iser, Wolfgang. "The Reading Process: A Phenomenological Approach." In *Modern Criticism & Theory: A Reader*. Edited by David Lodge. New York: Longman, 1988, p. 212-28.

Kamboureli, Smaro. "The Poetics of Failure in *Wilson's Bowl*." *Island*, 10 (Fall 1981): 84-88.

Keith, W.J. "Struggles with Silence." Review of *Wilson's Bowl*. *Canadian Literature*, 91 (Winter 1981): 99-102.

Knight, Lorna. "With all best wishes, high hopes and thanks: Phyllis Webb, Canadian Poetry, and Publishing in the Early 1950s." *West Coast Line* Number Six, 25, 3 (Winter 1991-92): 43-53.

Knutson, Susan. "Chiasmus, Chasm, Chi: Phyllis Webb's Semantic Geometry." *West Coast Line* Number Six, 25, 3 (Winter 1991-92): 118-24.

Kristeva, Julia. *Desire in Language: A Semiotic Approach to Literature and Art*. Edited by Leon S. Roudiez. Translated by Thomas Gora, Alice Jardine, and Leon S. Roudiez. New York: Columbia, 1980.

————. *Revolution in Poetic Language*. Translated by Margaret Waller; with an introduction by Leon S. Roudiez. New York: Columbia, 1984.

————. *The Kristeva Reader*. Edited by Toril Moi. Oxford: Blackwell, 1986.

Layton, Irving. *Love Where the Nights Are Long: Canadian Love Poems*. Selected by Irving Layton with drawings by Harold Town. Toronto: McClelland and Stewart, 1962.

Laing, R.D. *The Self and Others*. London: Tavistock, 1961.

————. *The Politics of Experience and The Bird of Paradise*. Harmondsworth: Penguin, 1967.

————. *The Politics of the Family*. Massey Lectures, Eighth Series. Toronto: Canadian Broadcasting Corporation, 1968.

Lecker, Robert, ed. *Canadian Canons: Essays in Literary Value*. Toronto: University of Toronto Press, 1991.

Macfarlane, Julian. Review of *Selected Poems*. *The Capilano Review*, 1 (Spring 1972): 53-58.

Mallinson, Jean. "Ideology and Poetry: An Examination of Some Recent Trends in Canadian Criticism." *Studies in Canadian Literature*, 3 (Winter 1978): 93-97.

Mandel, Ann. "The Poetry of Last Things," Review of *Wilson's Bowl*. *Essays on Canadian Writing*, 26 (Summer 1983): 85-91.

————. Review of *True Stories* by Margaret Atwood and *Wilson's Bowl* by Phyllis Webb. *The Fiddlehead*, 131 (January 1982): 63-70.

Marlatt, Daphne. "Musing with Mothertongue." *Touch to My Tongue*. Edmonton: Longspoon, 1984. Reprinted in *Gynocritics: Feminist Approaches to Canadian and Quebec Women's Writing*. Edited by/preparé par Barbara Godard. Oakville, ON: ECW Press, 1987, p. 223-26.

————. *Salvage*. Red Deer, AB: Red Deer College Press, 1991.

————. Letters to Phyllis Webb. November 22, 1982; January 18, 1983. "Phyllis Webb and Daphne Marlatt: A Selected Correspondence." *West Coast Line* Number Six, 25, 3 (Winter 1991-92): 89-94.

Mays, John Bentley. "Phyllis Webb (for Bob Wallace)." *Open Letter*, 2d ser., 6 (Fall 1973): 8-33.

McCarter, Ken. "Party Platforms and Manifestos in B.C. Provincial Elections, 1903-1975." Unpublished research project at the University of British Columbia, 1976. UBC Special Collections.

Nelson, Sharon H. "Bemused, Branded, and Belittled: Women and Writing in Canada." *Fireweed*, 15 (Winter 1982): 65-97.

New, W.H. "A Wellspring of Magma: Modern Canadian Writing." *Twentieth Century Literature*, 14 (October 1968): 126-27.

Nichol, bp. *the martyrology Books 1 & 2*. Toronto: Coach House Press, 1972.

Olson, Charles. "Projective Verse." In *The Poetics of the New American Poetry*. Edited by Donald Allen and Warren Tallman. New York: Grove, 1973, p. 147-74.

Pacey, Desmond. "A Group of Seven." *Queen's Quarterly*, 63 (Autumn 1956): 436, 442-43. Reprinted as Desmond Pacey, "A Group of Seven Poets." *Essays in Canadian Criticism, 1938-68*. Toronto: Ryerson, 1969, p. 112-13, 120-21.

————. *Creative Writing in Canada: A Short History of English-Canadian Literature*. 2d ed. Toronto: Ryerson, 1961, p. 241, 247.

Pearson, Alan. "Poetry Chronicle." *The Tamarack Review*, 39 (Spring 1966): 87.

Perloff, Marjorie. *The Dance of the Intellect: Studies in the Poetry of the Pound Tradition*. New York: Cambridge University Press, 1985.

————. *Radical Artifice: Writing Poetry in the Age of Media*. Chicago: University of Chicago Press, 1991.

Pound, Ezra. "Hugh Selwyn Mauberley." In *Selected Poems*. Edited with an introduction by T.S. Eliot. London: Faber and Faber, 1959.

Rich, Adrienne. *Of Woman Born: Motherhood as Experience and Institution, 1976*. Tenth anniversary ed. New York and London: W.W. Norton, 1986.

Rico, Gabriel Lusser. *Writing the Natural Way*. Los Angeles: J.P. Tarcher, 1983.

Ricou, Laurie. "Phyllis Webb, Daphne Marlatt and Simultitude: Journal Entries from a Capitalist Bourgeois Patriarchal Anglo-Saxon Mainstream Critic." In *A Mazing Space: Writing Canadian Women Writing*. Edited by Shirley Neuman and Smaro Kamboureli. Edmonton: Longspoon/NeWest, 1986, p. 205-15.

Riffaterre, Michael. "Compulsory Reader Response: The Intertextual Drive." In *Intertextuality: Theories and Practices*. Edited by Michael Worton and Judith Still. Manchester: Manchester University Press, 1990, p. 56-78.

Rosenthal, Helène. "The Luminous Web." Review of *Selected Poems 1954-1965, The Ubyssey* (University of British Columbia), September 14, 1971, p. 7-8.

Said, Edward. "Opponents, Audiences, Constituencies, and Community." In *The Politics of Interpretation*. Edited by W.J.T. Mitchell. Chicago: University of Chicago Press, 1983, p. 7-32.

Sartre, Jean-Paul. *Being and Nothingness: An Essay on Phenomenological Ontology*. Translated and introduced by Hazel E. Barnes. New York: Philosophical Library [1955].

Schweichkart, Patrocinio, and Elizabeth A. Flynn. "Reading Ourselves: Toward a Feminist Theory of Reading." *Gender and Reading: Essays on Readers, Texts, and Contexts*. Baltimore: Johns Hopkins University Press, 1986, p. 31-62.

Scobie, Stephen. "The Single Hook," Review of *Talking. Books in Canada*, 2 (November 1982): 23-24.

————. "I and I: Phyllis Webb's 'I Daniel.'" *Open Letter*, 6th ser., 2-3 (Summer-Fall 1985): 61-68. Reprinted in *Signature Event Cantext: Essays by Stephen Scobie*. The Writer as Critic Series, II. General editor, Smaro Kamboureli. Edmonton: NeWest Press, 1989, p. 127-31.

————. "Leonard Cohen, Phyllis Webb, and the End(s) of Modernism." In *Canadian Canons: Essays in Literary Value*. Edited by Robert Lecker. Toronto: University of Toronto Press, 1991, p. 57-70.

_____. "'Breaking': Extracts from 'The Keil Diary.'" *West Coast Line* Number Six, 25, 3 (Winter 1991-92): 125-38.

Sonthoff, Helen. "Structure of Loss: The Poetry of Phyllis Webb." *Canadian Literature*, 9 (Summer 1961): 15-22.

Souster, Raymond. *New Wave Canada: The New Explosion in Canadian Poetry.* Edited with an introduction and bibliography by Raymond Souster. Toronto: Contact Press, 1965.

Stevens, Peter. "Creative Bonds in the Limbo of Narcissism." *The Globe and Mail* (Toronto), December 4, 1971, p. 33.

_____. "Shaking the Alphabet." Review of *Selected Poems 1954-1965.* *Canadian Literature*, 52 (Spring 1972): 82-84.

_____. Review of *Wilson's Bowl*. *The Windsor Star*, March 21, 1981, p. E7.

Stevens, Wallace. *The Collected Poems.* New York: Vintage Books, 1982.

Story, Norah. "Webb, Phyllis (1927-)." *The Oxford Companion to Canadian History and Literature.* Toronto: Oxford University Press, 1967, p. 825.

Suzuki, D.T. *The Field of Zen.* Edited with a foreword by Christmas Humphreys. New York: Harper & Row, 1969.

Thesen, Sharon. Introduction to *The Vision Tree: Selected Poems by Phyllis Webb.* Vancouver: Talonbooks, 1982, p. 9-19.

Thompson, John. *STILT JACK.* Toronto: House of Anansi Press, 1978.

Torgovnick, Marianna. "The Politics of the 'We.'" *The South Atlantic Quarterly*, 91, 1 (Winter 1992): 43-59.

Tostevin, Lola. Review of *Wilson's Bowl*. *NeWest Review*, April 6, 1981, p. 15.

van Herk, Aritha. "And silence is also a nakedness (an inter-text to *Naked Poems*)." *West Coast Line* Number Six, 25, 3 (Winter 1991-92): 175-84.

Wachtel, Eleanor. "Intimations of Mortality." *Books in Canada*, November 12, 1983, p. 8-15.

Whalley, George. Preface to *Writing in Canada: Proceedings of the Canadian Writers' Conference held at Queen's University, July 1955.* Edited by George Whalley with an introduction by F.R. Scott. Toronto: Macmillan, 1956.

Whiteman, Bruce. "A New Webb." *CV II*, 6, 4 (August 1982): 16.

Williams, William Carlos. *The Collected Earlier Poems of William Carlos Williams.* Rev. ed. New York: New Directions, 1963.

Williamson, Janice. "Citing Resistance: Vision, Space, Authority, Transgression in Canadian Women's Poetry." PhD dissertation, York University, 1987.

_____. "The Feminine Suicide Narratives of Phyllis Webb." *West Coast Line* Number Six, 25, 3 (Winter 1991-92): 155-74.

Wolff, Janet. *The Social Production of Art 1981.* New York: New York University Press, 1989.

Woolf, Virginia. "The Leaning Tower." *The Moment and Other Essays*, 105-25. New York: Harcourt Brace, 1952.

Woodcock, George. "In the Beginning Was the Question: The Poems of Phyllis Webb." *Queen's Quarterly*, 93 (Autumn 1986): 527-45; reprinted in *Northern Spring: The Flowering of Canadian Literature*. Vancouver: Douglas and McIntyre, 1987, p. 246-65.

Worton, Michael, and Judith Still. Introduction to *Intertextuality: Theories and Practices*. Manchester: Manchester University Press, 1990, p. 1-44.

Index

Adamov, Arthur, 141, 142
Adaskin, Harry and Frances, 129
aesthetics, 128; imagist, 162; Kantian, 110; Dudek's, 133
agency, 29, 32, 43, 104
anarchism, 30
Amnesty International, 156
Atwood, Margaret, 76, 160; "Letters to Margaret Atwood," 79, 103
"The Authors Are in Eternity," 66-67
avant-garde, 91, 144

Barbour, Douglas, 121, 160
Barthes, Roland, 151; *Pleasure of the Text,* 69-70; siren signifiers, 100
Beardsley, Doug, 63, 151
Benjamin, Jessica, 97, 100, 107 n. 8
Beresford-Howe, Constance, 137
Benveniste, Emile, 78
Berliner, Lilo, 2, 4 n. 9, 36, 157-59
Bhabha, Homi, 3-5, 6, 31
binary: oppositions, 14-15, 55; thought, 40
Birney, Earle, 128, 131, 143, 145, 146
bisset, bill, 94, 145, 148, 159
"The Bowl," 151
"Breaking," 14-15, 77, 114
Brossard, Nicole, 87 n.1
Bryson, Norman, 7, 34 n. 8
Buddhism, 15-17, 131; *see also* Zen Buddhism
buddhist: philosophy, 21; values, 115
Butler, Judith, 5, 33 n. 4; 73 n. 5

Canada Council, 137, 146, 155, 160
Canadian Writers' Conference, 136, 139
Cartesian "I," 9, 80, 98; *see also* self
Carr, Brenda, 115, 108 n. 14, 121
Carr, Emily, 129
CBC (Canadian Broadcasting Corporation), 60, 131, 136-37, 143, 147-48, 152, 154
CCF (Cooperative Commonwealth Federation), 126-27, 130, 163 n. 1

centrifugal, 40-41, 91
centripetal, 40-41
chaos theory, 100
Chung Yung, 12
Civil Liberties Association, letter to, 154-55
Clifford, James, 53-55
clustering, 39-42
Cogswell, Fred, 113
Cohen, Leonard, 132, 161
"The Colour of the Light," 6-9
Confucian, 21, 115; *see also* Neo-Confucian
Corrington, John, 112
Creeley, Robert, 21, 59, 144, 146, 147

Daniells, Roy, 128, 143
dark, 25, 45, 52-53, 65; as other, 1-2; as female, 5, 26; grand dark, 37, 41, 46
Davey, Frank, 115, 122 nn. 6, 7, 123 nn.9, 10, 12, 145
Dickinson, Emily, 67, 68
Dorscht, Susan Rudy, 115, 121
Dostoevsky, Fyodor, 78, 99
"Double Entendre," 10-12, 138-39
Dudek, Louis, 131-32, 142, 145. 164 n. 10, 164 n. 12
Duff, Wilson, 30, 100, 157-59; "Nothing Comes Only in Pieces," 2, 157; *Images stone, b.c.,* 157-58
Duncan, Robert, 21, 22, 144, 146
DuPlessis, Rachel Blau, 95

"Earth Descending," 9-10, 133, 137
Easthope, Antony, 35 n. 13; 122 n. 3
Enlightenment 1, 112
erotic: female erotic, 25, 29; in inter-textual relations, 100, 107 n. 1; in language, 69; lesbian erotic, 22; Marlatt on, 61-62; in *Water and Light,* 120; in Webb's writing, 114
essentialist, 110, 118, 143
Estok, Michael, 70, 120
Even Your Right Eye, 13, 114, 131, 139

181